Helmut Schmidt
Perspectives on Politics

Helmut Schmidt
Perspectives on Politics

edited by
Wolfram F. Hanrieder

Westview Press / Boulder, Colorado

All materials originally in German were provided in English by agencies of the government of the Federal Republic of Germany.

All photographs appear courtesy of Bundesbildstelle Bonn.

Published in 1982 in the United States of America by
Westview Press, Inc.
5500 Central Avenue
Boulder, Colorado 80301
Frederick A. Praeger, President and Publisher

Library of Congress Cataloging in Publication Data
Schmidt, Helmut, 1918 Dec. 23–
  Bibliography: p.
  Includes index.
  1. Germany (West)—Politics and government—Addresses, essays, lectures. 2. World politics—1975–1985—Addresses, essays, lectures. I. Hanrieder, Wolfram F. II. Title.
DD259.7.S36A5   1982   327'.0904   82-6924
ISBN 0-86531-205-2   AACR2

Printed and bound in the United States of America

Contents

A combination of political forces is a bloodless and inhuman entity, and in the manipulation of these mechanical categories we seem to lose touch of the realities they conceal — the pulse and play of warm, live passions, the beating hearts of men who suffer and aspire. We are sometimes put off with phrases instead of explanations; and the language of cogs and pulleys fails, sometimes, to illuminate the workings of the spirit.

—F. M. Cornford, *Thucydides Mythistoricus*

Introduction

Wolfram F. Hanrieder

A public figure is inevitably a creature of his time and place. The circumstance of history is impressed upon a public life, and those who have gained high office are continually called upon to articulate a public response to the issues of the times. The result is a sort of dialectic, a more or less sustained dialogue between the personal attributes and sensibilities of a political leader and the historical imperatives that press upon the social order for which he has accepted partial and temporary responsibility. Public personalities evolve alongside historical developments, sometimes intersecting with them, other times remaining at a watchful distance or poised proximity—depending at least in part on the element of chance, of political *fortuna,* of being in the right place at the right time.

But the emphasis, or neglect, that public issues receive from a political figure are as much an expression of personal sensibilities and value judgments as they are a reflection of their objective historical importance. Although the requirements of governance, especially at the highest level, demand that the central preoccupations of the state be dealt with continually, there is ample latitude for a political leader to make choices of emphasis, to leave a personal imprint on the political process, and to confront issues with a unique style. Unyielding as they appear to be, even the imperatives of circumstance and of necessity permit a political figure to nudge them in one direction or another, to press against them in ways that are unique and personal. A political leader's public response to the challenges of his era is inevitably an autobiographical statement about himself—the historical process reflected in a temperament.

Helmut Schmidt, federal chancellor of the Federal Republic of Germany, is one of the most remarkable political figures on the contemporary world stage. One impressive aspect of Schmidt's career is the wide range of influential positions he has held prior to attaining the most important political office in the Federal Republic. Before he was elected to the office of federal chancellor by the Bundestag in 1974, Schmidt was a member of the Bundestag, senator for the interior of the city-state of Hamburg, floor leader of his party in the Bundestag, minister of defense, and minister of economics and of finance. He has held a number of high positions in the Social Democratic Party as well, making for a variety of experience that is unusual even in a European parliamentary system! At a time when national leaders, especially in the United States, are selected for qualities that often seem irrelevant for solving the problems they confront, Helmut Schmidt's long apprenticeship for the office of chancellor has prepared him well to deal with the range and complexity of political issues and has afforded the public a long and balanced look at the person and policies of West Germany's head of government.

The long public life of Helmut Schmidt coincides closely with the life span of the Federal Republic. He and West Germany grew into maturity together, and the variety of responsibilities that Schmidt undertook in the course of his public life are closely connected with many of the major preoccupations of the new state: the need to establish a viable democratic system and proceed with political and economic reconstruction; the task of making moral and financial restitution to the victims of Nazi Germany and returning Germany to the international community as a respected member; the quest for security within the Atlantic Alliance (and, in later years, for a constructive approach to arms control); the political and economic adjustments required by membership in an integrated European economic order; the painful necessity of dealing with the division of Germany and Europe, and with the problems emerging from the management of East-West détente in the 1970s and 1980s; and the search for an answer to the vexing question of the Federal Republic's appropriate posture in the North-South dialogue. There is hardly an important issue in West German foreign and domestic policy over the last decades in which Helmut Schmidt, at various stages in his public life, has not participated either in word or deed.

HELMUT SCHMIDT: THE POLITICAL CENTRIST

On many issues, Helmut Schmidt has located himself at the political center—that center being not only the crossing point of two extremes but also the core of public policy. When Schmidt joined the Social Democratic Party (SPD) in 1946, he was in many respects a representative of a new generation of Germans, a generation schooled by disaster that emerged from the daily lessons taught by the war and the Nazi regime with a deeply skeptical attitude toward ideological exertions and philosophical certitudes, a generation searching more for clarity and reason than for murky metaphysical meaning. Most likely, these were the years that shaped Schmidt's political temperament. "It is an illusion," Henry Kissinger has written, "to believe that leaders gain in profundity while they gain experience. . . . The convictions that leaders have formed before reaching high office are the intellectual capital they will consume as long as they continue in office."[2]

The public voice of Helmut Schmidt—one of the most articulate of our time—developed amid the substantive as well as personal abrasions of parliamentary debate. Since the Social Democrats did not participate in a German federal government until 1966, when they joined the Christian Democrats and Christian Social Democrats (CDU/CSU) in the so-called Grand Coalition, Helmut Schmidt's formative years as a parliamentarian were shaped while his party was in opposition. These were difficult years for the Social Democrats. Internationalist by ideological conviction and historical tradition, the SPD of the 1950s nonetheless opposed West European integration as well as the transatlantic security ties that Chancellor Konrad Adenauer was establishing with the United States. The SPD had no intrinsic objections to the idea of European integration and to Adenauer's policy of reconciliation with the West, but they also believed that the commitments resulting from such a policy—rearmament and membership in the Western Alliance—were detrimental to the cause of German unity. They were also very apprehensive about the prospect of a West European community that would be limited in membership and that exhibited strongly Catholic and conservative overtones.

These issues were critical, since the political and military commitments made by the Adenauer government—commitments that were the precondition for economic recovery and the restoration of sovereignty—affected not only the future of German foreign policy but also the direction and content of West Germany's domestic sociopolitical and economic order. Both government and opposition evaluated foreign policy projects in terms of the obstacles and opportunities that would be created for the social order they wanted to establish. Until the 1950s, the Socialists' blueprint for a new German socioeconomic and political order was Marxist-reformist, with pronounced antibourgeois and anticlerical overtones. But the strategists of the CDU/CSU had correctly counted on the moderately conservative temper of the electorate (the SPD made very disappointing showings in the 1953 and 1957 elections) and the objections to rearmament and the commitment to German reunification, although widespread, were more than balanced by practical considerations. The immediate requirements of economic reconstruction, the desire for an adequate standard of living after years of deprivation, and the gains promised in return for collaborating with the Western powers made opposition to rearmament and the call for German unity essentially emotional issues that had to face a daily test against expediency, the hope for "normalcy," and the constraints imposed by East-West tensions.

In response to these developments, and also because the prospects for German reunification became increasingly dim, a reformist wing emerged within the Social Democratic Party, made up of such members as Helmut Schmidt,

Fritz Erler, Willy Brandt, and Herbert Wehner. They planned to revamp the SPD's orientation and image and change it from a doctrinaire instrument of the "class struggle" into a broad-based party that would appeal to a wider constituency and demonstrate to the electorate that the party was capable of constructive participation in the governance of the Federal Republic. This brought the SPD closer to the European integrationist principles and NATO-oriented security policies of the CDU/CSU–led governments of Konrad Adenauer and Ludwig Erhard and ultimately created the basis for a measure of bipartisanship in foreign policy. The 1959 SPD party program further extended the party's readiness for political accommodation into the sphere of domestic socioeconomic issues. In these developments Helmut Schmidt was a key figure. He had become the party's expert and spokesman on security questions (an expertise also demonstrated in books on nuclear-strategic issues), and his personal attributes—a sharp intelligence, an apparently indefatigable capacity for work, an ability for rhetorical exposition, and a well-developed sense of the possible—lent themselves well to the style as well as the substance of the rejuvenated Social Democratic Party.

The Social Democrats' move toward the political center culminated in their joining the CDU/CSU in the coalition of 1966 and the Free Democrats (FDP) in the coalition of 1969. But the political accommodations required for sustaining the partnership with the Free Democrats, especially in the area of socioeconomic policy, made the left wing of the Social Democrats increasingly critical of what they began to view as an excessively conciliatory, "mainstream" political program of the party leadership. For several reasons, this division in the party became more troublesome after Helmut Schmidt replaced Willy Brandt as chancellor in 1974. First, the dynamics and drama of *Ostpolitik* (in which the German government had demonstrated its willingness for reconciliation with the East) had essentially run its course with the conclusion of a series of treaties in which the Federal Republic recognized the German Democratic Republic and the existing East European borders. Second, the Free Democrats gained an even larger voice in shaping the coalition's socioeconomic policies at the same time that foreign policy issues, which in the early 1970s had provided the most solid common ground for the coalition, receded somewhat into the background. Finally, Helmut Schmidt, located at the right wing of the party on domestic as well as on foreign policy questions, presented a more inviting target for the left wing's discontent than had Willy Brandt. As a result, on several key issues (for example, socioeconomic policy, arms control, and nuclear energy policy), Schmidt was closer to the SPD's coalition partner, and even to the opposition, than to the left wing of his own party. The centrist position that Schmidt managed to occupy in German politics thus became a source of contention in intraparty alignments and an element of weakness in the coalition politics of the government. It was a source of strength in the electorate at large, however, as Schmidt consistently ran ahead of his party in public opinion polls.

HELMUT SCHMIDT AND THE "SECOND" GERMAN ECONOMIC MIRACLE

Although Schmidt's centrist position was under attack from the Left as well as from the Right in Germany, abroad, the German chancellor became the personification of German economic and monetary prowess, the embodiment of what could be called the "second" German economic miracle.

The first German "economic miracle"—the rapid reconstruction of the ravaged postwar German economy in the 1950s—was as much a political as an economic phenomenon. As the European continent lay shattered and disillusioned, the United States provided goods and money for reconstruction and, as the possessor of the only viable nuclear force, guaranteed West European security without great immediate risk to itself. The economic reconstruction program advanced by the United States in the postwar years guided the West German economy on a course that the Adenauer government, in contrast to the Social Democrats, did not find onerous. It dovetailed neatly with the domestic economic principles of Ludwig Erhard's "social market economy"—a blend of laissez-faire with a dash of dirigisme—making for an agreeable combination of necessity and choice and resulting in the much-touted economic miracle of the 1950s. Moreover, this meshing of international and domestic economic principles was sustained by the entire range of German policies toward the West: economic recovery was skillfully complemented by Bonn's policies on political recovery and on security and rearmament.

A second German economic miracle, at least from the American perspective, took place in the 1970s when the Federal Republic managed much more successfully than other Western industrialized countries to adjust to the dislocations and "stagflation" caused by the quadrupling of oil prices in 1973-74. Especially in American eyes, Chancellor Schmidt became the representative of Germany's economic performance—not only because he was the German chancellor and a trained and articulate economist, but because his personal and political style reflected the new confidence and, to a degree, self-assertion of the Germans.

The Federal Republic's growing influence has come about by design as well as by opportunity: the Germans have become stronger in absolute terms through their own conscious efforts, and they have become stronger in relative terms through the default of others. The demise of the Bretton Woods international monetary system, the problems the United States experienced in managing transatlantic relations, the aftereffects of Vietnam and Watergate, the West's troublesome and costly energy dependence, the development of Soviet-U.S. nuclear parity, and a variety of other factors signaled a relative decline of U.S. influence and a new configuration of the global balance of power. Moreover, the constituent elements of the balance of power have been changing as well: the day-to-day realities of economic and monetary interdependence are partially supplanting such measures of power as military capacity. Although security has become a question of national survival in the nuclear age, in the 1970s and early 1980s a shift of emphasis began to take place in world politics away from the military elements of power toward its economic elements.

There is no question that the Federal Republic benefits from these developments, since they emphasize those aspects of international influence that are most susceptible to the application of German economic capacity. This has not been an unmixed blessing, however. Economic and monetary "language" has traditionally provided the West Germans with an excellent opportunity to translate political demands, which might have been suspect because of Germany's past, into respectable economic demands. But now that economic issues are themselves more charged with political meaning, economic language also has become less neutral and more subject to being interpreted as an expression of power politics. In the past decade, the Germans have gradually become more assured in voicing their views on what they consider an appropriate German role in the West European, transatlantic, and global configurations of power. Although they have not voiced these views stridently or sought to implement them heavy-handedly, their aspirations, real or imagined, have occasioned suspicion as well as confidence, criticism as well as approbation.

The articulation of German interests is also complicated by the deterioration of the Atlantic compact and the stagnation of European integration. In the past, German governments could express German aspirations in the language of Europe and the Atlantic Alliance rather than in terms of German national interests: being a good German was the same as being a good Atlanticist or a good Europeanist. But as the alliances diverged in purpose over the decades, and as the Federal Republic gained a role of leadership in the European Community and a larger voice in the Atlantic Alliance, Bonn's opportunities to advance national interests in the name of general international cooperation became less ample and convincing. The legitimizing ecumenical language in which German purposes could be expressed in the past is less suited to the new circumstances and requires the Germans to learn a new diplomatic vocabulary.

These are sensitive matters, and Chancellor Schmidt has addressed them in a forthright and circumspect manner. Although not immune to the temptations of delivering lectures on economic matters to U.S. presidents and other world leaders (a few of whom have found it difficult to forgive him for having been right too early) Schmidt is nonetheless aware that because of Germany's past the Germans must speak softly. As the views of the Federal Republic gain more and more authority, Schmidt has recognized the psychological fact that authority, although more than advice, is less than a command. As he has put it: "We are not small enough to keep our mouth shut, but we are too small to do more than talk." For Schmidt, restraint as well as self-assurance should define the dynamics of German economic and monetary prowess, and he has been careful to play down the Federal Republic's growing political influence, mindful of historic European misgivings and suspicions about the Germans.

The view of the Federal Republic as an economic giant has not remained unchallenged in Germany—independent of the question as to what political leverage derives from that stature. When Americans in the past suggested a Washington-Bonn political-economic axis or a locomotive role for the German economy, Helmut Schmidt (as well as other leaders in government and business) responded with self-depreciation, appealingly modest in tone and supported by statistics that attest to the vulnerability of the German economy to global economic disturbances, particularly those emanating from the United States. Indeed, the difficulties that the German economy experienced in adjusting to the second wave of oil price increases in 1979, the balance-of-payments deficits that the Federal Republic accumulated toward the end of the seventies, the weakening of the mark relative to the dollar in 1980 and 1981, and the fiscal and budgetary problems that assailed the German government in 1981-82 raised some questions about the economic and monetary position of the Federal Republic. High unemployment rates, in particular, raise sensitive political and moral issues for the Social Democrats, who are committed to the equitable sharing of economic burdens as well as economic benefits. Nevertheless, Germany's inflation rate has remained comparatively low, German exports remained highly competitive in the wake of a depreciating mark, and Germany's foreign reserve holdings remain comfortably high.

HELMUT SCHMIDT: CENTRIST IN EAST-WEST RELATIONS?

The increased role of the Federal Republic in world affairs is especially sensitive in the area of East-West relations. No other political issue (except for the fear of a German finger on the nuclear trigger) is as charged with psychological burdens as is the Federal Republic's policy toward the East. The suspicion that the Federal Republic is an actual or potential revisionist European power, prepared to unhinge the status quo if given the opportunity, is close to the surface of many of the issues—political, military-strategic, economic—that are contested between Bonn and other capitals. Even though Bonn's *Ostpolitik* followed rather than preceded other dynamic Western approaches to the East, their partners' response to *Ostpolitik* demonstrated to the Germans that their own approach to détente called for a delicate balance of movement and restraint. Too little readiness to support East-West accommodation had in the past brought charges of obstructionism (for example, when Bonn dragged its feet on arms control), and too much enthusiasm for détente raised fears that Bonn would weaken its ties to the West to create better prospects for German unity. Even today there is the question whether *Ostpolitik* is merely the remnant of former reunification efforts, the sum of past subtractions as it were, or the beginning of an evolutionary process intended to change the status quo by formally recognizing it. The Federal Republic's abiding concern with the question of German unity lends a somewhat unsettled (and, for some, unsettling) quality to its diplomatic dealings with the Soviet Union, Eastern Europe, and East Germany. As a consequence, German intentions are questioned more intensely the less they can be questioned openly. Both the Germans and their allies have learned that even between partners, confidence is suspicion asleep.

Chancellor Schmidt's Atlanticist credentials are impeccable and of long standing, and even his political opponents in Germany do not question his friendship with the United States. But the interests of the United States and the Federal Republic are not the same, and they will not become more congruent by pressing the Germans to make gestures of loyalty that they consider embarrassing and of little practical value, or to make choices of substance that for them are unpalatable and damaging. The disagreements between Bonn and Washington—on the nature of the Soviet threat, the efficacy and equity of economic sanctions directed toward the Eastern bloc, economic and monetary policies, the shape of a future European order, and the potential of East-West détente, to mention just a few—resist accommodation, not to speak of settlement, unless both parties arrive at an appreciation of their conflicting interests and at mutually acceptable ways of dealing with them. This process is not easy and is further complicated by the differing institutional characteristics and domestic political configurations in both countries. A case in point is the plan for the modernization of NATO's intermediate-range nuclear weapons, in which domestic and foreign policy considerations are connected in a particularly troublesome combination.

Chancellor Schmidt has, for all practical purposes, staked his political life on his government's commitment to the "double-track" NATO decision of December 1979, which he helped initiate. The decision envisages the deployment on German soil of modernized medium-range nuclear weapons and calls at the same time for earnest East-West arms control negotiations that would make the deployment unnecessary. This commitment, intended to redress the imbalance in the area of Eurostrategic nuclear weapons created by the deployment of an increasing number of Soviet SS-20 missiles, has placed a heavy burden on Bonn's relations with Moscow and is widely opposed in Germany because of the fear that only its first component will be implemented.

The advent of nuclear parity between the United States and the Soviet Union has deeply disturbing implications for Germany, more so than for any other U.S. NATO partner. Owing to geography and history, the Federal Republic has been from the beginning a NATO member with special inhibitions, obligations, and anxieties, and the problems plaguing NATO because of the waning American nuclear superiority have always been felt more keenly in Bonn than in other West European capitals. For France and Britain, Soviet-U.S. nuclear parity has strengthened the rationale for sustaining, and perhaps augmenting, their national nuclear arsenals. For the Federal Republic, the possibility of a national nuclear posture is foreclosed because of political, legal, and psychological reasons, and for the same reasons, an increase in German conventional troop levels would be equally troublesome. In the absence of a West European nuclear force, which would raise its own problems, the Germans have no alternative for their security dependence on Washington, nor have they given any indication that they are looking for one. Helmut Schmidt in particular personifies that commitment to the Atlantic security community.

But the Germans have an equally deep interest, also owing to geography and history, in détente. Complemented in the early 1970s by Bonn's *Ostpolitik,* détente has yielded the Germans political, humanitarian, and economic benefits to which they will continue to cling, even as Washington admonishes them that détente is indivisible and that the Alliance must stand united in the face of Soviet expansionism and suppression. One way of looking at *Ostpolitik* that would deepen U.S. understanding of its meaning is to see that it was from its beginning connected with Germany's security policy, not because it lessened the Federal Republic's strategic dependence on the United States or its allegiance to NATO, but because Bonn's readiness to legitimize the territorial status quo reduced Soviet incentives to apply military pressure outside the Warsaw Pact region. *Ostpolitik* tackled German security problems at their roots and thus became a complementary political part of Germany's military security policy—a combination of interests that is reflected in the dual components of the NATO "double-track" decision. Without impairing Germany's attachment to the West, *Ostpolitik* conveys to the Soviet Union a more constructive and conciliatory political intent.

Since the Germans have been the main beneficiaries of détente, they are committed to the evolution of a European order that will secure and broaden these benefits. Neither the United States nor the Soviet Union share those benefits or embrace that commitment. Both are disappointed with the results of détente. Both have for decades preferred the solidificaion rather than the alteration of the European status quo, especially with respect to the division of Germany, which they perceive to be its central stabilizing feature. Both have a tendency to exploit their nuclear strategic preponderance to compensate for political, economic, and diplomatic infirmities. Suspicious of the superpowers' political use of their nuclear arsenals, some Europeans believe that Washington and Moscow are primarily interested in arms control at a high plateau of balanced capabilities rather than in arms reduction and that (perhaps inaccurately with respect to the United States) U.S. and Soviet claims to superpower status can be sustained in the nuclear-strategic area only. Many Europeans see their basic security interests protected more convincingly through the political rather than the military-strategic balance of power, an attitude reflected in the reluctance of smaller NATO countries to accept modernized theater nuclear weapons on their soil. Chancellor Schmidt, who holds a much more balanced and considered view of these matters, thus plays an essential mediatory and supportive role in transatlantic relations, a role that clearly serves to strengthen, not weaken, transatlantic security ties.

The deterioration of East-West relations in the early 1980s, which also has led to a deterioration of German-American relations, has placed Chancellor Schmidt in a paradoxical and difficult position. Paradoxical because this genuine friend of the United States, an Atlanticist by temperament as well as by political conviction, is viewed by some on this side of the Atlantic as an irritating obstacle to a coordinated Western effort to contain the Soviet Union and not for what he is — a loyal ally, whose admonitions reflect concern and not animosity or a "neutralist" posture in the East-West conflict. Difficult because Schmidt's Atlanticist security policies have weakened his position in his own party, and because his conviction that the Federal Republic can and must play an interpretive role in a constructive dialogue between East and West is resented in Washington and plays into the hands of his formal opposition in Bonn.

In the 1980s, we shall see a new configuration of regional and global power relationships in which the Federal Republic will continue to play a significant role. Measured against German aspirations of the 1950s, the fading of the transatlantic and European compacts and the thwarting of Bonn's reunification efforts would have to be considered major foreign policy failures. Paradoxically, however, it is the absence of Atlantic unity, European unity, and German unity that has increased the political leverage of the Federal Republic, making it the object of the West's political and economic expectations and the East's inducements and pressures. The question is: to what use will this leverage be applied at a time when German foreign policy projects have become more prosaic, when less clear-cut choices are demanded of German foreign policy makers, and when the familiar guidelines of German foreign policy are becoming murkier even as Bonn's central security interests remain firmly tied to Washington and as its political fortunes in Europe remain tied to Moscow and Paris?

But it is precisely the absence of stark alternatives in European and German foreign policies that will maximize the impact of German policies on the coming European order, especially in the area of economic and monetary policy. Today, Europeans are not as preoccupied with the dramatic "high politics" of previous decades as they are with the much more technical economic and political tasks that confront them: economic growth and monetary stability, security of energy and other raw materials supplies, dealing constructively with the Third World, and adjusting European Community structures in order to implement much-needed reforms and accommodate new members. In all those tasks, which require coordinated and therefore incremental steps, economic policy will play a steady, fundamental, and perhaps decisive role, with large opportunities for the Federal Republic to translate economic and monetary capacity into political leverage. In addition, German economic policies suitable for shaping the European order can most likely command a wide domestic consensus if they continue to adhere to the principles of Germany's economic culture and sustain modest economic growth and stable price levels. For these external and internal political-economic tasks, Germany's present leadership is eminently suited.

It is indeed striking how the three great chancellors of the Federal Republic—Konrad Adenauer, Willy Brandt, and Helmut Schmidt—were politically and temperamentally prepared for their historical tasks. It was the great achievement of Konrad Adenauer to have fashioned a fundamental reconciliation of Germany with the West and the great achievement of Willy Brandt to have conveyed a similar readiness for reconciliation toward the East. Both acted in response to historical developments that have taken on, in retrospect, an almost inescapable quality yet were advanced as well by the personal sensibilities and characteristics of Adenauer and Brandt. The historical imperatives of the 1970s and early 1980s are less visibly formed and compel a less clearly shaped German response, not only because we are too close to them to gauge their meaning, but also because their inherent complexities and contradictions yield no clear-cut alternatives. For such times, in which new configurations of power and purpose are gradually evolving, the temperamental and political attributes of Helmut Schmidt are well suited. This has less to do with Schmidt's qualities of caution and "pragmatism" than with the range and depth of his thinking, his breadth of experience, his stature as a statesman, and his personal integrity. The experiences of his life have provided Schmidt with a measured view of what is necessary as well as of what is possible—and a sense of the necessary is the essence of civic duty, while a sense of the possible is not an obstacle but the prerequisite for a larger vision.

* * *

The adroit use of language, essential for most political figures as an instrument of advocacy and persuasion, has characterized Chancellor Schmidt's political career from the beginning. In presenting to an English-speaking readership a collection of Helmut Schmidt's speeches, interviews, and essays, it was my intention to have the selections reflect, in the range of their topics, the range of his experience, concerns, and political temperament. Many of these concerns are about important practical matters of public policy, but in the more philosophical essays of this collection, the reader will also find Helmut Schmidt speaking in a reflective and contemplative voice that reveals how his response to the issues of the day are informed by a moral sensibility and a view of public life that connect the world of thought with the world of action.

NOTES

1. For a more detailed account of Chancellor Schmidt's political biography, see the essay by Hans Georg Lehmann in this volume.

2. Henry A. Kissinger, *White House Years* (Boston: Little, Brown, 1979), p. 54.

1

Germany in the Era of Negotiations

(October 1970)

The rationale of West German foreign policy is very simple: the postwar era has ended. Its hallmarks were high hopes for Western political structures on the one hand, and high tension between East and West on the other. Now a new epoch is in the offing. In the West it is going to be characterized by less ambitious objectives and more pragmatic approaches. The achievements of the fifties and sixties will not be dismantled, but the aims for the immediate future will be lowered. Dreams of "Atlantic Union Now" or "Instant Europe" must give way to expectations more closely geared to realities: wider and deeper cooperation, without necessarily institutional perfection. Between East and West the new era could be one of diminished tension and growing détente, of more cooperation and less confrontation. Not unlike President Nixon, the Bonn government is also trying to "build agreement upon agreement" without in any way deluding itself that this could be a process easily or speedily accomplished.

There is no conflict between these policies. They are not mutually exclusive; indeed, they complement one another. The Federal Republic of Germany is firmly rooted in the West — both in the Atlantic Alliance and in such European institutions as the Western European Union and the Common Market. These Western ties are beyond question.

II

It is an undeniable fact that the North Atlantic Treaty Organization (NATO) has fully served its purpose during its twenty years of existence. In Europe, it has created a military balance vis-à-vis the Eastern bloc, and thus maintained the peace through grave international crises: first Korea, then Berlin and Cuba,

Reprinted by permission from *Foreign Affairs* 49 (October 1970):40–50.

finally Prague. And there has been more reasonable reform in recent years than many critics are willing to admit.

In the seventies as well, NATO will retain its lasting value as a safeguard against any revival of communist aggressiveness. After all, the lesson of Czechoslovakia in 1968 has been that the era of East-West crises is not yet a thing of the past. By means of the Brezhnev doctrine, Moscow has brutally collectivized the sovereignty of the East European nations. At the same time, the Soviet military are coolly debating the question whether war has really ceased to be an instrument of politics in the nuclear age.

Without the North Atlantic Alliance, there can be no security for Europe. Without it, the main threat to the West cannot be eliminated: namely a political stranglehold which could suffocate individual areas such as West Berlin, or bring pressure to bear on the Federal Republic or the NATO countries located on Europe's northern and southern flanks.

By the same token, without a firm foundation in NATO, there can be no sensible policy of détente in Europe. The maintenance of an effective defense depends on the continuity of a balance of power as does the improvement of East-West relations.

From all this, three conclusions can be drawn: for Germany, for Western Europe, and for the relationship between Europe and its two North American allies, especially the United States.

For Germany, an exclusively national policy of deterrence would lack both credibility and effectiveness. As Chancellor Willy Brandt said in his policy statement on October 28, 1969, "For our security we need friends and allies, just as they need us and our contribution for theirs." Let me repeat here what I said recently before the North Atlantic Council: "The new German government will continue the previous policy, both within the Alliance and toward the Alliance. We will not diminish the German defense effort, either in quantity or in quality, but will improve our contribution by a program for modernizing and reforming our armed forces. . . . Our defense contribution of 460,000 men under arms will remain unaltered."

For Europe, the necessity remains to keep up an effective defense. The buildup of the Soviet fleet, and of a Soviet naval presence in the Mediterranean, is growing at an undiminished rate. The military potential of the Warsaw Pact is continuously being reinforced and modernized in the western part of the USSR and in communist Eastern Europe in such manner and strength that we have no alternative but to maintain NATO forces now in Western Europe, in sufficient strength and of adequate quality. In this context, one has to at least *raise* the question whether Europe could not do more than it has done in the past to combine its various national efforts in the fields of defense, of arms procurement, and of technology, and to make them more effective by streamlining them without an increase in expenditure.

For the United States, given the strategic implications of the military potential of the Soviet Union and its continued effort in this respect, it remains an unquestionable fact of life in our time that there is no substitute for the role and function of the United States in the balance of strategic power.

Against this background, we actively support European efforts which would facilitate the continued and unquestioned presence of sufficient U.S. troops in Europe. The Euro-Group in Brussels and some other cooperative ventures are first steps on the road to what may, in time, become the consolidated defense establishment of a politically united Western Europe.

But we are still far from that goal. And we know too well that the alliance with the United States continues to be indispensable for maintaining that balance in the defense and deterrence capabilities which lead the other side to a rational handling of its foreign policy. The alliance with the United States is kept alive by the military presence of the United States in Europe and must remain so for some time. Also during this decade the fundamental asymmetry between East and West in Europe has to be brought into balance by a U.S. military presence in Europe itself.

It is only this presence, by the way, which underpins the strategy of "flexible response." It has taken the members of the Atlantic Alliance many years to reach agreement on this strategy. It is reasonable and credible. There is no alternative to it. A return to massive nuclear retaliation would be incredible, as would be a fallback on purely "tactical" nuclear defense—the former being unimaginably cruel to the Americans, the latter to the Europeans. The strategy of flexible response is the only one which combines credibly effective deterrence with nonsuicidal defense, sharing the risks of warfare in a fair way between North Americans and West Europeans.

This fact is not accepted with happiness—either on this or on the other side of the Atlantic. However, it must be taken into account with all the implications it carries in many fields. It is with intense concern that we follow the course of events in the United States and Canada, and the development of thoughts suggesting a lessening of foreign policy commitments of the United States, in particular concerning Europe. Past experience gives rise to the hope that notwithstanding the pressing domestic issues a wide consensus will emerge to reaffirm the responsibilities of the United States as a vital and fundamental backbone for the strategic balance.

Certainly, substantial changes in the international environment would justify a reassessment of the number of American troops necessary in Europe. It is not Holy Writ that U.S. forces will have to remain in Europe at present strength forever and ever (already the American garrison in Germany has been reduced by 20 percent over the past four years). We are hopeful that future conditions will allow for modifications of their role. Major changes, however, have not yet occurred. They may be looming on the horizon, but they may never become palpable political reality if the West throws away its cards before going to the conference table or before getting agreements on mutual force reductions.

There are many convincing arguments against precipitate or premature American troop withdrawals from Europe. In the first place there is the conventional military argument. U.S. ground troops man one-fourth of the European dividing line; the U.S. Air Force furnishes between 70 and 80 percent of all flying units in the 4th ATAF [Allied tactical air force] covering southern Germany, and about the same percentage of HAWK and NIKE [missile] batteries in that area. Were any of them thinned out or pulled out, grievous gaps would be created and the concept of forward defense turned into a shambles. Moreover, substantial U.S. withdrawals would sorely undermine public confidence not only in the reliability of the American commitment but also in the basic feasibility of European defense. An opinion poll recently conducted in West Germany bears this out. Sixty-six percent of those polled — and 79 percent of all Bundeswehr soldiers — felt that without American troops Germany would be overrun in the event of a communist aggression. Thus, an American pullout might indeed cause a psychological landslide and impel a despondent Western Europe toward its first major reorientation since the end of World War II.

Finally, nobody can deny that Western Europe, even if it were willing and able to put a European soldier in place of every GI withdrawn, could never make up for the deterrent effect inherent in American troops and their immediate link with the strategic deterrence. In the balance of power that obtains between the two superpowers one cannot replace the soldiers of the American superpower by French, British, or German soldiers. This is true for the Seventh Army; it also goes for the Sixth Fleet. Unilateral American withdrawals would accentuate rather than attenuate the structural imbalance of the present situation.

For obvious reasons, West Germany could not man the breach. By the same token, increased German payments for continued undiminished American presence offer no way out, because they would have to come from the German defense budget. The best way to help the Americans stay in Europe lies therefore in a joint European effort to facilitate the presence of U.S. troops here, and I hope that sufficient agreement can be effected among our European partners in this new venture.

III

The political unification of Western Europe continues to be a principal goal of our foreign policy. But the desire for institutional perfection is now tempered by a decade of sobering experience. Too many high-flying plans and projects have foundered on the mountains of national self-interest. The European Defense Community, a European Political Community, European Union along the Fouchet pattern — all of these projects were eminently sensible and desirable, yet they failed. The European nation-states were not ready for them.

Each failure, however, caused a grievous loss of dynamics and confidence and threw Europe back by several years. The lesson is obvious: West European unification is jeopardized if its architects aim for the unattainable. Pragmatism and gradualism offer better chances.

West Germany still wants to see Western Europe unified. It was, after all, Chancellor Brandt who engineered a decisive breakthrough when, at the Hague Conference in December 1969, he convinced France's President Pompidou of the necessity to get Europe moving again. Meanwhile, talks about the entry of new members—first and foremost the United Kingdom—into the Common Market club have begun. They will no doubt be protracted, but they are off to a felicitous start. The Europe of the Six is evolving into a Europe of the Ten. And the Community is now moving toward increased integration as well.

Though some would argue that more members and more integration are incompatible aims, we have learned the hard way that integration takes time. If we cannot have all, at least we should work for all that is possible—for strengthened consultation procedures in the first place, for less-than-perfect forms of union in the second. The Common Market nations must consider themselves lucky if they can complete their economic and currency union by the end of the seventies. So why not include in that process those willing and able to join? Why not take them along on the road to political union that lies beyond the horizons of 1980?

Others contend that you cannot simultaneously pursue integration in Western Europe and rapprochement with Eastern Europe. But these are not the fifties any longer. Then it was possible to plan for a Carolingian Western Europe for which Eastern Europe was nothing but a heathen adversary. But now, the Carolingians have passed away; the East has been put on the map. Whatever structure the West Europeans are going to create, it will certainly not be one without windows, doors, and passageways to the East Europeans. President Pompidou put it very bluntly in his Strasbourg speech last June: Western Europe would not come into existence unless it developed its relations with the countries of Eastern Europe; France, at any rate, would not go along if it were otherwise. Seen in this light, an active Eastern policy would appear to be a prerequisite of a West European renewal.

IV

Three preliminary remarks must be made about our *Ostpolitik,* the Eastern policy of the new West German government.

(1) It is not the result of a radical break with the past but rather the logical outcome of an evolution that started in the mid-sixties under Foreign Minister Gerhard Schröder; it found a first expression in the Peace Note of March 1966 and was assiduously developed by the Grand Coalition.

(2) It is firmly embedded in the fabric of a strong Western alliance. It is in

no way an attempt to break away from that alliance, but rather an attempt to engage the political strength of the alliance in order to overcome the sterile confrontation of the past decade. The Paris Treaties of 1954 and our commitments to NATO are beyond question—and so is our constitution. West Germany will not become a "wanderer between the two worlds," as Chancellor Brandt has repeatedly stated. It is no "floating kidney."

(3) Bonn's Eastern probe fits into the wider pattern of Western policy vis-à-vis the communist powers. Its basic aim is to find out what room and readiness there are in the East for compromise and conciliation. Like other Western probes—the Strategic Arms Limitation Talks (SALT), for instance—ours is also governed by the basic consideration that if it fails we must not find ourselves in a worse position than before. We shall not embark on any adventure from which our friends will have to bail us out.

The impelling motive of our Eastern operation was the recognition that security through deterrence is only one essential element of stabilizing the framework of international relations and that security through lessening tension is a supplementary one, no less essential. The ultimate goal of this undertaking is the healing of the rift that has divided Europe for more than twenty years. Since the partition of our continent and our country cannot be overcome, at least we must want to overcome the separation of the peoples; since borders cannot be shifted about any longer, we must bend all our efforts to render their presence more tolerable. This, basically, is what *Ostpolitik* is all about.

Our method is that of patient, persevering, matter-of-fact diplomatic dialogue, carried on in a spirit neither euphoric nor frustrated. That dialogue is being launched simultaneously with the Soviet Union, with Eastern Europe, and with East Germany.

We see the situation realistically, as it is. Nothing important can be accomplished in Eastern Europe that Moscow does not agree to; it would be foolish to try to drive wedges among the members of the Warsaw Pact. Nevertheless, Warsaw, East Berlin, Prague, and the others are not mere satellites without a will of their own and without any influence. We recognize that they are not. Therefore, we started an exchange of opinions with Poland and the German Democratic Republic (GDR), at the same time that we opened talks with the Soviet Union. We hope that later there will be conversations with other member states of the Warsaw Pact as well. In each case, we consider the proposal to conclude an agreement on the renunciation of force a useful organizational framework for addressing the different bilateral problems.

With Moscow we have had and still have intensive and serious talks and negotiations. At the time of this writing, the outcome so far has been a preliminary agreement on the substance of a renunciation-of-force agreement. In addition, several points of understanding relating to matters of mutual interest were put on record. The Soviets refrained from insisting on their previous maximalist positions. "Recognition" of all existing frontiers was no longer demanded, "respect" accepted instead; they were declared "inviolable" but not necessarily "unalterable." Moscow accepted the German view that treaties previously concluded with third parties should not be affected; this is especially important with regard to the Paris Treaties, our membership in NATO, and our European Community ties. Moreover, the Soviets showed themselves willing to accept a letter from the Federal Government to the effect that self-determination for the entire German people remains the goal of our policy. While Berlin is not an object of talks or arrangements between Bonn and Moscow, the Soviets took note of our view that a general détente must include and is intimately linked with a satisfactory settlement of the situation in and around Berlin. The ultimate result remains still to be seen. At present one can at least say that the Soviets are negotiating as seriously as in SALT.

The dialogue with Warsaw has also taken an encouraging turn since the Brandt administration took office. The Federal Republic does not feel able to recognize formally and finally the Oder-Neisse Line as Poland's western border; this is a decision which even the architects of present-day Poland reserved to a peace treaty with Germany. But we are willing to do everything possible short of an eventual peace treaty. We have made the Poles a twofold offer: first, to concede in no uncertain terms that, in its view, the Oder-Neisse is the western frontier of Poland; and second, to commit itself to the inviolability of this frontier. There is real hope that an agreement can be reached along these lines.

The third area in which we aim at normalization is the relationship between the two German states. Here it is our primary goal to end a development that, in the past twenty years, has ever more deepened the rift between the two Germanys. This will not be made possible as long as they adhere unequivocally to maximalist claims and arguments. The people in both parts of Germany want practical solutions that would permit the nation to live together more easily than it can at present.

The communist leadership of the GDR obviously finds it difficult to budge from its formalistic position. It demands the final and definitive recognition of East Germany in terms of international law as a prerequisite to any negotiations over normalization. And it leaves nobody in doubt that the relations between East Berlin and Bonn should be no different in character from those between, say, Belgium and Poland.

Bonn, in turn, has made it clear that it is ready to adopt a sensible, forthcoming attitude. We think it is useless to continue pretending there is no GDR; not that we approve of the regime or of the social system it has imposed on the East Germans, but neither do we call its existence in question any longer. We are eager to talk with East Germany, as the Erfurt and Kassel meetings between Chancellor Brandt and Chairman Stoph have proved. We shall cooperate with them wherever they are ready for it. There is one thing, however, which we refuse to do: recognize the other part of Germany as a foreign country. The Germans are one nation and will remain so. If the GDR should one day be ready to normalize its relations with the Federal Republic on the basis of this principle, then we on our part will no longer object to the GDR establishing relations with third countries or participating in the activities of international organizations on the basis of equal rights. But such an attitude cannot be taken prior to an agreement on a modus vivendi between West Germany and East Germany. It could be aimed at in the wake of détente, but cannot precede it.

In all of this, of course, Berlin plays a crucial role. It is still an international tinderbox. All our efforts to achieve détente can remain futile if the situation there continues insecure and unsecured. Berlin (East and West) cannot remain an island of the cold war in a Europe of cooperation. To be sure, it is primarily a responsibility of the Four Powers, and the Federal Government clearly recognizes the special rights and responsibilities which these powers still hold with regard to Berlin and Germany as a whole. At the same time, however, West Berlin is in many important ways a warden of the Federal Republic, tightly interwoven, as it is, with the social, economic, monetary and legal fabric of West Germany. For this reason, the Federal Government cannot fail to make its voice heard whenever the fate of Berlin is at stake. Our point of view is very simple: as developments have confirmed the existence of the GDR, so developments have confirmed as a fact the special relationship between West Berlin and the Federal Republic. Both of these realities are equally real. If this is not recognized by both sides, confrontation cannot be replaced by cooperation.

V

The vast implications of the endeavors to reach agreements with the Soviet Union on strategic armaments are not only widely understood in the United States but also in the other allied countries. Corresponding with these endeavors, which among other things envisage a continued nuclear deterrence sufficiency for the West, we should seek Western efforts to engage the Soviet-bloc countries more deeply in the policy of mutual balanced force reductions (MBFR) which would, if implemented correctly, reduce the burdens of defense without increasing security risks.

The Federal Government attaches high importance to this topic. We would like to see it introduced as a priority issue into East-West relations and also make it an important point on the agenda of any international conference on the security of Europe, if and whenever such a conference comes about. Within NATO, we have favored an early Western MBFR initiative; and we are pleased to note that the demarche decided upon at the Rome Council meeting in May 1970 has met with a less unsubtle and more forthcoming response on the part of the Warsaw Pact than might have been expected.

There are, of course, still plenty of snags ahead, but in the face of ever more pressing Asian preoccupations and growing internal demands, the Soviets might now indeed be more favorably inclined to balanced force reductions in Europe than at any other time. Paradoxically, the Czechoslovak tragedy may have helped them to come around; for in August 1968, they proved to themselves as well as to their unfortunate allies that presence on the ground is not absolutely necessary for controlling an area—potential presence, quickly able to be mobilized in a crisis, weighs just as heavily on the scales. Remote control can function as effectively as control on the spot.

The important point is that we treat mutual and balanced force reductions not as a narrowly military exercise but as an eminently political operation. It might well be the European way of lowering the levels of uncertainty, cost, and potential violence in the East-West confrontation, comparable to SALT on the strategic plane. Mutual balanced force reductions would make it possible to reduce the U.S. troop presence in Europe without changing the correlation of forces and without diminishing Western Europe's confidence in the American commitment. The Americans would neither leave Europe completely nor loose themselves from it; the part of their forces to be withdrawn would depart under circumstances which would minimize the probability of their having to return in order to meet a major contingency. American troop withdrawals would not come as a retreat but rather as a contribution toward the evolution of more cooperative and less confrontational patterns of relationship in Europe.

This, in my view, would also be the chief difference between the disengagement ideas of old and the more recent MBFR project. Then the Americans were to be crowded out of the Old World, in which case the balance would have been tipped in favor of the East; now they will retain a foothold. This is important, for peace in Europe can only be preserved, and efforts to achieve détente will only be successful, if the relative balance of forces which we have today continues to be maintained. The point of MBFR is that the balance would be lowered, not changed.

In all of these fields, West German policy is characterized by a combination of persistence and realism. We know what the goals are but we are flexible when it comes to mapping out the routes that will take us there. It is no longer all or nothing, take it or leave it. Nobody is waiting for spectacular acts to change the world overnight. The important thing is to get processes started which will, in due time, lead either to solutions of our unsolved problems or to agreed-upon nonsolutions which the world can live with more easily than with the dangerously unstable status quo.

2

The 1977 Alastair Buchan Memorial Lecture

(October 28, 1977)

The Alastair Buchan Memorial Lectures have been established as a tribute to the Institute's first director. The 1977 Lecture was delivered by Helmut Schmidt on October 28, 1977.

In his address the chairman of the Institute's council, Professor Ernst van der Beugel, welcomed the speaker as follows:

"Mr Chancellor, to govern implies a keen sense of priorities. The priority you have chosen in delivering the second Alastair Buchan Memorial Lecture is a very high tribute to Alastair's memory and a great privilege for this Institute. Our welcome is twofold. We, of course, welcome you as Head of Government of the Federal Republic. We are, however, proud to welcome you also as Helmut Schmidt, member of this Institute since 1959. In welcoming you as Federal Chancellor, we would like to express our conviction that what happens in the Federal Republic will, to a very great extent, determine the fate of Europe and of the Western Alliance. We admire your achievements; we trust your policies; we share your concerns; you inspire our confidence, not in the least with regard to that central moral problem of Government: to strike a just and effective balance between freedom and authority. In welcoming our member, Helmut Schmidt, we think of the many intellectual contributions you have made to the work of this Institute by preparing papers and by participating in our discussions. In spite of the enormous burden of your high offices — Parliamentary Leader of your Party, Federal Minister of Defence, Federal Minister of Finance and, finally, Federal Chancellor — you have always found time for this Institute.

"Alastair was primarily a scholar, but, at the same time, deeply interested in acts of policy. . . . It is, therefore, more than fitting that a man of action,

Reprinted by permission from *Survival*, Vol. XX (Jan./Feb. 1978):2–10. Published by the International Institute for Strategic Studies, London.

dedicated to the conceptional basis on which policy should rest, honours with his Lecture this afternoon the scholar who never lost his link with concrete acts of policy."

It is a privilege and a challenge for me to deliver to you today the 1977 Alastair Buchan Memorial lecture.

I consider it a very special privilege because in this way I can pay tribute to Alastair Buchan and at the same time indicate my appreciation and admiration for the work carried out by the International Institute for Strategic Studies [IISS]. Alastair was a brilliant thinker on subjects concerning war and peace. He was an outstanding journalist. He was also a good pedagogue. When I first participated in an international meeting organized by the IISS there were several working groups among which was one on nuclear strategy and another on conventional warfare. I had volunteered for the latter but Alastair said, "No, you go to the first one because this is what you have to learn." And so I did. He was the fine director of the Institute when I became a member eighteen years ago; I came to be his friend because I shared his deep concern about maintaining world peace and global security as a major prerequisite for human freedom and happiness.

At the same time I consider it a challenge to try to analyze within the short space of this memorial lecture some important aspects of Western security. I know that there are many in the audience today who have devoted more time and intellectual power to the dimensions of Western security about which I propose to speak: strategic and political aspects on the one hand, economic and social aspects on the other.

NEW DIMENSIONS OF SECURITY

In preparing for this lecture I picked up again Alastair Buchan's book *Power and Equilibrium in the 1970s*.[1] It is an important and a very thoughtful book in which Alastair analyzed the structure of world politics only five years ago. His main concern was with the balance of power between the United States, Western Europe, Japan, the Soviet Union, and China. Brilliant thinker though he was, he did not at that time devote much attention to the economic, the social, and the internal aspects of Western security, which I will discuss today as new dimensions of security. These aspects do not replace the earlier models of balance and imbalance of power around the globe. But I believe that they must be added to those concepts which, in time, they will change and modify. I know, of course, that Walter Bagehot once stated: "One of the greatest pains of human nature is the pain of a new idea." Yet I believe that it is in the best interest of a tradition established and promoted by Alastair to try to understand these new dimensions of security now rather than to discover in the future that we made the wrong decisions because we failed to understand them and take them into consideration.

What are these new dimensions? First, economic development. By this I mean the necessity to safeguard the basis of our prosperity, to safeguard free trade access to energy supplies and to raw materials, and the need for a monetary system which will help us to reach those targets. There was a feeling not too long ago that we had few problems in this field. However, the oil crisis, the phasing out of the Bretton Woods agreement, worldwide inflation, unemployment, and inadequate economic growth, have together changed the picture and have created widespread feelings of insecurity.

Second, social security. By this I mean the necessity to achieve and maintain social peace at home, making goods and jobs available for our people and at the same time telling them bluntly that there are limits to what the state can do for them. It is in this connection that I would like to congratulate my friends Jim Callaghan and Denis Healey on their success in fighting inflation and restoring confidence in sterling. The battle is not yet over, but you, the British, have come a long way since last year and I firmly believe that the outlook is good.

Third, domestic security. By this I mean the necessity to strengthen and defend our society against terrorists whose sole aim is to destroy its fabric with acts of brutal killing and kidnapping. You have had your share of terrorist activity in this country and you have faced up to it. Now we in Germany are faced with a different, but equally ugly, form of terrorism. So are the Dutch and other nations. We are determined to put an end to it without sacrificing the liberal qualities of our society. In connection with this I would like to point to and applaud the work done by the IISS in analyzing terrorism, and I want to urge more international cooperation to stop terrorist activities.

J. B. Priestley in his book *The English* quotes himself—because he believes his idea is important, and I fully agree—to the effect that foreigners often only see the walls around the gardens of Britain and fail to appreciate the beauty of what lies within them. Here indeed is one of the main reasons why many foreigners misjudge Britain and the British. But in the framework of this lecture the analogy has another application: in the past we have all worked toward maintaining and mending our outward defenses but have possibly neglected the economic structure of our gardens, the importance of the well-being of its plants and the threats to their roots. Therefore, while I do not mean to suggest that we should drop our guard of outward defense, I shall devote most of this lecture to the internal considerations of Western security. I shall concentrate on the economic dimensions, but first I shall analyze some current strategic and political issues.

THE NECESSITY OF ARMS CONTROL

Most of us will agree that political and military balance is the prerequisite of our security, and I would warn against the illusion that there may be grounds for neglecting that balance. Indeed, it is not only the prerequisite for our security but also for fruitful progress in East-West détente.

In the first place we should recognize that—paradoxical as it may sound—there is a closer proximity between a hazardous arms race, on the one hand, and a successful control of arms, on the other, than ever before. There is only a narrow divide between the hope for peace and the danger of war.

Second, changed strategic conditions confront us with new problems. SALT codifies the nuclear strategic balance between the Soviet Union and the United States. To put it another way: SALT neutralizes their strategic nuclear capabilities. In Europe this magnifies the significance of the disparities between East and West in nuclear tactical and conventional weapons.

Third, because of this we must press ahead with the Vienna negotiations on mutual balanced force reductions (MBFR) as an important step toward a better balance of military power in Europe.

No one can deny that the principle of parity is a sensible one. However, its fulfilment must be the aim of all arms-limitation and arms-control negotiations and it must apply to all categories of weapons. Neither side can agree to diminish its security unilaterally.

It is of vital interest to us all that the negotiations between the two superpowers on the limitation and reduction of nuclear strategic weapons should continue and lead to a lasting agreement. The nuclear powers have a special, an overwhelming responsibility in this field. On the other hand, we in Europe must be particularly careful to ensure that these negotiations do not neglect the components of NATO's deterrence strategy.

We are all faced with the dilemma of having to meet the moral and political demand for arms limitation while at the same time maintaining a fully effective deterrent to war. We are not unaware that both the United States and the Soviet Union must be anxious to remove threatening strategic developments from their relationship. But strategic arms limitations confined to the United States and the Soviet Union will inevitably impair the security of the West European members of the [Western] Alliance vis-à-vis Soviet military superiority in Europe if we do not succeed in removing the disparities of military power in Europe parallel to the SALT negotiations. So long as this is not the case we must maintain the balance of the full range of deterrence strategy. The Alliance must, therefore, be ready to make available the means to support its present strategy, which is still the right one, and to prevent any developments that could undermine the basis of this strategy.

At the meeting of Western heads of state and government in London last May I said that the more we stabilize strategic nuclear parity between East and West, which my government has always advocated, the greater will be the necessity to achieve a conventional equilibrium as well.

Today, again in London, let me add that when the SALT negotiations opened we Europeans did not have a clear enough view of the close connection between parity of strategic nuclear weapons, on the one hand, and tactical nuclear and conventional weapons on the other, or if we did, we did not articulate it clearly enough. Today we need to recognize clearly the connection between SALT and MBFR and to draw the necessary practical conclusions.

At the same meeting in May I said that there were, in theory, two possible ways of establishing a conventional balance with the Warsaw Pact states. One would be for the Western Alliance to undertake a massive buildup of forces and weapons systems; the other for both NATO and the Warsaw Pact to reduce their force strength and achieve an overall balance at a lower level. I prefer the latter.

The Vienna negotiations have still not produced any concrete agreement. Since they began the Warsaw Pact has, if anything, increased the disparities in both conventional and tactical nuclear forces. Up to now the Soviet Union has given no clear indication that she is willing to accept the principle of parity for Europe, as she did for SALT, and thus make the principle of renunciation of force an element of the military balance as well.

Until we see real progress on MBFR, we shall have to rely on the effectiveness of deterrence. It is in this context and no other that the public discussion in all member states of the Western Alliance about the "neutron weapon" has to be seen. We have to consider whether the "neutron weapon" is of value to the Alliance as an additional element of the deterrence-strategy, as a means of preventing war. But we should not limit ourselves to that examination. We should also examine what relevance and weight this weapon has in our efforts to achieve arms control.

For the first time in history arms-control negotiations are being conducted when there exists a weapon capable of destroying all living things. Failure of such negotiations can no longer be compensated for by banking on military victory. That is why it is of such crucial importance that all should realize the seriousness of the Vienna negotiations, and why results must be achieved there. I would like to list seven "musts" and "must nots" for these negotiations:

1. Both sides, all participants in the MBFR negotiations, must state their willingness to bring the negotiations to a positive conclusion and to be party to reductions on an equal basis.
2. Priority must be given to the aim—and it must be achieved without delay—of preventing any further increase in the military confrontation, and thus dispelling apprehensions.
3. The threat of a surprise attack must be eliminated.
4. The confidence-building measures voluntarily agreed on at the CSCE [Conference on Security and Cooperation in Europe] must be accepted with binding effect.
5. It must remain the principal objective of MBFR to achieve, by means of reductions, a balance of forces at a lower level.

With officers of the British Army of the Rhine, April 1977.

6. Force reductions must be oriented to the principle of parity and must be verifiable. Parity and collectivity must be recognized as the fundamental and determining principles.

7. The capability of both Alliance systems to organize their defense must not be impaired.

We should also consider whether it is necessary to extend the confidence-building measures beyond the agreed scope. Even if we should achieve conventional parity within the MBFR reduction area, this will still fall considerably short of parity of conventional forces in Europe as a whole. This is underlined by the fact that the Soviet Union has substantially increased her strategic reinforcement capabilities and could rapidly bring forward forces concentrated outside the reduction area whereas American forces, if reduced in MBFR, would be cut off from Europe by the Atlantic.

Since the West formulated its double strategy of deterrence and détente ten years ago, progress along the road to détente has been respectable. The *Ostpolitik* of the Federal Republic of Germany, based firmly on the Alliance, has promoted and helped to shape this development. The Quadripartite Agreement on Berlin has been another step toward stability and security in

Europe. Berlin, once a major source of crisis, is not the problem it was. Security in Europe has been reinforced by bilateral agreements in which the parties undertake not to resort to force.

The American commitment to Europe no longer stems solely from rights and obligations arising from World War II. Rather, that commitment rests on the security interests of the United States and Western Europe alike. The Soviet Union and her allies have explicitly recognized this fact by putting their signatures to the Final Act of the CSCE in Helsinki. For us in Germany, the German question remains open; we are called upon to achieve the reunification of Germany. But the German question cannot, and must not, have priority over peace. This is a contribution of the Federal Republic of Germany to stability in Europe.

WORLD ECONOMY AND SECURITY

The need for deterrence and détente cannot, however, detract from the fact that a sound economy—and for me this includes full employment just as much as social justice—is the foundation of all security. This is true in two ways: unless our economy flourishes we can maintain neither the military equilibrium nor the stability of our free and democratic institutions. The Western economies have been profoundly shaken by the serious recession following worldwide inflation, the collapse of the international monetary system, and the oil crisis. Today our primary task is to restabilize the economic foundations of the democratic state and thus not least the foundations of our common security policy. Let me stress what Henry Kissinger said in his 1976 Alastair Buchan Memorial lecture before this Institute: "A world that cries out for economic advance, for social justice, for political liberty and for a stable peace needs our collective commitment and contribution."[2]

Today, just as in the immediate aftermath of World War II, the economic and military aspects of our security policy are again on a par with each other. In 1947 George Marshall called for a working economy to establish the political and social conditions under which free institutions can exist. That task presents itself anew today under different conditions. Since the end of World War II the Western democracies, favored by constant economic growth, have experienced the full effects of democratic equality; they have transformed themselves into open societies with more social justice. For the individual citizen, the state is today the guarantor of social security and social justice. Never before has the working population had so large a share of the nation's economic prosperity.

We have to ask ourselves, however, whether this redistribution process has not cut profits unreasonably and thus caused the decline in investment and capital expenditures in recent years. One cause of our economic problem—that of insufficient investment and capital expenditure—lies, I believe, in the greater risks for companies arising from the faster rate at which the world economic structure is changing, rising oil and energy prices, and the partial saturation of important markets in the industrial countries.

Owing to the development of the social security network, public expenditure in this area has risen at a faster rate from year to year than the gross national product. Today we have, I believe, reached the load limit in many of our countries, at least for the time being.

On top of this, the developing countries are stepping up their demands on the Western industrial world. They demand both full control over their raw materials and higher prices, they demand more development aid, they demand the biggest possible share of the benefits of Western investment in the Third World, and they demand unrestricted access for their industrial products into our markets. In the last analysis, these are claims on the gross national product of the Western industrial countries.

For years the Western countries have been exposed to the pressure of inflation, the result of excessive demands on their GNP. It was the monetary crisis of 1971 that exposed challenges, which existed earlier, in concrete form. In the following years inflation was fueled by an unprecedented boom in the commodity sector, and ultimately by the price policy of the OPEC cartel. All this led to a structural upheaval in the global balances of payment network, to a structural upheaval in world trade, in world demand, and thereby in employment.

The dangers of inflation are still with us today. Throughout the world, the days of cheap energy and raw materials are over: prices are very likely to continue to rise in real terms, and this means relative to the price of the goods which the industrial countries manufacture and export.

The answer to our problems cannot lie in dismantling our social achievements, in rolling back social progress. The stability of liberal democracy depends on the extent to which we can secure greater social justice. If the Federal Republic of Germany is today enjoying considerable stability it is because she has made social justice a broad reality.

There are three problems which the West will have to resolve in the economic sector, not least for the sake of its security.

The first is to construct and safeguard a liberal, flexible, and hence working world economic system. The international economic order we created after 1945 enabled the Western democracies—and also some developing countries—to expand their economies at a speed and with a constancy which have no parallel in economic history. Through their free trade and capital transactions the Western countries have grown more and more into one vast market. The ever-increasing international division of labor was, and still is, the main source of progress and prosperity. National economies have thus become increasingly interdependent. But this interdependence, of a hitherto unknown degree, has not only provided stronger impulses for growth in an expanding world economy, but has also now led to greater inflation and recession. The effects of the world recession have been greatest for those countries whose economic structure is least flexible and whose political management has been least able to adjust to the new situation. This crisis has deepened the disparities between the Western countries. It has exacerbated the divergence of rates of inflation and created payments imbalances which have grown steadily worse.

The recession has thus become a great threat to our world economic system: the tendency to try to solve problems unilaterally with protectionist measures has increased and is increasing daily. We must ward off this threat in a united effort.

Protectionism offers no solutions. World economic interdependence has led to a synchronization of economic fluctuations between all nations. Where, as in the countries of Western Europe, exports in important branches of industry account for half or more of total production, no single country can free itself from the vortex of world economic recession by its own efforts. In practice, nations have lost their economic autonomy. An attempt to return to unilateral national measures would be disastrous. The only way out is through closer economic cooperation.

The Western democracies are about to embark on this road. Since the beginning of the recession we have successfully intensified our efforts to coordinate economic policy. We have agreed to pursue growth and full employment without repeating the old inflationary mistakes.

To achieve this consensus is essential. Let me make this point clear: there are no economic panaceas which can be recommended to, or prescribed for, governments by majority decisions, as it were. Each government must, in consultation with its partners, take those steps which take into account the special situation of its country.

In this joint effort a major aim must be to restore foreign trade equilibrium. The present payments imbalances originate only partly from the oil price explosion. In the three years of 1974–76, the accumulated OPEC surplus amounted to 145 billion U.S. dollars, whereas the deficit countries were in the red on current account to the amount of 210 billion. The oil price explosion can, therefore, explain only part of the deterioration of the global balance of payments network.

The current account deficits of the oil-consuming industrial and developing countries in relation to OPEC cannot be rectified by traditional instruments of adjustment. The prime remedy is to consume less oil. Other measures are the development of alternative sources of energy and the stepping up of exports to the oil-exporting countries in line with their own development and the increase in their capacity to absorb goods from the industrial oil consumers.

In the meantime we must provide adequate facilities for financing these deficits but in a way which does not delay the reduction of non-oil deficits. The creation of the Witteveen facility is an important step to this end.

Today, the structural modification caused by the progressive international division of labor coincides with other structural changes, such as in demand, or technical changes on the supply side. This has no doubt led to an aggravation of the employment situation and a strengthening of protectionist forces.

However, we must realize that trade policy cannot serve as a national instrument for creating jobs. Such a solution could only have short-term success — that is, only until such time as the trade partners take countermeasures. These considerations apply to Europe in particular. The European Community, being the world's biggest exporter and importer, depends on open markets. To yield to protectionist temptations would be suicidal for Europe.

Markets must be kept open for industrial exports from the Third World as well. The Western countries need cooperation with the Third World on a basis of trust, and it is in their own uppermost interest to integrate the developing countries fully into the system of world trade.

What is more, in view of saturation in our own markets, the markets of the developing countries with their unlimited demand potential could become an important pillar of our future growth. However, if one wants to export one must import as well. We should therefore enable the developing countries, by more imports and greater transfers of capital, to buy more from us.

The OECD countries have so far, on the whole, withstood the temptation of protectionism and kept their markets open. This success is of crucial importance. It contrasts our present situation with that of the 1930s when the Western countries, by destroying free world trade, drove each other into a state of permanent depression and permanent unemployment.

As far as my own country is concerned, we are resolved to continue to keep our markets open. On July 1, 1977, the West-European Free Trade Zone was implemented. It is the world's largest free trade area for industrial products. The open system of world trade must be maintained.

ACCESS TO RAW MATERIALS

The second major task which confronts us is to ensure our raw material and energy supplies. Let us bear in mind that whereas the Eastern industrial countries are self-sufficient as a group, at least in raw material and energy supplies for the time being, the West, apart from foodstuffs, consumes more raw materials and oil than it produces. The Western countries depend on massive imports from the Third World.

There are thus two sources of danger for our raw material supplies. These supplies can be endangered, for one thing, by the outbreak of war or civil war in Third World regions and, for another, by insufficient production due to insufficient investment in the Third World.

We have all been conscious of the first source of danger since the Middle East war of 1973 and the oil crisis. Another region which is of vital importance to the security of our raw material supplies and which has become a trouble spot in international affairs is southern Africa.

Conflicts in the Third World give the Soviet Union an opportunity to expand her influence. Imagine the implications for Western economic security if the Soviet Union, with South Africa and Rhodesia as her allies, were to monopolize, for example, world chromium supplies. To avert the dangers arising out of Third World instability the West has to pursue a policy aimed at the peaceful solution of conflicts and a peaceful conciliation of interests in those regions.

The conflicts in the Middle East and southern Africa have long attracted the attention of Western foreign policy. The United States is making every effort to mediate in the Israel-Arab conflict. Europe supports this by an effort of its own and by its willingness to play an active part in the economic reconstruction and development of the region following a peace settlement. In Rhodesia, London and Washington in particular are trying to bring about a peaceful transfer of power to the black majority; in Namibia the five Western members of the Security Council are trying to find a solution. The Federal Republic of Germany is playing an active part there. The Western powers are endeavoring to convince South Africa of the need for fundamental and rapid reforms.

Even if political stability can be assured, however, one can only import what has been previously produced. Here lies the second source of danger for our raw material supplies.

Raw material investment in developing countries is no longer financed and promoted as it once was. In the mining sector in particular, exploration and prospecting in the Third World have largely come to a standstill. There can be no doubt about the long-term consequences. Henry Kissinger warned at UNCTAD IV against an explosion of raw material costs — he should rather have said prices — should the current investment trends continue. The lead-time for large-scale mining projects is six to eight years and sometimes more. In other words, the said danger to our raw material supplies does not hit us today — but it is today that we must act.

The indispensable cooperation between industrial and developing countries in the exploitation of raw material resources must be restored and intensified. To provide stable and close cooperation between industrialized and developing countries it is, I believe, necessary and justified that guarantees for those private investments should be given by the host countries. This should become a general rule and, in the framework of the North-South dialogue, a necessary quid pro quo.

How should we ensure our energy supplies? If there is a cardinal problem for the economic security of the West, it is that of energy. More than half of the Western world's energy requirements are at present being met by mineral oil. But we must face a fact which no policy can change: this is the exhaustion of world oil reserves which is now becoming apparent. Recent studies by the

OECD, M.I.T. [Massachusetts Institute of Technology] and EXXON agree that predictable oil supplies may not even suffice to cover requirements in the 1980s. And I am afraid this fundamental fact will not be notably changed even by the new oil fields which you in Britain have discovered in the North Sea.

The main consequence is that the wasteful use of energy, of which we have made a habit, must stop. We must be quick to make decisive progress on energy conservation and the development of new types of energy.

In this situation the industrial countries cannot afford to forego any option for energy policy. This is particularly true for nuclear energy. But I would add that a key role in this respect falls to the United States who uses half of the energy consumed by the Western world. It is therefore in our interest that President Carter should be successful with his energy conservation program.

TRADE WITH THE EAST

The third major task of Western security policy in economic terms is to establish balanced and stable economic relations with the communist state trading countries of the East.

Since 1970 East-West trade has practically quadrupled. The Federal Republic of Germany is the most important Western trade partner of each of the communist Eastern countries. This strong intensification of trade and cooperation is the result of political détente and also of the economic interests of both sides. The economies of the communist East have reached a stage of development where their growth also depends more and more on an increase in productivity. That is why the East has a strong and lasting interest in importing Western technology.

The East, due to its large potential of raw materials and energy, affords the West the possibility of diversifying, to a certain extent, its raw material and energy imports. At the same time it offers markets which are especially attractive for the West because they are not, or not fully, involved in the synchronization of Western business cycles. In 1975, for instance, due to the world recession, German exports dropped by almost 4 percent in nominal terms whereas the exports to the Soviet Union rose by 46 percent, thus making a valuable contribution toward improved use of capacities and a better employment situation in my country.

Who, then, derives the greater benefit from East-West trade? There are critics in the West who say that the West, by its technology exports, indirectly helps the Soviet military buildup. Critical voices in the East will probably object that helping the West to preserve jobs is supporting the capitalist system. I believe that these conflicting arguments in themselves indicate that East-West trade benefits both sides. And so, after all, it should and must be.

A couple of decades ago the American writer Ambrose Bierce said, "Calamities are of two kinds: misfortune to ourselves and good fortune to others." I do not think that this applies in modern economic conditions of interdependence. I would say today: economic misfortune to others will cause calamity to ourselves. And good fortune to others will also cause good fortune to ourselves.

If the Western countries act jointly, the development of trade relations and of industrial cooperation with the East can, I am convinced, be essential for both our own economic security and the safeguarding of peace.

Another urgent task I have often mentioned is to get the East to assume a constructive role in the North-South issue. So far, the Soviet Union and her allies have supported verbally the demands of the developing countries, but as regards financial support they have been trying to pin the responsibility entirely on the West. The development aid of the East is negligible compared with its economic potential, and even more so compared with Western contributions. In 1976, for instance, the amount of official development assistance transferred by the Federal Republic of Germany alone was two and a half times as high as the total transfer made by the Soviet Union plus all the other Eastern bloc countries together. Or to give you another example: the official development assistance of all the OECD countries in 1976 was twenty-seven times as high as that of the Comecon countries including the Soviet Union.

The integration of the Eastern countries into the world economic system has already progressed so far that they can feel the direct impact of inflation and recession in the Western industrial countries. They should recognize, therefore, that world economic stability is in their own interest. But this stability, and ultimately the stability of world peace, can no longer be ensured unless hunger and distress in the Third World are overcome. This is a goal which requires the joint efforts of all industrial countries. The Eastern bloc countries can no longer retain the role of disinterested onlookers in the North-South dialogue, limiting their support to the supply of military weapons.

TERRORISM

Finally, let me say a few words about the deep shock we have all felt over the last four weeks as a result of terrorist action. The focal point of the events themselves was my country, but from day to day it became increasingly clear to people in all corners of the world that terrorism is not a problem of exclusively German concern but an international problem of global dimension.

In my country, we have experienced with gratitude what it means in such a situation when other countries rally round with advice, with active assistance. And it has been an exercise and a very fine experience in practical solidarity. During those days, gestures were made, I feel, for cooperation among the world's nations and for a common stand, a common effort to overcome the plague of international terrorism with its contempt for human life and with its aim of destroying democratic society.

I would like to express the hope that this terrible experience will prompt the United Nations to adopt quickly the convention which we have proposed against the taking of hostages. Nobody today can any longer make light of terrorist violence as the work of people who have simply been led astray by allegedly political motives, and on top of that grant them political asylum. Jonathan Carr in the *Financial Times* wrote the other day: "The German terrorist cannot really be classed with any political wing. If they can be compared to anything it is to Dostoievski's devils, people who by their own admission are ready even to throw acid into a child's face if it will help their cause. What is that cause? Beyond destroying society it is impossible to say."[3] I think he is right. Moreover, the effect is not only on domestic politics. In extreme circumstances terrorism might even trigger off international conflict.

Therefore, we should act together to confront the blindness of terrorist killers with the steadfastness of our democratic convictions. Let us together continue to defend human dignity and human rights as inviolable and inalienable values; and let us defend the right to live and to enjoy personal freedom, rights we all identify as inalienable principles.

Ladies and gentlemen, I have tried to outline the dimensions of a policy aimed at establishing and maintaining a state of affairs in which our free democratic institutions can survive and prosper.

The industrial democracies of the West produce 65 percent of the world's goods and their share in world trade is 70 percent. They are the motive force of world economic growth and technological progress. The power and moral superiority of our belief in the freedom and dignity of man is evident.

This is why, inspired by a constructive will for reform, all of us endeavor perpetually to renew democracy. Only in this way can we remove weaknesses, obsolete conditions, and injustices.

The industrial democracies of the world must further intensify their cooperation: in the European Community, in the Atlantic Community, and in the Trilateral Community formed by Europe, North America, and the Pacific region embracing Japan, Australia, and New Zealand. This cohesion is of crucial importance for peace, for economic growth, and for the cause of freedom, justice, and human dignity.

No less decisive, however, is the relationship between the two big powers, because on them depends how much of the surface of our globe will be covered by the policy of détente and to what extent its substance will be strengthened by a policy aimed at preserving peace. We feel encouraged by the statements made by the two leading personalities of both sides.

Jimmy Carter gave the assurance that in the search for world peace the United States will be found in the forefront and stand by her commitment to the freedom of man. The following passage from his speech before the United Nations on October 4, 1977, appears to me to be of particular significance.

We must look beyond the present, and work to prevent the critical threats and in-stabilities of the future. If the principles of self-restraint, reciprocity and mutual accommodation of interests are observed, then the United States and the Soviet Union will not only succeed in limiting weapons, but will also create a foundation for better relations in other spheres of interests.[4]

Leonid Brezhnev said early this year:

The allegations that the Soviet Union goes beyond its defense requirements and is seeking military superiority to be able to deal the first blow are malicious and un-founded.

And in the same speech Brezhnev rightly stated, "There is no more burning and vital task than that of making peace durable and indestructible." He added, "As far as the Soviet Union is concerned, we shall not be found want-ing."[5]

In our quest for security and peace in Europe and worldwide, we shall take the two statesmen by their word. For, in the last resort, the survival of mankind depends on the strengthening of world peace.

NOTES

1. *Power and Equilibrium in the 1970s* (London and New York: Praeger, 1972). The Russell C. Leffingwell Lectures, 1972.

2. "The 1976 Alastair Buchan Memorial Lecture," *Survival*, Vol. XVIII (Sept./Oct. 1976):194. (Published by the International Institute for Strategic Studies, London.)

3. *The Financial Times*, October 24, 1977, p. 16.

4. Address by President Carter to the UN General Assembly, October 4, 1977 (USIS).

5. Leonid Brezhnev, "Outstanding Exploit of the Defenders of Tula," *Pravda*, January 19, 1977.

3

A Policy of Reliable Partnership

(Spring 1981)

The beginning of the 1980s has been difficult, and the problems will be mounting as the decade goes on. Judging from the experience of the past year, the Western democracies' firmness, their resolve to stand their ground, and their willingness to cooperate will be tested, above all, in the following areas:

(1) *Confrontation and cooperation between East and West.* With its arms buildup the Soviet Union has been departing from the principle of military balance. In Afghanistan it has provoked the entire community of nations. At the same time, though, it is apparent that General-Secretary Brezhnev wants to keep the door to talks and negotiations open.

(2) *Independence and nonalignment of the Third World nations.* Today these are decisive factors in the world's political balance. They are, however, threatened by unsettled political conflicts, the taking of East-West confrontation to the Third World, and by the disastrous consequences of the oil price explosion and unchecked population growth.

(3) *The structure of a working world economy.* The consequences of the oil price explosion on the world economy affect all nations: in the West, and East, and above all the developing countries. They limit almost every government's room for maneuver in the areas of economic policy and finances. In many countries they are endangering social and political stability. In the process of the necessary reconciliation of differing economic interests, the danger of conflicts and tensions is growing within nations and in international relations.

In this situation there is little on which we can depend in shaping our policy. There are no simple solutions. The search for stability, or at the least calculability or dependability, has been a continual theme in the statements of all politicians at the beginning of this year. At the same time, though, we know that, again and again, political and military balance, as well as economic

Reprinted by permission from *Foreign Affairs* 59 (Spring 1981):743–755.

stability, must be reestablished, that conflicts must be contained or settled in rapidly changing circumstances, and that all nations must soon jointly tackle the great challenges to the future of mankind in spite of all conflicts dividing them.

In the final analysis, stability will only be possible in the unsteady world situation in the 1980s to the extent that governments and politicians, but also businessmen, bankers, and working people, can depend on each other's calculability. In view of the dual threat of nuclear catastrophe on the one hand, and economic and ecological catastrophe on the other, it will be of vital importance that nations and governments do not allow themselves to be swayed from a steady and moderate course by conflicts and tensions which are often of only artificial topicality.

                                          II

The most important factor contributing to stability is and remains the partnership between Europeans and Americans. This historic partnership remains a constant of our policy. Our basic foreign policy orientation is not negotiable. Our American and our European friends as well as our partners the world over can depend on it. In addition, on no occasion have I left any doubt about this point in the minds of the Soviet leaders. In a ceremony at the Paulskirche on the occasion of the bicentennial celebration of the United States I said:

> German-American friendship and alliance . . . have been a major and to us very tangible and lasting achievement in those thirty years. It is at the same time one of the factors that has helped maintain world stability, a factor which everyone can rely on and — with reference to third quarters — has to reckon with.

The European-American partnership, and thus the alliance founded on it, to us is not just a matter of power politics. To be sure, that is part of it. The Atlantic Alliance and partnership, however, above all reflect the fact that a community of nations shares the same fate — a fact which no politician could ignore even if he wished to do so. I should like to quote from my speech in the Paulskirche once more:

> Apart from our historical and cultural ties, it is above all the human links that have engendered on both sides of the Atlantic that large measure of identity of political and social values that is today the solid foundation of our friendship.

Thus not only we Germans but all West European allies welcome the new self-confidence and determination which are becoming apparent in the United States. After the American elections, President Giscard d'Estaing and I, as well as the other heads of government in the European Council, were agreed that

With President Ronald Reagan, Oval Office, the White House, May 1981.

Europeans could not but be happy to see an America which is determined to accept its international responsibilities to the full.

We Europeans are aware that only in its alliance with Western Europe can the United States meet its responsibility as a world power. America's political and military presence in Europe is an indispensable condition not only for the security of West Europeans but also for the American role as a world power. Only in close cooperation, mobilizing each partner's potential for the common cause, will Europeans and Americans be able to make their contributions to the world's political and economic balance.

We know from our own experience that it is difficult enough to set and maintain a clear foreign policy course within a democratic system. A parliamentary consensus and acceptance by various social groups often depend on factors other than foreign policy interests. This also applies to foreign policy cooperation among democracies. Basic national trends which influence elections and government opinion are sometimes in opposition to each other. Pacifist tendencies, national protest, isolationism, or neutralism can occur simultaneously in different countries. The human weakness of blaming others can easily become a national tendency and cloud one's view of others' achievements.

We can learn from experience: a successful partnership among democracies calls for a high degree of sensitivity to the requirements of the democratic opinion-forming process in partner countries. In addition to the demanding task of domestic leadership, leading politicians are faced with the difficult task of coordination and consultation outside their countries. It was therefore an encouragement to me that President Reagan, who at that time had just been elected, and I were in complete agreement on the central role of early and close consultation among allies. I was also impressed by the fairness and openness with which Secretary of State Alexander Haig and others, in Senate hearings, expounded upon the vital contribution of the allies to our common security.

I have no doubts as to the West's ability to cope with its challenges and tasks. And I see no reason to abandon the Alliance's dual strategy of defense capability and willingness to cooperate. In the fourteen years since the Harmel Report the political and military integration of the Alliance has increased. We Germans have thrown our full political and military weight into the scales of the West, in three ways:

First, through our *Ostpolitik* we have, in constant consultation with our allies, settled difficult conflicts originating in the legacy of Hitler's war of conquest. Without our treaty policy there would have been no Quadripartite Treaty on Berlin. This treaty has made a substantial contribution toward reducing the danger of a clash of the nuclear powers in the heart of Europe. It was only on this foundation that it was possible to conclude the Conference on Security and Cooperation in Europe (CSCE) in Helsinki, in opposition to the original Soviet aims, with the explicit confirmation of North America's responsibility for European, and thus also for Atlantic, security.

Second, we have increased the size of the federal armed forces to a total of 500,000, consistently raised our defense budget by about 3 percent in real terms annually, and attained the capacity to arm and have ready for combat within a few days 1.2 million trained soldiers. Today we have at our disposal more than twice as many trained soldiers, in proportion to the population, as the United States. We provide about 50 percent of NATO's land forces in central Europe. More of the Alliance's military facilities are concentrated in German territory than anywhere else. We contribute more defense aid to our partners Turkey, Greece, and Portugal than any other partner in the Alliance with the exception of the United States.

Third, along with our partners in the European Community we have made progress in working out common positions on major international issues. Western Europe's weight and influence in world affairs and its contribution to political balance between East and West have grown. The decisions by Greece, Portugal, and Spain to join the European Community also significantly strengthen democracy in Europe.

I might add that the Germans and the French as well as the other European partners are aware that the great political and economic achievements of the European Community are unthinkable without German-French cooperation—an *"entente parfaite et sans faille,"* as President Giscard called it. This was, historically, the core of the new Europe, and so it remains. The statements which President Giscard and I issued in February 1980 and again in February 1981 contain the substance of a joint foreign policy, a European contribution to today's Western policy on world affairs. What Henry Kissinger said in 1976 in his Alastair Buchan Memorial lecture is true now more than ever: "A vital and cohesive Western Europe is an irreplaceable weight on the scales of global diplomacy. American policy can only gain by having a strong partner of parallel moral purposes."

III

Western policy continues to center on maintaining a balance of military forces. The members of the Alliance are faced with the urgent task of reestablishing the balance which the Soviet Union upset through its advance in two spheres: in the Third World and through the rapid development of a new nuclear medium-range capability for which there is no adequate counterbalance on the Western side.

There is no doubt about this: our security depends, among other things, on a secure supply of energy and other raw materials. The Soviet advance in Afghanistan, Yemen, Ethiopia, and Angola affects Western security interests for which the Atlantic Treaty does not give exhaustive geographical definition.

For us Germans, however, military contributions outside the contractually defined NATO territory are subject to limitations which will be understood by everyone who is familiar with our more recent history and our constitution, which drew the appropriate conclusions from that history. As our allies know, we shall not, however, be inactive in the Alliance while other allies protect interests which we share outside the NATO area. Through an active policy of economic and political partnership, we shall moreover help the countries of the regions concerned to maintain their independence. I am thinking of our support for Pakistan or for Somalia and the nations of southern Africa.

A vital question in Europe is the implementation of the NATO dual decision of December 1979. We cannot do without the stationing of American medium-range weapons in Western Europe as long as the Soviet Union, with its new SS-20 missiles, poses a threat to the whole of Western Europe, the Mediterranean countries, and the Middle East, as well as important parts of Asia. Owing to their limited range, the SS-20s are directed not at the United States but practically only at countries which cannot reach the Soviet Union with similar weapons. Thus the Soviet Union has upset the military balance in Europe and created for itself an instrument of political pressure on the countries within the range of the SS-20, for which the West so far has no counterbalance.

The partners in the Alliance have linked the necessary decision on modernization with an offer to negotiate with the Soviet Union at the same time on limiting land-based nuclear medium-range missiles. This was done to prevent an arms race, to prevent mutual increases to higher and higher levels, which would create new dangers, provide no additional security, and demand of both sides unjustifiable economic sacrifices. The intention is to clear the path for the Soviet Union to remedy the dangerous mistake it made by upsetting the balance.

At the same time, the members of the Alliance owe it to their own public to show that they are doing everything in their power to stop the uncontrolled growth of nuclear arsenals, the dangers of which, for geographical reasons, are particularly apparent in my country. Only a policy which aims at the necessary military balance at the lowest possible level—to be agreed upon jointly—can count on the public's full approval in the countries of Western Europe. Our people expect preparation for the stationing of American medium-range weapons to be accompanied by the active implementation of the second part of the dual decision. This is why I made the following comments before the Bundestag:

> This dual decision by the Alliance is, militarily, an indispensable part of Western strategy and, politically, a test of the Alliance's solidarity. Whoever, in the current world situation, calls this dual decision or one of its two parts into question calls the Alliance into question.

Since the federal government regards the dual decision as vitally important for the security of Europe, it has strongly supported arms-control negotiations between the superpowers. It has always supported a continuation of the SALT process. During my talks in Moscow last summer the Soviets gave first indications of a willingness to respond to the NATO offer of negotiations on medium-range weapons. The talks began last fall in Geneva, and I hope and trust that they will be taken up again this year. I can only concur with President Reagan's statement in his message to Congress on February 18:

> We remain committed to the goal of arms limitation through negotiation. I hope we can persuade our adversaries to come to realistic, balanced and verifiable agreements. But, as we negotiate, our security must be fully protected by a balanced and realistic defense program.

Thinking about our security I inevitably find myself coming back to the principle of balance. An approximate balance of forces is and remains a necessary element in maintaining peace. That alone, however, is not sufficient as a condition for peace. The willingness to talk to one another and to be open to others and their interests is also necessary. That is, practically, the will to stabilize the balance politically.

In the present circumstances this approach seems to me to be promising, provided that two conditions are met: the first is basic agreement that security can only rest on the balance of forces. This precludes, as stated in the German-

French statement of February 6, 1981, "the acceptance of a position of weakness as well as the quest for military superiority." Confidence-building measures in the military sphere which we are striving for with the aid of a conference on disarmament in Europe, about which negotiations are currently being held in Madrid, could politically prop such a basic agreement. The fact that General-Secretary Brezhnev has now declared his fundamental willingness to apply such measures in all the European part of the Soviet Union represents substantial progress. The second condition is that the West give convincing signals of its determination to allow no shifting of balance in favor of the Soviet Union.

In view of the difference in political systems it is inevitable that the Soviets speculate on what must appear to them to be the weakness of Western democracy: our public debate on questions of security and defense. We can demonstrate that the democratic decision-making process also means strength. The European partners in the Alliance must give the first signal by making the necessary preparations for the implementation of the dual decision. At the same time, though, the United States must vigorously work toward arms limitation talks between the superpowers.

IV

The troubled beginning of the 1980s has made it apparent that the will for independence, self-reliance, and nonalignment has become the strongest political force in the countries of the Third World—perhaps the only one uniting them. Traditional psychological strains on their relations with the West are therefore becoming less prominent. The totally inadequate development aid by the Soviet Union, its lack of cooperation in finding peaceful solutions to conflicts, and above all its invasion of Afghanistan have opened the eyes of many in the Third World. This important political and psychological turning point in the developing countries is, at the same time, a confirmation for the West that it is on the right path with a policy of equal partnership as well as with its material aid, its political support for peaceful solutions to conflicts, and its active participation in the United Nations. It is now up to us to increase and turn to best advantage this political capital, which we have accumulated at the price of great effort and material sacrifice.

The Western democracies' status and prestige in the countries of the Third World are not simply a function of East-West confrontation. We need not allow the Soviet Union and its helpers to dictate how we are to act. There is no reason at all for us to share the burden of the Soviet Union's inappropriate development policy, for example by unnecessarily putting the label of East-West confrontation on conflicts in Third World countries. We must respect the Third World countries' desire for nonalignment as well as their will to bring about genuine reforms. This is in keeping with our own conception of worldwide cooperation in partnership. It does not preclude the possibility of Western democracies helping their partners in the Third World to safeguard their state of nonalignment through their own defense capability. But the decisive contribution of the Western democracies to worldwide partnership must be made in the field of worldwide economic cooperation and by providing political assistance in the peaceful settlement of regional conflicts.

We Germans were delighted over the happy solution to the hostage affair in Tehran and appreciate the recognition which our contribution to the release of the hostages found in America. But this was a solution to only one of the many conflicts standing in the way of worldwide cooperation in partnership. I think that the Western democracies' position and influence in the world can be used even more systematically to contain conflicts and find peaceful solutions to them. We have not yet exhausted the means of cooperation—in the international organizations, in coordinated bilateral action, and, particularly, by sharing the load of responsibility. Here, too, credible support for the independence and self-reliance of Third World nations will stand us in good stead.

Support in the development of regional structures for economic cooperation and security seems to me to be especially important. This offers, in the long run, the best prospects for effectively containing regional conflicts and keeping alien powers out of them. Here Western Europe can offer the benefit of its own experience. Economic cooperation between the European Economic Community and the Association of Southeast Asian Nations (ASEAN), for example, is now being supplemented by consultation and the intensive exchange of political views. The wide network of cooperation agreements between the EEC and most Third World countries also opens up channels of political communication. In southern Africa we now have the chance, after Zimbabwe, to help Namibia also to achieve independence. With their diplomacy in the framework of the United Nations, the five Western countries have made substantial progress. They should now carry on their efforts even more vigorously.

In the Middle East, Americans and Europeans have built up close relations with all of the nations of a region whose political stability plays a central role in the supply of energy and in the world's political balance. I cannot predict if and when the rigid fronts in the Middle East conflict will become more flexible. But I think the time will come for Americans and Europeans to consider together how, through concerted, if not necessarily identical, diplomatic action they can contribute to a comprehensive, just, and lasting peace settlement.

V

In the world economy we must cope with the fact that the OPEC nations achieved a balance-of-payments surplus of more than $100 billion last year, which means that the other nations had a deficit of the same magnitude.

As a result, signs of crisis are perceptible in all industrial countries: marketing and trade difficulties, problems of financing, protectionist tendencies, and, above all, unemployment. Everywhere we are faced with the need for painful structural changes, for an expensive adjustment to alternative production techniques conserving energy and raw materials and to new energy sources, as well as meeting the requirements of a worldwide division of labor. If we do not now resist the temptation to isolate ourselves with our problems and to seek refuge in protectionist formulas, we will be in danger of drifting together into a world economic crisis of unknown dimensions.

First priority should therefore be given to the task of maintaining a working world economy. The Western industrial nations will very soon have to coordinate their policy in that field. But in the long run this coordinating mechanism is not enough. The oil-exporting nations must be involved, above all Saudi Arabia, whose annual current-accounts surplus of $40 billion indicates its position as the world's largest energy supplier and creditor. The Soviet Union, too, as a large industrial nation will not be able to remain in splendid isolation but, increasingly, will have to face its responsibility for the world economy (as well as its moral and economic obligations to the developing countries). After all, Poland's economic problems are not only a result of domestic factors.

Those who are most severely affected by the structural crisis of the world economy, however, are the oil-importing developing countries. According to estimates by the International Monetary Fund, the current-accounts deficit of these countries will grow from slightly over $62 billion in 1980 to almost $70 billion in 1981. This means that the total amount of development aid (ODA) by the Western industrial nations can only play an inadequate role. In 1980 it amounted to slightly over $23.5 billion while the annual increase in the developing countries' oil bill from 1979 to 1980 amounted to almost $24 billion. Moreover, there are the catastrophic effects of too-rapid population growth in many of these countries. That which in the industrial countries leads to unemployment, painful structural change, and problems in economic growth means increased hunger and starvation in the developing countries.

We regard overcoming hunger and want and promoting the economic development of disadvantaged regions of the world as both a humanitarian necessity and a necessary contribution toward securing peace on a long-term basis. There are no simple formulas for future cooperation between North and South, nor for the North-South dialogue. This dialogue must, above all, see things as they are. This leads to the following priorities:

(1) No nation in the world can refuse its share of common responsibility, neither the developing countries, nor the state trading countries of Eastern Europe, nor the oil-producing countries, nor the large Western industrial nations.

(2) A solution to energy problems is of vital importance. Here the OPEC countries are called upon not only to make direct investments, to provide grants and make contributions to the recycling process, but also to be willing to engage in a dialogue between oil producers and consumers. The industrial countries are called upon to cut down on the use of oil and develop and utilize new energy sources and technologies.

(3) Population growth control is unavoidable. We cannot hope to ensure a life in dignity for six billion people in twenty years or for ten billion people thirty years later.

(4) Official aid by the industrial nations continues to be necessary. Equally important, however, is private investment, at the same time the most effective instrument for the transfer of technology. And still far more important is the progressive integration of the developing countries in international trade relations which, in turn, requires the willingness of the industrial nations for structural change in their own countries.

(5) Equally important is the willingness of the developing regions for multilateral cooperation.

These questions are to be discussed at the proposed North-South summit meeting in Mexico. That summit should not negotiate, nor should it be considered a matter of political prestige. What it should do is clarify political priorities among heads of government and provide political impulses for a realistic North-South dialogue.

VI

Ten years ago . . . I wrote the following on East-West relations: "Not unlike President Nixon, the Bonn government is also trying to 'build agreement upon agreement' without in any way deluding itself that this could be a process easily or speedily accomplished." In February of 1980—after Afghanistan—President Giscard and I had to conclude that "détente would not survive another blow of this kind." A year later we repeated this in view of the situation in and around Poland. This time, unlike 1970, we were able to invoke the duty of political moderation which the Final Act of Helsinki imposes on all signatory nations. It has now become a resource for all Europeans in East and West.

After the experiences of the last ten years we must conclude that West-East policy still contains elements of confrontation which require great vigilance. However, it also contains essential elements of cooperation which make the dialogue seem promising. In practical terms this means cooperation on the foundation of a balance of military forces. I should like to expound on this in the light of the experiences of the difficult past year.

Last summer I went to Moscow because I was convinced that, particularly in times of crisis, contact must not be lost. I made it very clear to the political leaders in the Kremlin where we Germans stand and what our views are. I was able to do this because our positions had been previously coordinated with our partners in the Alliance. I listened and tried to gain an impression of the persons involved and of political opinion making in the Kremlin. It was my impression that the understanding of the leaders in the Kremlin for the long-term tasks of world economic and political cooperation is growing. The present generation of leaders in the Kremlin is still aware, from its own experience, of what war means. My conclusion is that, precisely because relations are difficult and extremely complex, we need not less communication but more. A meeting between President Reagan and General-Secretary Brezhnev at the appropriate time would thus be a logical step in current East-West relations.

The German treaties of the past ten years with Moscow, Warsaw, and Prague, the Basic Treaty with the German Democratic Republic, and the Quadripartite Treaty on Berlin are, along with the Final Act of Helsinki, a strong foundation for admittedly limited yet dependable cooperation. I know from a great number of talks what this means for the citizens of the countries of Eastern Europe. It also means a great deal for a nation and a divided people in Germany's geographical and political situation. A leading statesman from the Third World wrote the following to me after a visit to the Federal Republic of Germany last year:

> Soviet armed forces on the FRG's borders for the last 35 years have taught the Germans to adopt a foreign policy that does not oscillate between arrogant assertiveness and humiliating acquiescence. As a result many people have come to recognize that the FRG can be depended on to chart a firm middle course, one that eases East-West person-person and state-state relations, without tilting the balance in favor of the Soviets in the longer run.

My conclusion is that treaties and agreements between East and West can lead to admittedly limited, but, as a whole, dependable cooperation between treaty partners.

Economic exchange with the East is in the interest of both sides. There is truly little danger of one-sided dependence: only some 2 percent of our exports go to the Soviet Union. Our volume of trade with Switzerland, for example, is twice as great as that with the Soviet Union.

In the longer term, I regard two considerations as important: First, cooperation in energy policy which can reduce Western Europe's heavy dependence on the Middle East and concentrate the interest of the Soviet Union on Siberia's sizable gas and oil reserves. In this connection it goes without saying that we do not want to exchange one kind of dependence for another. Second, gradually bringing the Soviet Union to accept its share of responsibility for a working world economy and a reconciliation of interests between industrial and developing countries.

My conclusion is that carefully balanced economic partnership is in the interest of both sides.

VII

We will only be able to meet the challenges of the 1980s effectively if we orient our policy, beyond the necessities of day-to-day politics, on the longer term standard of reliable partnership.

This policy of reliable partnership begins with and is based on cooperation among democracies. It should help us to translate the internal strength of democracy into effective foreign policy. I, for my part, have never shared the fainthearted belief that democracies, in their foreign policy, must always vacillate between unpolitical credulity and the equally unpolitical demand for punishment of the other side. In a democracy, too, one can understand that world politics is always power politics, especially between nations which are rivals in their political convictions, social structure, and size.

I appreciate the fact that President Reagan has repeatedly promised frequent and close consultations with the allies. It would also be desirable to agree on a global concept for Western policy, with shared responsibilities, to face the challenges of the 1980s.

Finally, reaching beyond the necessary confrontation, I think the elements of cooperation which have been built up in the last ten years with the Soviet Union and its allies must be developed further. Thus we must carefully see to it that longer-term chances for cooperation are not spoiled by the necessary short-term confrontation or even tests of strength. This is why I believe that, in addition to the further development of contractual and economic cooperation—on the basis of balance—we should also take to heart the elements of international crisis management which I named in May 1978 before the United Nations:

— avoiding provocation;
— clearly explaining to the other side the choices and options open to us;
— defusing dangerous situations through willingness to compromise;
— enabling those involved to save face.

4

Speech Before the Tenth Special General Assembly of the United Nations

(May 26, 1978)

Mr. President,

I consider it a particular privilege to address this august assembly today under your distinguished presidency. Our two countries enjoy cordial and friendly relations and we are happy to see you at the helm of the important work of the United Nations General Assembly this year already for a third time. My delegation is, therefore, confident that this special session will come to a mutually agreed and satisfactory close.

1. INTRODUCTION

On behalf of my country and its people I wish to say: it is our desire and we are doing everything in our power to make it come true that the nations of the earth will find their way to lasting peace. We sincerely desire peace because we have experienced two world wars which claimed millions of victims. We desire peace because we are most directly affected by the fact that large areas of the world are suffering from military conflicts.

The Federal Republic of Germany, therefore, welcomes the fact that the United Nations by convening this special session of the General Assembly are making the world more deeply aware of the dangers of the arms race. We have supported the initiative of the nonaligned countries from the very beginning. The United Nations are thus intensifying the efforts to achieve disarmament and arms control, subjects which have been on the agenda at this forum for the past thirty-two years.

I am speaking on behalf of a country that cannot and will not act as a big power. We are, however, aware of our share of the responsibility for peace.

The treaties we have concluded have in many ways made manifest in binding form our renunciation of force.

2. NUCLEAR WEAPONS AND PEACE

With the invention of nuclear weapons, mankind has entered a new age. It is fundamentally different from all previous ages. The revolution in military strategy brought about by the nuclear weapons has created new conditions for war and peace.

Every conflict between states or alliances equipped with nuclear weaponry therefore implies a risk that has no equivalent in history.

Nor is that risk confined to parties to a conflict but it threatens their neighbors and whole continents, and, in the extreme case of a global war with nuclear means of mass destruction, the entire planet — predictably with catastrophic consequences for several generations.

Ever since, we have lived with a system of mutual nuclear deterrence of the superpowers. Three and a half decades of nuclear peace do not yet give a final answer to the question how peace without fear can be achieved.

This is too short a span of time to already draw conclusions of historical significance.

Yet, armed peace since 1945 has lasted in an epoch that has abounded with profound differences and conflicts of interests between those who hold nuclear power.

However, the efforts since the Second World War to achieve disarmament and arms control, which began with the Baruch plan, have fallen well short of the original expectations of the peoples.

Still, several important results have been achieved — with regard to the political nuclear test ban, the nonproliferation of nuclear weapons, and the limitation of strategic nuclear weapons. The Disarmament Decade proclaimed by the United Nations at the beginning of this decade is not without positive results.

On the other hand, the result of efforts to reduce conventional forces and armaments have so far been disappointing.

Outside the system of deterrence and the alliances protected by nuclear weapons, political conflicts since 1945 have led to a number of new wars in many parts of the world that have been fought with modern, non-nuclear weapons with great destructive power.

In the interest of peace we need today a comprehensive political partnership for security. Only in this way will it be possible to set in motion a process of genuine arms limitation and reduction. At this juncture I wish to pay my respects to President Carter for the energy and the force of conviction with which he has promoted this process.

3. BASIC ELEMENTS OF SECURITY POLICY

The concept for a more stable peace consists of four elements:

- First, a policy of political, strategic, and military balance;
- Second, a policy of détente, of conflict containment, and of reconciliation of interests;
- Third, the capacity for effective crisis management;
- Fourth, the predictability and the calculability of political and military conduct.

We know from experience, however, that in a world full of mistrust and radical conflicts there is no simple and no quick recipe for achieving these four basic elements of partnership for security on a stable basis. Disarmament can only come about where trust prevails, and trust will only develop where security prevails.

Security policy as a policy for peace must today be global in scope if it is to prove successful. Events in the Middle East, in the Eastern Mediterranean, in Africa, or in Southeast Asia concern all of us because they hamper, indeed place gravely in jeopardy, the process of détente and mutual trust which is growing slowly.

It is not enough to give our attention exclusively to nuclear weapons. Worldwide agreements among the nuclear powers themselves cannot prevent the outbreak of conventional regional wars. Such wars can escalate and culminate in a clash between the big powers.

The prohibition of the use or threat of force embodied in the Charter of the United Nations must therefore apply to all weapons, both nuclear and conventional. Whoever is the first to take up arms of whatever kind and resorts to or threatens military attack violates this prohibition. I repeat: this prohibition is comprehensive, either it applies totally or not at all. Those who try to restrict this prohibition to the first use of certain weapons must ask themselves whether they would consider an attack launched with other weapons less prohibited. Should a country which is threatened by a neighbor heavily armed with conventional weapons be less protected than others by the prohibition of the use of force?

Regional agreements on conventional forces and armaments must therefore be sought on a par and simultaneously with efforts to limit armaments in the nuclear sphere; not only in Europe but in all regions.

4. BALANCE

Balance is the most important principle from which all efforts to achieve arms control and disarmament must start. For as long as a world government with a world police force and a monopoly of weapons appears utopian, the stabilization of balance will remain our principal task. Balance is today an indispensable element of a strategy for safeguarding peace.

Attempts to reach agreement on arms limitations that are not aimed at establishing a stable balance offer little prospect of lasting success. Arms limitations must therefore serve to create a stable balance of forces at a lower level.

Though progress toward arms limitation has up to now been modest, it has brought one important strategic result at least: the superpowers have redefined their own security requirements. They no longer regard the unilateral growth of nuclear power automatically as an increase in their own security. I consider this to be a great step forward.

Insecurity will be generated if one side exposes a potential adversary to growing uncertainty. Concern about increasing inferiority or imponderabilities, fear or political miscalculation, could lead a state that, rightly or wrongly, feels inferior to panic and act irrationally. The more the awareness of this spreads and encourages governments to draw appropriate conclusions in the field of armaments the more will it be possible to gain recognition for the principle of a balance of forces.

Balance is not a one-time but a continuous task. Economic and social change can create instability and hence new dangers. This aspect must not be neglected.

Military balance need not necessarily take the shape of total arithmetical identity of all kinds of armed forces and weapons. But parity must be established overall in terms of security policy. It must also be understood and accepted psychologically as such by the peoples.

A policy of balance can by no means be confined to the military sphere. Balance must rather be sought in foreign policy, in the economic and in the social fields for the sake of domestic peace in our countries and peace between states.

5. DÉTENTE AND CONTAINMENT OF CONFLICTS

A fruitful policy of détente and the containment of political conflicts either presupposes the existence of a considerable degree of balance in terms of security policy, or it goes hand in hand with the establishment of such balance.

We have learned in Europe that there is a very close link between military security and détente. Since the Western Alliance formulated its strategy for defense *and* détente a decade ago in the Harmel Report, encouraging results have been achieved on the road to détente.

On this basis the German *Ostpolitik* has, since 1969, fundamentally improved the relationship between the Federal Republic of Germany and its Eastern neighbors in a process of normalization and reconciliation. And it has also been possible to stabilize the situation in and around Berlin.

Such efforts to reduce political conflicts must be intensified and extended to other regions. The fear that in each case the other side wants arms limitation only so that it can secure a political advance for itself can only be overcome in a long confidence-building procedure.

6. CRISIS MANAGEMENT

Even given the mutual will for balance and détente, acute, unforeseen conflicts can bring on a crisis situation. That is why the capacity for effective crisis management is necessary. It presupposes first of all that communication between the parties to a conflict is not broken off at any time. The world's statesmen must talk to one another; hence they must know each other.

Crisis management demands the political will:

- First, to avoid provocations;
- Second, to make one's own options unmistakably clear;
- Third, to defuse dangerous situations through readiness for compromise;
- Fourth, to enable those concerned to save face.

Recent history has furnished several examples of successful crisis management. I recall the Berlin crisis of 1961 and the Cuba crisis of 1962.

The mastering of those serious crises has, by the way, had a long-term effect. It has initiated the process of rethinking by the big nuclear-weapon powers and created the psychological bases for the policy of détente and disarmament. Without the experience gained in these crises, which had led for the first time to the direct confrontation of the nuclear powers, the Partial Test Ban Treaty, the Non-Proliferation Treaty, and SALT would have been difficult to achieve. The Treaty of Tlatelolco of 1967 should be numbered among these agreements. I welcome the fact that the Soviet Union has now acceded to Protocol II of this treaty.

Because even the most successful peace policy can never rule out sudden conflicts entirely we must all, by means of constantly improving methods of crisis management, ensure that conflicts remain manageable.

7. CALCULABILITY

The greater the calculability of the political and military conduct of those involved, the less the danger of acute crises. The prime condition of calculability is openness and transparency.

The anxiety about unpleasant or dangerous surprises can be considerably allayed by more transparency of the military capacities but also of the arms production. The fact that in the meantime the concrete data of the military potential on both sides are being disclosed in SALT and at the Vienna negotiations is a big step forward in building mutual confidence.

The disclosure of such force data by those concerned will make possible a reliable assessment of the military options of the other side and of its capabilities.

An unequivocal data base can generate the confidence which in due course should also permit of a verified and balanced reduction of military spending. The Federal Republic of Germany has made its contribution to the preparatory work undertaken by the Secretary General of the United Nations regarding the comparability and disclosure of military budgets.

The observance of agreements concluded must also be made transparent. One's own security is enhanced when the security requirements of others are respected in this way.

My country has in major treaties subjected itself to transparency and international inspection. This concept which is supported by our people will remain our policy.

But if in the name of peace arms control were to be abused for hegemonic power politics or for the purpose of creating a discriminatory class system of international law, it would not meet with approval. Attempts to impose restrictions on nations which had no part in bringing them about would not meet the requirements of peace.

The element of predictability, necessary for security and peace, must go far beyond the transparency of military capabilities. It must apply above all to the basic concept and the objectives of political strategies. The better future developments can be predicted, the less the danger of surprise and, as a consequence, the greater the prospects for international security. Anyone who acts unpredictably is liable to create hazards.

8. NUCLEAR ARMS LIMITATION

SALT I was the first effective limitation of nuclear arms. This limitation became feasible only because the problem of international verification could be left aside due to the existence of satellites. We hope that SALT II will soon be brought to a successful conclusion.

In the Non-Proliferation Treaty, the two great powers, too, have explicitly undertaken to reduce their nuclear armaments. We must take them by their word.

The Non-Proliferation Treaty has definitely proved valuable in limiting nuclear armaments. It has so far on the whole halted the geographical proliferation of nuclear weapons.

On the other hand, nonproliferation policy must not become an obstacle for the peaceful use of nuclear energy. To many countries not possessing sufficient sources of energy, nuclear power is indispensable. In its Article IV, the Non-Proliferation Treaty gives the signatory states an explicit assurance for the peaceful use of nuclear energy. This assurance in the treaty was the determining factor for ratification by our Parliament, and that assurance must be upheld without subtracting from it.

The growing use of nuclear energy makes it necessary, however, to strengthen international measures to prevent its misuse, and this is especially true for the use of plutonium. For this purpose effective improvements of the present nonproliferation regime must be borne by a broad international consensus. This treaty—an important instrument of the nonproliferation policy— might otherwise be jeopardized.

In acceding to the Non-Proliferation Treaty over a hundred countries have given an internationally binding commitment to renounce nuclear weapons and thereby rendered a substantial contribution to international security. By doing so they have acquired a claim which must be fulfilled.

9. ARMS LIMITATION IN EUROPE

In Europe détente has progressed considerably in the course of this decade. The treaties concluded by the Federal Republic of Germany with the countries of Eastern Europe, the Quadripartite Agreement on Berlin, and the CSCE Final Act of Helsinki have given concrete expression to the prohibition of the use or threat of force embodied in the Charter of the United Nations. There exists today a greater measure of mutual trust in Europe than at any time in past decades. This is, I hope, an encouraging experience for other regions as well. It is the result of a joint endeavor in which, apart from the two great powers, all members of the two alliances as well as the neutral and nonaligned countries of Europe have constructively participated.

Yet the fact remains that in Europe the biggest accumulations of arms and armed forces confront each other. What now needs to be done is to establish a military balance at a lower level and thus make security more stable.

At the MBFR negotiations in Vienna which began five years ago we aim, together with our allies, to establish parity by means of balanced reductions. The result of the negotiations should be common collective ceilings on both sides.

During the recent visit to my country by General-Secretary Brezhnev both sides stated—for the first time in a joint East-West declaration—that they deem it most important that neither side should seek military superiority and that approximate equality and parity suffice to safeguard defense, and here I agree with Foreign Minister Gromyko.

We consider this declaration to be a major conceptual contribution to the safeguarding of peace. The more so because the Soviet Union has shown in this declaration its willingness to discuss weapons up to now not covered by the SALT negotiations, such as medium-range missiles.

These weapons, owing to their huge destructive power, are as lethal a threat to Europe and to other regions as are the strategic intercontinental weapons to

International summit meeting, Puerto Rico, June 1976. From left to right: French President Valéry Giscard d'Estaing, Chancellor Helmut Schmidt, Japanese Prime Minister Takeo Miki, President Gerald Ford, British Prime Minister James Callaghan, Canadian Prime Minister Pierre Trudeau, Italian Prime Minister Aldo Moro.

the superpowers. They therefore cannot be ignored in a system of military balance. It is against this background too that we are studying President Giscard d'Estaing's proposals with great interest.

10. GERMAN CONTRIBUTIONS TO
INTERNATIONAL SECURITY

Considering the devastating consequences which the Second World War unleashed by Hitler had for our people and for many other European peoples, no one can doubt our existential interest in arms control and disarmament.

As far back as 1954 my country renounced the production of nuclear, biological, and chemical weapons. We agreed then that the observance of this pledge should be subject to international verification.

The Federal Republic of Germany considers the conclusion of a convention on an effective and comprehensive ban on chemical weapons to be particularly urgent. It welcomes the ongoing bilateral talks between the Soviet Union and the United States which aim at a joint initiative.

We are convinced that it is possible to work out an international verification system, including on-site inspections, which would not prejudice the legitimate interests of industry and research.

Our experience as a country which has renounced the production of chemical weapons and submitted to international control shows that such controls can be effective and without harm economically and that their cost can be reasonable.

We are ready to make our experience in this field generally available. Therefore I invite all interested states to come to the Federal Republic of Germany and see for themselves that it is possible to adequately verify a ban on production.

The Federal Republic of Germany hopes that it will soon be possible to draft a convention prohibiting all nuclear weapon tests. We are ready to participate in the seismological verification of a comprehensive test ban and to make our institutions available for this purpose.

From what I have just said you can see that my country has served the aim of maintaining stability and security through arms limitation by a broad range of different treaty commitments and that it is determined to continue to do so.

The defense contribution which the Federal Republic of Germany makes to the North Atlantic Alliance as one of its members serves the aim of security through balance. This collective defense alliance is—in view of the overall situation in Europe—indispensable for the security of my country. I wish to emphasize that my country has integrated its armed forces fully into the joint organization of the Alliance.

The North Atlantic Alliance is exclusively oriented to collective defense. A few days from now it will again demonstrate its will to secure balance and to maintain collective self-defense, but equally its will for détente and arms limitation. It is a reliable factor in the international partnership for security which I spoke of earlier on.

The European Community of the Nine, on the other hand, is a partner regarding political and economic stability. Its establishment is one regional answer to historic experience and to the challenges of our time. From the outset its establishment was one of the essential aims of the policy of my country.

11. STRENGTHENING INTERNATIONAL CONFIDENCE

In view of the obstacles in the way of rapid progress toward internationally agreed arms limitation, I think a confidence-building offensive is called for. And it is quite feasible.

The confidence-building measures contained in the Final Act of Helsinki have proved to be valuable. In my opinion they should be made binding upon all states in Europe. We therefore welcome the proposals in this direction made by the French president. Over and above this, confidence-building measures in all parts of the world could serve to improve the political climate for disarmament and arms control. They should in each case make allowance for regional conditions. Consideration should be given in this connection to the notification of military exercises, exchange visits of members of the armed forces, and invitations to governments to send observers to military exercises. Such regional agreements could form the basis for a future worldwide convention on confidence-building measures. We welcome the fact that confidence-building measures are contained in the draft joint Program of Action.

The growth of confidence cannot, of course, be confined to the sphere of military security. The elimination of mistrust, fear, and hostility is an all-embracing and universal task. This is a perspective which ranges into the future and which concerns young people. It is up to the older generation to make the younger generation in our countries more appreciative of this perspective. This is a task of great consequence which the United Nations should take upon themselves. We are willing to make a material contribution toward a United Nations program aiming to foster understanding among the young generation of all nations. We shall present our proposals to such a program in the course of this year.

12. ARMS LIMITATION AND DEVELOPMENT

In connection with this special session of the General Assembly many references have been made to the disproportion between expenditures for military purposes on the one hand and for agricultural, infrastructural, and industrial development purposes by the great majority of nations on the other. These references are justified; the facts give just cause for concern. There are highly productive countries who have a large military potential, and who make exceptionally heavy financial outlays for it—but who at the same time make a totally inadequate contribution to the transfer of capital and technology to developing countries.

Weapons supplies are no substitute for economic development. On the contrary, the transfer of weapons has assumed proportions that have made it one of the most serious international problems. It is President Carter's merit that he drew attention to this with great urgency last year. Regulating the international transfer of armaments must feature prominently in our efforts to achieve arms limitation. I wish to express my full agreement with Vice-President Mondale here.

Initiatives in this direction will bear fruit if both, suppliers and recipients, agree to exercise restraint. With this aim in mind we support the proposal embodied in the Program of Action for a study of the related problems. In particular, I would very much like all countries who export armaments to undertake to disclose their supplies.

However, dangers arise not only from arms supplied by governments but also from the commercial exploitation of discarded military equipment. Consequently, the study must also cover the possibilities of controlling private trade in military equipment.

I would like to take this opportunity to outline my own country's policy in this field. We refuse as a matter of principle to grant aid for the export of weapons. Only in exceptional and on the whole very limited cases do we allow any weapons at all to be supplied to countries outside our own alliance. According to analyses prepared by the Stockholm Institute of Peace Research, German supplies of weapons to the Third World account for only three-hundredths of one percent of our gross national product. According to our estimates this is the equivalent of two-tenths of one percent of our total exports. We strictly do not allow weapons to be exported to areas of international tension.

On the other hand, we have massively increased our development aid budget, so that it is now the equivalent of more than one-tenth of our defense effort. If every country in the world could say this of itself, many people in the developing countries would be better off. Those who build up their armaments beyond what is needed for their defense are limiting their capacity for material aid to others.

Material want, hunger, and poverty are intolerable in many places. Only healthy economic and social development serves the cause of peace. Social justice is not merely a domestic but just as much an international necessity. If we succeed in limiting armaments and cutting our military expenditures we shall be releasing funds which can be used to make additional transfers to the developing countries.

My country will continue to increase the scope of its development assistance, although I prefer to speak of economic cooperation rather than aid, since we are all dependent on one another. That is why we expect solidarity to be reciprocated with solidarity.

13. SUMMARY

The task as we see it with regard to armaments—nuclear and other weapons alike—is to bring about balanced and verifiable limitations, to effect specific and balanced reductions, and hopefully one day to bring about the total elimination of arms. Complete and internationally controlled disarmament remains the goal.

If it is to be successful this process requires a comprehensive security policy based on the following guidelines:

- Political, strategic and military balance;
- Détente, containment of conflicts, and reconciliation of interests;
- Capacity for effective crisis management;
- Predictability and calculability of political and military conduct.

With these guidelines in mind we are cooperating in the talks at Geneva and Vienna with a sense of commitment and initiative. This special session of the United Nations General Assembly on disarmament has an opportunity to demonstrate the credibility of international efforts in the field of disarmament and arms control. We hope this special session will avail itself of this opportunity. To this end it is necessary that we will be able to discuss the existing problems frankly but without polemics and to reach our decisions by consensus. That would be a demonstration of our ability to work together in a global framework to strengthen peace and security.

With this aim in mind we put forward the following proposals:

First: Our experience with the verification of our commitment not to produce chemical weapons is at the disposal of other nations.

Second: We shall make available our seismological facilities for the verification of a comprehensive test ban.

Third: We support restrictions on the international transfer of conventional arms.

Fourth: We support efforts to increase confidence through a greater degree of transparency in military expenditures and activities.

Fifth: We shall have reached our goal only if the nations succeed in trusting each other. Here much will depend on the young people. This is why we are in favor of the United Nations to consider specific ways of bringing the youth of different nations into closer contact.

It has been the general experience that all-embracing concepts for global disarmament hold out no prospect of success. What we need instead are many individual advances, progress step by step. And all of them taken with the determination to harmonize conflicting interests.

Anyone who dismisses the idea of compromise in principle is not fit for peace. If he is not prepared to meet others half way he cannot expect them to move toward him. Anyone who cultivates enemy stereotypes and prejudices will himself be regarded as an enemy.

There is far too much enmity in this world. What we need instead is partnership. Such partnership must ensue from the recognition that no one can guarantee his security and peace by himself.

The historical experiences of nations differ from one another, their ideologies even more. My experience of the World War made me a committed member of a political movement in my country which has fought for arms limitation for the past 115 years. For the past 20 years I have devoted my energy to this cause with determination, with realism, and with a sense of commitment.

I have done so because I know that the horrors of the past must not be repeated. We Germans know that preventing this is to a large extent *our* task.

The world can be confident: we Germans will live up to that task.

5

Speech in Moscow

(June 30, 1980)

Mr. General-Secretary, Mr. Chairman of the Council of Ministers, Ladies and Gentlemen:

Thank you for the words you have just addressed to us, Mr. General-Secretary. At the same time I should like to thank you and the other members of the Soviet leadership, also on behalf of Foreign Minister Genscher and the entire delegation, for the invitation to visit Moscow and for the hospitality extended to us this evening. This is my fifth visit to Moscow. In view of the current grave international situation I consider it a very important visit. We are able, Mr. General-Secretary, to follow on from your visit to the Federal Republic of Germany in 1978 and the various high-level talks that have been held since then.

The relations between our two countries, which we set on a sound foundation about ten years ago with the German-Soviet Treaty of August 12, 1970, must prove to be stable, durable, and capable of development in difficult times, too. Otherwise we would not be able to live up to the obligations we have assumed in the treaty itself and in our joint declarations of 1973 and 1978. In this context I also mention the Quadripartite Agreement of 1971 which has noticeably eased the situation in and around Berlin.

The Federal Republic of Germany abides firmly by the agreements it has concluded. We adhere strictly to the multilateral conventions which form a link between us. In particular I have in mind the CSCE Final Act. We still have to do some work together to bring about its realization. In coordination with our allies and through intensive consultations with all participants in the conference we are preparing ourselves for the Madrid Follow-up Conference at which political and economic issues, certain security aspects, as well as human rights will feature prominently. The Madrid Conference can also bring about important decisions in the field of arms control. We can hope for greater

This speech was made on the occasion of a series of meetings between Soviet and German heads of state.

security in Europe if we succeed in elaborating confidence-building measures which are of military relevance to the entire European continent and binding on all the participants. (A conference on the military aspects of security in Europe would be a suitable forum for the commencement of negotiations on this subject.) We hope that a substantive mandate for negotiations can be agreed on in Madrid. The preamble to the CSCE Final Act refers to détente which is "universal in scope" and to "recognizing the close link between peace and security in Europe and in the world as a whole." And in our Joint Declaration of May 6, 1978, we pledged ourselves to respect the "indivisibility of peace and security throughout the world."

ALARMING DEVELOPMENT OF INTERNATIONAL RELATIONS

The alarming development of international relations during recent months has demonstrated quite clearly how important this statement is. The Afghanistan crisis is casting a broad shadow on East-West relations in Europe. It is causing deep concern and great anxiety particularly in the states of the Third World, in the nonaligned countries, especially the Islamic ones.

We must respect the voice of these people whose security, freedom, and self-determination are at stake. World peace depends increasingly on all peoples — even those not belonging to an alliance — being able to rely on their sovereignty and independence being ensured. Nonalignment has now become a real factor of international peace.

In the matter of the Afghanistan crisis, my government supports, together with France, with its partners in the European Community and the participants in the Venice Summit of June 22 and 23, and with the overwhelming majority of the international community, the United Nations General Assembly resolution of January 14, 1980, as well as the position expressed by the Islamic Conference at its last two meetings.

The common objective of these resolutions and initiatives is to restore an independent, nonaligned Afghanistan, free from foreign troops — an Afghanistan in keeping with the wishes of the Afghan people and the legitimate interests of Afghanistan's neighbors.

I am sure that you, Mr. General-Secretary, would make a vital contribution to defusing this dangerous crisis if you could declare that the announced withdrawal of some Soviet troops from Afghanistan is the beginning of a movement which will be continued until withdrawal is complete.

I am also concerned about the stagnation in the peace-keeping efforts as regards the Israeli-Arab conflict. Acts of violence intensify the danger emanating from this area of conflict for the entire region. Together with its European partners my government is pressing for progress in the quest for a just, lasting, and comprehensive settlement.

Here, too, it is the recognition and realization of fundamental principles of the international community which are involved: the right to security of all states of the region, including Israel, as well as justice for all peoples; i.e., also the legitimate rights of the Palestinian people, including their right to self-determination.

These principles must also gain acceptance in southern Africa if the nations of the region and the world as a whole are to be spared bloody racial warfare. Developments in Zimbabwe show that conflicts can be resolved by peaceful means. My government will do everything possible so that Namibia acquires its independence on the basis of Security Council Resolution 435. It supports without reservation those who advocate self-determination and human dignity. In South Africa, racial discrimination must give way to a policy of equality for all.

The hostage-taking in Tehran concerns all nations, not only the Americans who can count on us in their patient endeavors to obtain the release of the hostages. The international community expects each state to do its share in pressing for an early humane decision by the Iranian authorities.

In former Indochina, there is still no peace after the great suffering of the Vietnam War. Millions of people have become victims of grave internal and external conflicts. Together with our European partners, we support ASEAN's responsible commitment to regional security and cooperation.

Only recently in the preface to the German edition of your speeches and interviews you, Mr. General-Secretary, pointed out that crises occurring anywhere in the world today have far-reaching repercussions on international relations as a whole. I share your view. In addition to regional conflicts which we must seek to resolve by peaceful means there are global tasks which we can only resolve jointly.

RECONCILIATION OF INTERESTS BETWEEN INDUSTRIALIZED AND DEVELOPING COUNTRIES

The necessary reconciliation of interests between North and South, between industrialized and developing countries, has been made increasingly more difficult but also more urgent by the population explosion in the Third World and the explosion of the oil prices.

We are all called upon to assist in mastering this task of the century—for moral reasons and because we bear a joint responsibility for world peace. That means Western and Eastern industrialized countries, the large oil-exporting countries, but then also the developing countries themselves.

Those who care for peace in this world must refrain from imposing their own political, social, and economic ideas on the Third World. The countries of the Third World have a right to plurality, to run their own internal and external affairs, and to be free from domination.

We must give priority to ensuring internationally secure, adequate energy supplies. Or else there will be the danger of a worldwide struggle for the distribution of energy with devastating effects. The industrialized countries, the oil-producing countries, and the non–oil-producing developing countries are dependent on one another if they want to develop their own potential for economic advancement and prosperity. Our two countries can achieve a great deal through their cooperation. From the outset I welcomed your proposal, Mr. General-Secretary, for an all-European energy conference and I shall continue to support it.

MILITARY BALANCE OF POWER

However, we can only do what is expected of us if we feel secure and are, in fact, secure. The military balance of power, both regional and global, i.e., in Europe and in the world as a whole, is an indispensable key element for a peaceful future.

The preservation of equilibrium where it already exists and the creation of equilibrium where it does not yet exist must, therefore, be a priority issue of our cooperation. We must find ways of stopping the arms race which is both futile and irresponsible. The East and the West must therefore intensify their efforts to achieve agreements on arms control and arms limitation.

The American-Soviet SALT treaty of last June is, in our opinion, a vitally

With Soviet Prime Minister Alexei Kosygin and General-Secretary Leonid Brezhnev, Moscow, June 1980.

important step along this path. We hope that it will soon be ratified and shall continue to advocate its ratification. The two superpowers bear a special responsibility for peace. We hope, therefore, that the United States, which has expressly said so, and the Soviet Union abide by the provisions of the treaty even without formal ratification.

In the field of medium-range nuclear missiles, there has, unfortunately, been a continuing development which runs counter to the gain in stability from the conclusion of SALT II. Foreign Minister Genscher and I myself have repeatedly drawn attention to this dangerous development, both publicly and in our talks with the Soviet leadership. Nobody could or can be in doubt about our concern.

From 1978 onward the Western Alliance had to prepare concrete steps to counter the imbalance in this important field. The outcome of the lengthy and responsible deliberations is well known: the NATO decision of December 1979, which comprises both a decision of defense and a proposal for arms limitation. I am appealing to our Soviet hosts not to cast aside this offer of negotiations.

We have read the declaration of the Warsaw Pact states of May 15. In it they state their readiness to negotiate on all weapons systems. Put this willingness into practice by agreeing to begin preparatory negotiations on medium-range systems without prior conditions.

PRESERVATION OF PEACE

Mr. General-Secretary, Ladies and Gentlemen, I have had to talk about crises, areas of tension, and conflicts. Many people in my country — and not only there — are concerned about the preservation of peace. Precisely for that reason, two things are important:

First, we must ensure that particularly in difficult times the communication between those holding political responsibility is maintained and intensified. We must undertake even greater efforts in future to find ways and means of preventing conflicts, at least of making them manageable. Second, political action must be marked by great circumspection and a firm resolve for peace.

My government's will for peace is demonstrated by its calculable policy, which is based on a realistic assessment of the situation and on clear-cut premises. I would like to name the three underlying elements:

- The firm integration of the Federal Republic of Germany in the Atlantic Alliance and the European Community, in the knowledge that it shares common values and interests with the United States of America and the other allies.
- The policy of détente and cooperation with our Eastern neighbors.

- The policy of partnership on equal terms with countries of the Third World.

The German and the Soviet people both have vivid memories of the horrors of war, of death, expulsion, and destruction. We have both, Mr. General-Secretary, spoken repeatedly of the particular responsibility of the generation we belong to, which consciously experienced the entire war. We Germans in the heart of Europe could only lose everything and gain nothing from another war. The people in my country are aware of this. They therefore agree on the basic course of our policy. And it is precisely this consensus which makes our political course stable and clear: a course aimed at peace.

COOPERATION BETWEEN EAST AND WEST

But there is not only cause for concern—there is also cause for hope. The cooperation and contacts between Germans on both sides of the river Elbe have improved. Last year I visited Bulgaria, Poland, and Hungary. I experienced the measure of cooperation we have achieved and I know that nobody wants to question the achievements.

It is gratifying to note that particularly in our relations with the Soviet Union we have achieved an exchange of views and consultations of remarkable intensity. We are thus able to gauge the interests and problems of the other side better. Our long-term economic cooperation also helps to safeguard peace.

Between our two states there exists a problem which still causes great human suffering: I am referring to the plight of the divided families. I am appealing to you, Mr. General-Secretary, to make possible a similarly favorable development with respect to the reunification of families. This is not so much an issue based on reason, but a matter of heart.

Our bilateral relationship is, I feel, a good illustration that problems can be settled, conflicts resolved, and tension alleviated by a readiness for negotiation and by a will for the reconciliation of interests. In this way the governments of our two countries have made a contribution toward equilibrium and stability. It is now paramount to prevent new dangerous imbalances arising which could jeopardize our joint achievements. I therefore welcome this opportunity of direct negotiations. I wanted to present our own views, which are based on positions shared by our friends and partners. But I also wanted to hear the views of the Soviet leadership. I hope that we can—above and beyond our bilateral cooperation—contribute toward finding solutions to problems besetting us and our partners.

Mr. General-Secretary, I propose a toast to your personal health, to the well-being of the Soviet leadership, to good relations between the Soviet Union and the Federal Republic of Germany, to the peaceful resolution of conflicts, and to peace in Europe and the world which we all need so urgently.

6

The Struggle for the World Product: Politics Between Power and Morals

(April 1974)

Anyone who, in these weeks and months of the "oil crisis," is asked to forecast the future development of international economic relations and who looks for fixed data and reliable trends to support his forecast will soon run into serious difficulties. Even after the mid-February Energy Conference in Washington, the impression, disturbing in many respects, remains that the world economy has entered a phase of extraordinary instability and that its future course is absolutely uncertain; it may bring stability, but also still greater instability. More integration, closer cooperation, an improved division of labor may increase the overall prosperity of nations. But the future course may just as well be characterized by disintegration, national isolation and the search for more self-sufficiency, thereby enhancing the contrasts already existing in the world.

It would be wrong, of course, to believe that the oil price explosion was the only cause of instability. But the massive increase in oil prices has clearly revealed the actual fragility of this elaborate system of economic relations among the nations of the world, from the structure of their balance of payments to their trade policy. To use energy nomenclature: just as a high-energy neutron breaks through the electrical shielding which surrounds the atom and penetrates into the nucleus, oil has shaken the very foundations of the present world economic system. And just as the neutron may induce oscillation and shatter the nucleus, oil may shatter the laboriously built structure of the world economy. The oil crisis may touch off a chain reaction of destructive forces,

Reprinted by permission from *Foreign Affairs* 52 (April 1974):437–451.

but—if properly harnessed and controlled—it may just as well help to improve international cooperation, if all those concerned join in the efforts to find the common denominator of what is going on these days between the Libyan desert and the Gulf of Maracaibo, and if they build a policy of reason on that common denominator.

II

At this present stage there can hardly be any doubt that, long before the explosive rise in the prices of almost all raw materials, international economic policy was moving toward a critical phase. It is no longer possible to ignore the fact that difficulties have recently multiplied, bit by bit, and what is astonishing is that this has happened during a period of worldwide new production records. Whereas, on the one hand, the world economy was experiencing a fantastic boom, there was, on the other hand, growing uneasiness about the institutions, particularly the slowness with which they were adapting to changing conditions, to new tasks and objectives, in order to ensure a greater equality of starting conditions among nations and to enable an undistorted exchange of goods and services among them. The crisis toward which the world economy was moving was not so much one of production as a crisis of its institutions in structural respects. In particular, the rules governing the exchange of goods and services were questioned on an increasing scale.

The protracted ill-health of the Bretton Woods system was one of the most significant symptoms of this development. Under the impact of the cumulative effects of inflation and speculative crises, this system finally collapsed and thus ceased to exist as an integrating factor. Ultimately, the system broke down because it failed to provide the framework for an orderly exchange of goods and services. Bretton Woods benefited some countries more than others—particularly the strong more than the weak—and above all it burdened the international monetary system with the payments deficits of the superpower. And thus it is not astonishing that, finally, a system that initially had been so successful should have produced interventionist policies on an increasing scale rather than greater economic freedom.

Even with imagination and expertise, it is difficult to establish a new and better system. It is difficult to create a supranational standard of value which is not at the same time a national currency, like the dollar, or a commodity used for speculative purposes, like gold. The Special Drawing Right, as an artificial numeraire without a market price, and with official parities only for transactions between central banks, was to be declared a primary currency reserve and to be made so strong that it could win the necessary confidence. There were to be fixed but adjustable exchange rates. In addition, it was intended to ensure that the extent and duration of payments imbalances should be appreciably reduced, that the facilities for financing such imbalances should be limited rather than expanded. All countries were to be obliged to settle payments balances from their own reserves.

The process of evaluating the pros and cons of the proposed monetary rules is still under way. What has so far emerged, after lengthy negotiations in some of the most beautiful cities of the world—including Nairobi, the modern metropolis in East Africa, and Rome, the ancient metropolis of Western civilization—is at least a basic concept. Luckily, there has also been found an interim solution to the important question of the valuation of the Special Drawing Right: the yardstick is to be the average value of a "basket" of major currencies instead of the U.S. dollar. On the other hand, however, there has so far been no decision on the question of how to finance the payments deficits of the less-developed countries; this question, though at first glance it appears to be of secondary importance from the point of view of monetary policy, is actually very important in the light of recent developments. It is certainly true to claim that, despite open flanks, the understanding for the common cause has increased and that therefore the continents have moved closer together in certain fundamental views. But even if all moral accessories are left aside, nobody—including the author of these lines—would be able to say just when the new system can be put into operation. For nobody, in view of the still incalculable effects of the dynamic changes in the terms of trade, can confidently claim to be in a position to determine new fixed parities and afterward defend them against market forces.

There are more symptoms of this struggle for new and better rules—e.g., in commercial policy. Last year we witnessed a peculiar, and largely unnoticed, formalistic dispute both within the European Community (EEC) and between the latter and the United States as to whether and in what form a connection was to be established between the reform of the international monetary system and the new multilateral trade negotiations (GATT) in Tokyo. France had initially requested that the new GATT Round should not begin until fixed parities had been reintroduced. The other European countries advocated concurrent efforts toward further liberalization of trade *and* monetary stabilization. The United States, on its part, was ready to support this formula of concurrent efforts only if it was clearly expressed that an efficient monetary system also called for a commercial policy prone to adjustments.

All this looked like a dispute on formal issues only. But, at the same time, it was the expression of fundamentally different positions: monetary matters first and trade afterward; or monetary matters and trade at the same time; or trade promoting monetary matters—these are concepts which may call for different approaches on the part of the nations concerned, and possibly the acceptance of economic disadvantages or sacrifices. Meanwhile, this dispute has taken on a purely academic character.

The conference held last September in the Japanese capital was an example of the above-mentioned concurrency and its ultimate results are still largely incalculable. The opening declaration of Tokyo is by no means the Magna Carta of an open world economy based on division of labor, although any reasonable person will accept the objective that the new GATT Round should promote the further liberalization of international trade in order to raise the standard of living and increase the prosperity of nations. He will likewise endorse the general claim that existing customs barriers should be lowered further and other trade barriers reduced or removed.

But the bureaucratic infighting behind these fine words is still going on, as is the struggle over the prices of raw materials. The wrangling is about tariff headings, preferences and counterpreferences, the purpose and extent of protectionist measures. Here, too, as in monetary matters, national interests play a prominent role. Not all countries, for instance, are as vitally interested in the largest possible degree of freedom for world trade as the Federal Republic of Germany. Thus, countries which have only just begun to build up industries at enormous social cost will not be too eager to enter into free competition with the powerful combines of industrialized countries. On the other hand, even in highly developed countries there are certain sectors whose competitiveness is limited; a case in point is the German clothing industry, which is complaining about low-priced shirts being imported from Formosa and Hong Kong. Such sectors cannot stand up to international competition and genuine social problems are created in the countries concerned when economic activity is running at a low ebb.

Agriculture will probably continue to be a further reservation in the system of a free exchange of goods and services. Agriculture is the spoiled child of protectionism, not only because governments vie for farmers' votes, but also because—understandably—every country is anxious to preserve its own minimum basis for feeding its people. This statement can be proved by hard-and-fast figures if one looks behind the scenes of European as well as U.S. agricultural policy. To the outside observer, the policy of European integration appears to be a puzzling tug-of-war over egg prices or wine quotas. Both in Europe and in the United States, the baffled consumer will often have the impression that relationships between the two are determined exclusively by soybeans and Arkansas chickens. Those who resent the economic power of the United States speak of the American challenge, and there may even be such strange excesses as the claim that the consumption of American chickens results in impotence.

Nor can we be certain that free capital movements are welcomed everywhere. Did not American newspapers, for instance, publish malicious reports on an allegedly unlimited stream of German capital into the West? Some people already saw the place swarming with Teutonic roughriders lassoing American cattle. And was not the United States somewhat vexed about the association policy of the EEC, which was even alleged to be striving for hegemony over the United States? Someone even invented the malicious quip that the Sixth Fleet in the Mediterranean would probably soon have to file an application for association.

Meanwhile, however, it will have been realized from New York to San Francisco how difficult it still is for Europeans to translate their dream of a political union into reality. It is not without protracted and painful labors that the Regional Fund is being created, which so far is the latest of the instruments of European unification, following the Agricultural Fund, the Social Fund, and the somewhat ill-fated monetary "snake." And it is conceivable that Europe's failure to tackle the oil crisis by pursuing a common policy will have an impact on the further process of unification.

III

What is the reason for this state of affairs? Why is it that thirty years after Bretton Woods the urgently needed reform of the international monetary system makes so little headway? Why is it that nations find it so hard to soften their protectionist trade systems and to give their trade policies a new, open, and equal structure? Why is it that after almost two decades of effort toward European unification, European political union is still unfinished? What is the reason for these disputes about quotas, customs tariffs, and posted prices? And the oil problem which now creates new and very strong tensions, is its nature not basically the same?

David Ricardo would certainly not like this state of the world economy and its institutions if he saw it. But he might congratulate himself on the skepticism and foresight he showed in discussing the consequences of the free trade thesis of his teacher, Adam Smith. Admittedly specialization, division of labor, and free trade across national boundaries have increased the wealth of nations and caused an immense supply of goods in the same way as the division of labor increased production within a single nation. But the main problem then is to define the laws which determine the distribution of this enormous output; it might be added: which determine the "fair" distribution, the "equitable" price, the "proper" value.

Even today, these "laws" have not yet been defined. The most ingenious theories of distribution in most cases explain only parts of the problem or are infeasible in actual practice. What remains are resourceful bickerings over the results of the joint efforts, a game full of ruses and little tricks, with strategies of threats, attrition and fatigue, of overnight conferences and dissolved meetings, a game of coalitions and cartels. What we are witnessing today in the field of international economic relations — in the monetary field and now in the field of oil and raw material prices — is virtually the same as what is going on between trade unions and employers' associations on the national level. It is a struggle for the distribution and use of the national product, a struggle for the world product.

But whereas the struggle for distribution has hitherto been fought within the framework of monetary and commercial rules, it has now become a struggle over prices as well and has thus taken on a new and in many respects dangerous dimension. The struggle over oil prices may be followed tomorrow by a similar struggle over the prices of other important raw materials. And since what is at stake is not just pawns on a chessboard, but the peaceful evolution of the world economy and the prosperity of the nations of this world, we need a politically sound philosophy if we are to win this dangerous fight.

IV

It would be a mistake to approach the oil problem with illusions, with a swashbuckling rattle of the sword in the manner of a past century's gunboat diplomacy or in an egotistical overbearing manner. This is no way in which to conduct the distribution combat! Each side, the oil-producing and the oil-consuming countries, must learn to understand and appreciate the other's interests, means, and possibilities, since there is no other way of avoiding abortive actions and corresponding reactions. The hectic events of the past nine months appear to indicate that this point has by no means been fully grasped.

Oil consumers would be well advised to examine the oil producers' motives impartially. It is true that, in the Middle East, current political issues have a bearing and that, to this extent, oil is considered a political weapon. But, in essence, the oil price issue is not one of a clash over the Suez Canal, the West Bank, or Jerusalem. What the oil producers, and not only the Arab ones, have in mind is to increase their share in that portion of the world product which is created with the aid of oil, the most important raw material for years to come. And they are able to do so to the extent that increased oil prices push up the import figures of oil-consuming countries at a rate higher than that at which the latter are able to step up their prices of exports.

The oil consumers would do well to grasp that this is exactly what is intended and not to allow certain facts to be repressed into the subconscious mind, especially the present distribution of wealth between industrialized countries on the one hand and oil-producing countries on the other. If, for instance, U.S. per capita income in 1971, i.e., a year prior to the start of the present price measures of the OPEC countries, were taken to be 100, the latter countries' figures for 1971 would be as follows: Kuwait 75, Abu Dhabi 49, Qatar 45, Libya 28, Venezuela 21, Saudi Arabia 11, Iran 9, Iraq 7, Nigeria 3, Indonesia 2.

And these figures are by no means a true reflection of the actual level of wealth attained in those countries; the disparity, in real terms, for the bulk of the population can well be assumed to be greater than these figures reveal. And it is this gap in incomes or wealth that alone should be taken to motivate the oil countries' policies.

Seen from this angle, the Western industrialized countries, including Japan,

With Crown Prince Fahd in Riyadh, Saudi Arabia, April 1981.

being oil consumers, can hardly avoid acknowledging the merits of the oil countries' claim, seeing that cheap oil was in the past a major factor in the former countries' growth. They should not blind themselves to the fact that the times of cheap oil are past and gone. A posted price of $1.80 per barrel of Arabian oil from the Persian Gulf, as it prevailed in January 1970, will not recur. It will not do so because oil producers, following ten years of systematic OPEC policies and aided by twenty years of careless energy policies on the part of the consumer countries, now have the power—in the form of the OPEC cartel—to achieve by increasing their prices the distribution pattern they desire. They have the power of those who control resources in short supply, resources which are of importance, in limitative respects, to a multitude of production lines in industrialized countries. There is so far absolutely no substitute for oil and its derivatives available at short notice; at the most, a sort of fringe substitution might be possible in alternative fuel power stations. Certain economies in quantities consumed are, however, possible at short notice and that alone would involve considerable changes in consumer habits. In other words: as a short-term proposition, the elasticity of demand for oil and its derivatives is very slight, and thus the conditions are right for an independent price policy.

On the other hand, oil producers would do well not to regard the new independence and power they have in pricing to be a device which is devoid of all limitations and consequences, especially in view of the effects this may have on the very existence of the developing countries. They should proceed with care when marking out their field of action. In doing so they should above all not allow this newly grown consciousness to mislead them when assessing the industrialized countries' economic possibilities. For although there is only a very slight possibility of substitution for oil at short notice, there is a limit to the price that can be charged. In the short run there is at least a point beyond which economic stability would be in jeopardy. And that point is reached whenever the industrialized countries are confronted with intolerable adaptation and reorganization problems incapable of being solved at short notice and are thus driven into employment crises or toward an even higher rate of inflation. In this context, I do not wish even to contemplate a point—at least theoretically conceivable—beyond which the irrational use of force might ensue.

But if we think in terms of five to ten years, the elasticity of the demand for oil will rapidly increase. Oil used for heat-producing purposes will become substitutable as soon as the price of oil equals or exceeds that of alternative sources of energy. However, scope for substitution is smaller in certain sectors of transportation and of the petrochemical industry. In the long run, though, oil could be replaced by electricity even in the field of transportation, for instance if nuclear energy were available to a greater extent, and long before that coal will have been assigned a larger role as a basic material in the chemical industries.

For these reasons, oil-producing countries would not only be gravely misjudging the power they wield but also be jeopardizing their own interests if they were to try to attain maximum absorption on a short-term basis. It would run counter to their own long-term interests if oil-producing countries were to pursue a price policy that would drive Western industrialized countries onto the verge of, or even right into, crises: you do not kill the goose that lays the golden egg. Extreme, supermonopolistic absorptions simply are not sensible strategy if the object is to narrow the income gap between the group of industrialized countries and the group of oil-producing countries. But the most important aspect is that such a policy would force the industrialized countries to resort to sweeping crash programs designed to direct their entire resources, their entire sophisticated technology to the substitution of oil or to the exploitation of unused oil reserves (sands, shales). Consequently, in the long run the effect for the OPEC countries might well be reversed. As far as the interests of the oil-producing countries are concerned, the optimum solution would therefore not lie in a *short-term maximum* absorption but rather in an absorption that is *achievable and tolerable on a long-term basis.*

With this in mind, a major question mark remains over the present oil-price policy. Price increases have been so exorbitant that, as a result of changes in incomes and demand, serious repercussions, particularly on employment, cannot be ruled out. In addition, the oil-producing countries have obviously been unaware of the strain which they impose on a fragile monetary system through their sudden withdrawal of purchasing power.

Therefore, even if one recognizes—as I do—that producer countries have a good case for claiming a greater share, there will have to be negotiations on the size and terms, because a new equilibrium cannot be the result of monopolistic practices and mechanisms, but will have to be brought about by balanced judgment and advance planning. Producer and consumer countries will have to sit down at the same conference table. In those talks, the oil-consuming industrialized and developing countries should not be forced at short notice to lower their standard of prosperity at the expense of their social stability. It should on the contrary be in the interest of the oil-producing countries, as well, to ensure that they can satisfy their requirements by being able to draw upon industrialized countries' national products that are in a process of growth and possibly even undergoing structural changes for the better.

At the same time, the problem of the use of the enormous monetary purchasing power now accruing to the oil-producing countries should be discussed, since this will have repercussions on the employment situation in the industrialized countries and on the extent of unavoidable structural changes. The search for solutions will certainly not be facilitated by the fact that there is no homogeneity of interests in either group. Some of the oil-producing countries such as Iran and Venezuela will—at least on a medium-term basis—be in a position to utilize the accruing purchasing power for, say, internal investment projects destined to expand their own production capacity. To this extent they will become importers of industrial goods and consequently trigger off a corresponding demand for export goods in the industrialized countries. Here lie welcome chances for economic and technological cooperation aiming at an accelerated industrialization of the oil-producing countries; this approach will require the development of coordinated programs. Other countries such as the sheikdoms of the Persian Gulf, Saudi Arabia, and possibly Libya will—even on a medium-term basis—not be able to absorb the additional purchasing power within their own frontiers. They will, in other words, not increase their imports and consequently not bring about an increase in demand for export goods; they will invest their monetary capital in other countries rather than spend it. This will result at first in the accumulation of huge, readily disposable amounts running in billions, which could well flow back to the industrialized countries as capital imports. Such amounts might also be made available to countries of the Third World which in turn could use them for buying export goods from industrialized countries.

The situation on the part of the oil-consuming countries is equally differentiated. Some of the industrialized countries are more seriously affected than others, the degree varying primarily according to the extent to which they are dependent upon oil imports and according to the previous position of their current account and their balance of payments in general, and finally, according to their export capacity. Countries with a current account surplus, i.e., countries which have so far not used their entire national product internally for consumption and investment, but have made part of it available to other countries, thereby acquiring monetary claims, are hardly expected to run into difficulties. This applies, for instance, to the Federal Republic of Germany, whose current account surplus is quite substantial. For the Federal Republic, even the increase in oil prices will presumably not result in a current account deficit. German export industries enjoy a high reputation in potential purchasing countries. In addition, the deutsche mark is backed by a very large monetary reserve so that any lean period could easily be overcome. The effects of the increases in oil prices on income will of course also be felt by countries with a strong monetary position.

Other countries whose balance of payments have hitherto been in equilibrium or have already shown a deficit, particularly a number of less-developed countries, may well run up such huge deficits on current account that they might very shortly be facing enormous financial gaps resulting in an immediate and urgent necessity either to step up exports or to reduce imports. Such a situation is extremely dangerous for the future of the whole world economy. But it would be a great mistake if each individual country within the group of oil consumers were now selfishly to try to solve its payments and employment problems by pursuing beggar-my-neighbor policies at the expense of its trading partners. Any relapse into largely bilateral bartering would be just as dangerous as any reintroduction of trade restrictions. Nor should there be any competitive devaluation. After the Washington Conference, we can only hope that, however justified the concern about specific national problems may be, the common interest will not be forgotten. Otherwise, an arrival at the point of no return cannot be ruled out.

The present flexibility of exchange rates may well facilitate the adjustment process, but it should not be allowed to lead to excessive downward floating. Any current account deficits that would remain if a compensatory increase in exports cannot be achieved at short notice might well be financed from the surpluses of oil-producing countries. The point would be to release capital flows of more or less the same size as the various current account deficits of oil-consuming countries. A large-scale concentration of investments in a few individual countries would create well-nigh insurmountable difficulties both for the latter countries and for those which fail to balance their current accounts for lack of capital imports. Should the earnings of the oil-producing countries, rather than being invested on a long-term basis, remain "mobile" as a whole and be capable of being moved at short notice out of one currency into another and from one investment outlet to the next, there would furthermore be new serious risks for the monetary situation.

Of course, a certain portion of the investment-seeking oil funds will find its way to consumer countries automatically: in the form of direct investments, investments in securities, credits, and bank deposits, either direct or via existing or new Euromarkets. Countries which would not automatically obtain an adequate share of these monies might remedy the situation by offering investment incentives or possibly by issuing foreign currency bonds, though there should be no free-for-all in the field of foreign bonds.

If, in the choice of countries in which to invest oil funds, preference were to be given to those with strong currencies, the latter's private sector investment outlets might prove insufficient. If so, it might be advisable to examine whether public investment outlets could be expanded. Above all, the countries concerned would have to ask themselves whether they were in a position to act as "marshalling yards" for international capital flows. They would have to try to offset inflowing liquidity by capital exports and this might entail the willingness to accept financial risks. Two countries that might be capable of undertaking this very difficult task could, for instance, be the United States or even the Federal Republic of Germany. Such a "marshalling yard" could help to direct the capital outflow selectively into those countries which—as a result of the oil crisis—are faced with major balance-of-payments problems. In the first place, however, this task would be a matter to be tackled by multinational institutions.

V

No matter what action the industrialized countries may take to wipe out balance-of-payments current-account deficits, the fundamental problem as such will remain unsolved. A process of shifts in patterns of income has been set in motion on a huge scale. The questions facing the industrialized countries are what strategy they should reasonably pursue and whether they are well advised to rely on capital imports in attempting to come to a long-term solution of their internal employment and financial problems. During a transitional phase this surely should be possible and might even be necessary in order to give the industrialized countries concerned time to adapt.

What will probably be unavoidable in the long run is a process of structural changes which would, among other things, increase the export capacity of those industrialized countries whose exports now flow at a low level. This results from the pressure of the Third World's dire needs. These would increase if the now-beginning process of transfers of purchasing power were to be strictly confined to industrialized countries on the one hand and oil countries on the other, especially if the released investment-seeking oil billions flow back in the opposite direction. The developing countries are in danger of being left high and dry. Their very existence is threatened by increasing oil prices because they do not have as high a net product as the industrialized countries to draw upon. For those who view the prosperity gap between the rich and the poor of this world with concern, every effort must be made to see that the oil producers place that portion of their additional purchasing power which they are unable to absorb at home directly at the disposal of developing countries to make effective the latter's demand for imports from industrialized countries.

The international organizations, too, will have to join in the efforts to channel the investment-seeking funds of oil countries to where they are needed to lessen the differences between levels of income. The International Monetary Fund (IMF), the World Bank, the International Development Agency and the regional development banks will in the future have to rely on those countries much more than before when seeking to obtain lending funds, even if—as I hope—the industrialized countries do not reduce their development assistance below its present level.

In the long run, therefore, the oil countries will also be facing the problem which now is accompanying development assistance rendered by industrialized countries. Mere financing of credit to developing countries will not be sufficient in the long run. The rate at which most countries of the Third World are accumulating capital resources of their own is so low that it is hardly possible to set in motion an accelerated process of self-development merely by offering them assistance in the form of credit, because most of their gain in productivity is eroded by their commitments to pay interest on, and repay the principal of, loans.

Thus, in the long run, there will have to be more genuine transfers of real resources in order to provide the less-developed nations with a genuine basis for continued self-development and thus also to decrease social and political tension. The oil-producing countries are now successfully making the most of their market position for obtaining a larger share, in real terms, in the world product. This share is considerably larger than all the development aid being provided by industrialized countries. Thus, some of the oil producers are automatically beginning to share in responsibility, a responsibility that they cannot shirk.

Obviously, the developments sparked by the increase in oil prices can hardly be brought under control unless there is a change in consciousness of the matter in public opinion. What is needed is a fundamental change in patterns of behavior both among individuals and among nations. This also applies to the question of a less wasteful use of each country's own resources and its attitude toward economic growth. The richer nations will have to realize that the product of national labor will not invariably be fully available for domestic distribution. It will not be easy to make the general public lastingly conscious of this fact.

Developments along these lines have already started in Europe. Of course, the model of the European Community is not capable of being applied automatically to other parts of the world. European integration is a historically necessary process that must be measured against European criteria. In principle there is already a substantial levelling out of differences in resources between the countries of Western Europe. The huge gap between incomes in the industrial centers on the line from Hamburg via the Rhine to the Rhône, including Northern Italy, on the one hand, and major parts of Southern Italy, Ireland, and Scotland on the other, will stand up to a comparison with the corresponding gap between certain industrialized countries and certain developing countries. The United States has a comparable North-South problem. From the very outset of the move toward European unity there was no doubt whatsoever regarding the fact that political integration would have to keep step with a planned and controlled transfer of funds from the stronger to the weaker nations. Up to and including 1973, for instance, the Federal Republic of Germany, the main provider of finance for the European Community, had paid some DM 9.5 billion—or approximately $3.5 billion at the current rate of exchange—net to other nations out of tax revenues. My country, whose financial capacity should not be overtaxed in the process, looks upon such payments as the cost of the integration venture.

On a worldwide scale, it will not be possible to reduce the differences in the levels of wealth unless the more advanced industrialized nations develop their own resources in close coordination with one another and with the primary-producing countries. If they fail to do so, the result might be social storms which could even seriously jeopardize world peace. If it can be assumed that most of the developed countries with a high level of prosperity have a great preference for peace, and that most of the less-developed countries have a high preference for increased wealth, there must be a level on which a convergence of preferences would stabilize the international political situation at a higher level of prosperity for both the wealthier and currently poorer countries. It would, therefore, serve the efforts to maintain peace on a worldwide scale if a comprehensive policy of economic cooperation were to be pursued rather than a policy of economic "apartheid."

Seen from this angle, time is short for working out sensible new rules for monetary affairs and trade. And seen from this angle, the cost of the peaceful development of the world economy will now have to be charged and paid.

7

Europe and Africa— Partners with Equal Rights: Speech Before the Nigerian Institute for International Affairs

(June 27, 1978)

Europe and Africa are not only geographical neighbors but natural and ideal economic partners. This in itself explains why the Federal Republic of Germany cannot pursue any policy toward Africa that is oriented exclusively to our own interests. It must rather be embedded in the interregional political and economic relations between Africa as a whole and the European Community.

What interests do we as Germans and Europeans have in Africa? We want an Africa undergoing steady economic and social development on a basis of political stability. Our own recent past has taught us that revolution and war are no suitable means of resolving political and economic problems. The safeguarding of peace is therefore the main pillar of our foreign policy.

FAIR BALANCE OF INTERESTS

But peace and stability can only blossom on the basis of genuine independence. Liberation from colonial rule does not give true freedom, however. It has to be consolidated by the constantly developing rule of the people within secure boundaries that are respected by one's neighbors. Thus our development aid contributions stem not from charity but from sober

Excerpts from Chancellor Schmidt's speech in Lagos. From June 26 to June 30, Chancellor Schmidt held talks in Nigeria and Zambia; he was the first German Chancellor to pay an official visit to Black Africa.

self-interest: we want to help the nations of Africa to become strong economic partners with whom we can trade to our mutual advantage. We call for the peaceful solution of conflicts in Africa and want to help as far as we can and as far as our African partners want us to. For this reason we support the observance of that extremely important principle of the Charter of the Organization of African Unity — the inviolability of the existing boundaries.

WAR WEAKENS AFRICAN PARTNERS

We in Europe are following with deep concern the escalation of tensions in several crisis areas in Africa, but above all in southern Africa, where developments are crucial to future Euro-African relations. Wars among African peoples can bring us no benefit whatsoever. On the contrary, they weaken our partners and impede the common development effort which is difficult enough as it is. Worse still, tensions in Africa threaten to allow non-African power-political interests to establish themselves on African soil. When two elephants fight the grass underneath then suffers. In other words, the basis for the growth of the African economies is destroyed.

NO SUPPORT FOR WARLIKE ACTIVITIES

Speaking for my government, I can assure you that we will not support any activities designed to spark off or spread armed conflict in Africa. Hardly any other industrial country pursues such a restrictive arms policy as the Federal Republic of Germany. Our constitution forbids us to deploy forces or arms in areas outside the scope of the alliance we have joined for our own defense. The African peoples and states could, therefore, never see the Federal Republic of Germany as an adversary; they should always see our country as a partner seeking cooperation on an equal basis. What we want is indivisible détente all over the globe.

NORTH AND SOUTH IN ONE BOAT

If we analyze the causes and effects of the world economic recession, or to put it more aptly the structural crisis, we must conclude that North and South are sitting in one boat: we are all still suffering under inflation in the industrial countries, the sudden rise in energy prices and abrupt fluctuations of other commodity prices, growing unemployment, slower growth rates both in North and South. The two forthcoming summit conferences will focus on the following three questions: How can economic growth be stimulated? How can monetary stability be improved? How can unemployment be reduced?

These questions cannot be answered simply by looking toward the industrial countries. They affect both the situation and the policies of the developing countries. A great deal depends on the growth of demand in the developing countries, on their ability to import from the industrial countries. And much depends on their degree of cooperation, their price policy regarding their own products, and their investment. On the other hand, low economic growth in the industrial countries is also bound to affect the economic situation of the developing countries, and they in particular are dependent upon a constantly increasing volume of exports. Growth in the industrial countries is a major prerequisite for the development of the Third World. On the other hand, the developing countries themselves are exercising increasing influence on this process.

GERMAN DEVELOPMENT AID

Reconciling the interests of North and South is one of the most urgent world political and economic problems with which we are faced. The Federal Republic of Germany is prepared to play its part in resolving this problem. We realize that this will mean sacrifices for the people of my country: larger contributions to the developing countries through granting them wider access to German markets, through more extensive financial cooperation, through capital exports and direct investment.

The financial contributions of the Federal Republic of Germany to developing countries can stand comparison. Here are just a few facts:

1. The total flow of resources from the Federal Republic of Germany to the developing countries accounts for 1.12 percent of our GNP, which is more than the 1 percent target set by the United Nations.

2. The Federal Republic of Germany's share of the European Community's foreign aid expenditure amounts to 25.9 percent. We meet some 11 percent of the World Bank's expenditure in the field of development assistance, which makes us its second largest donor of capital after the United States.

3. Our development budget now equals 10 percent of our defense expenditure. If other industrial countries, such as the Soviet Union, were to follow this example many developing countries would now be better off.

4. Last year the Federal Republic of Germany provided official development aid exceeding 4 billion deutsche marks. This is two and a half times more than the communist states of Eastern Europe—including the Soviet Union—together. We have repeatedly called upon our Eastern neighbors to do more for economic development and not to concentrate on supplying weapons to the Third World. No industrial country should shirk its contribution to the balancing of interests between North and South.

5. We lead the field in terms of per capita imports from developing countries.

Apart from official aid, transfer of private capital is of vital importance, especially to the more advanced developing countries. This brings not only

On the occasion of the state visit of Kenya's President Daniel arap Moi to the Federal Republic, February 1980.

capital but managerial experience and technology. Both sides have to contribute to this. The industrial countries must give the developing countries easier access to their capital markets. The developing countries, however, will only attract private investment if they provide sufficient legal protection and in this way create a climate of confidence.

My country is playing an active part in the discussions and negotiations on additional commodity agreements that are currently being conducted in Geneva within the scope of UNCTAD. We have a clear view of the problems facing many developing countries who are exposed to fluctuations on the world market.

We have been jealous champions of the Lomé Convention which guarantees fixed prices for a number of commodities, and I suggest that both developing and industrial countries seriously consider extending the principles of Lomé to more commodities and more countries in order to make greater allowance for the needs of the developing countries in particular.

UNION OF EQUAL PARTNERS

Global economic interdependence and the achievement of a balance of interests between North and South call for imagination and action. Interdependence is and must be understood as a reciprocal relationship: the suppliers of industrial goods and the suppliers of commodities must not seek domination or tutelage over one another.

In spite of their mutual dependence, a union of equal partners can and must be established between North and South without either side dominating the other. Equal treatment economically and equal rights politically — these are the goals each country should strive to attain for itself but at the same time acknowledge the right of others to do the same.

8

Speech Before the Society for the Family of Man

(November 19, 1980)

Ladies and Gentlemen:

It is with deep gratitude that I today accept the 1980 Family of Man Medallion. I see this as a recognition of the contributions which my country and my government have made toward peace, freedom, and justice.

I am particularly glad to receive the award here in New York, a great city in a great nation with whom we Germans are allied and with whom we are linked by bonds of friendship. The message I bring to you, my American friends, from Germany this evening is one of solidarity and amity. At the start of a new decade which has begun with tremendous worldwide political and economic problems and crises, my personal message is also one of confidence.

Your society stands for a high and noble cause. And you practice what you preach. Through your community-oriented services you offer help, particularly to young people in the depressed areas of this city.

The ideals you serve are also reflected in the maxims of your society: "All mankind is one family under God" and "A system of ethics is fundamental to all human engagements." These maxims are to me a genuine expression of Christian ethics, of humanism, of enlightenment. That is the spirit that animated the founders of your nation more than 200 years ago, the spirit which they worded so beautifully and so forcefully in the Bill of Rights and in your Constitution.

We Germans, especially our writers and philosophers, have over the generations played an important part in the development of that spirit. But you Americans were the ones who translated it into political reality. And we Germans have twice in our history taken your Constitution as our model: the first time in 1848 with not too great a success, the second time after 1945—actually in 1949, when the Federal Republic of Germany was founded on the basis of a new constitution which we call the Basic Law. We then adopted the civil rights enshrined in your Constitution and incorporated them in our own.

Since you informed me of your generous intention to present me with your Medallion, I have asked myself how governments can best promote the idea that this earth is inhabited by one family—the family of man.

The conclusion was: We must not act against the rights of men and women as individuals. We must not act against the rights of nations. But out of a sense of common responsibility statesmen all over the world must pursue the common aims and aspirations of men.

We must not act arrogantly against people, against our social or our natural environment. But we have to act out of responsibility toward other people, toward future generations who will inhabit the planet earth, and that also means out of responsibility toward nature.

Everything in line with this fundamental unity of purpose of the family of man I consider wise. Conversely, everything that aggravates national, racial, ideological, or economic differences dividing the family of man, everything that sets nation against nation, I consider out of step with the progress of mankind—and this I say as the representative of a people which was cruelly out of step during the period of Nazi rule.

Now, Robert McNamara has just used the word "interdependence." I think it is a key to the understanding of the fabric and the problems of the globe today. The word not only describes the real conditions of existence of nations and states and economies, but must also be seen as the underlying concept of their mutual relations. The concept of interdependence means, for instance, that a very powerful nation like the United States must be sensitive to the aspirations and interests of other nations who are inevitably affected by U.S. decisions. Or, in broader terms, it means that many problems can no longer be solved by one nation alone, not even by a group of nine nations like the European Economic Community, but require the cooperation of very many nations.

The awareness of interdependence among people and among nations is one of the most hopeful phenomena of our times. But it is the acting out of this awareness which gives meaning to the recognition of this key factor in world politics. We need the spirit of good neighborhood, of human solidarity. And we need family feelings.

The idea of the United Nations does correspond to the concept of a family of man—at least insofar as practically all states on earth are members. However, this universal political organization is sometimes lacking in family spirit, as some people at this table might have witnessed.

But despite such shortcomings, the United Nations is an indispensable organization, in fact the only one which offers a worldwide framework for cooperation. It must be used more as a platform for tackling world problems than as a platform for tackling each other in an exchange of polemics.

My country became a member of the United Nations only in 1973. Ever since we have tried to engage ourselves in the global efforts of this organization—but we have not involved the United Nations in controversial issues between my country and the others, i.e., the German Democratic Republic.

We proposed an international convention against the taking of hostages, which was approved by the General Assembly in December 1979. We suggested a broad discussion in the General Assembly on refugees. We have advocated an international register on the export and import of military arms.

As we are one of the younger members of the United Nations, we consider it an outstanding honor and a welcome acknowledgment of our efforts that our ambassador has been elected president of this year's General Assembly.

In recent years the United Nations has welcomed many new members from the Third World. It has provided a forum for them to voice their grievances and their hopes.

I think it is wrong to believe that these countries want to be difficult. They are in a difficult — in some cases extremely difficult — situation. This we must understand, and we must try to help them.

Our task is clear and easily stated: We must try to narrow the ever-widening gap between the rich and the poor countries — by improving the lot of the poor countries and also by setting more modest material targets in the rich countries than we have become used to in the sixties and even in the seventies.

I have no blueprint for success to offer — but some ideas and practical suggestions which might be helpful. One example is the second Lomé Convention between the European Community and fifty-seven developing countries in Africa, the Caribbean, and the Pacific. It shows how a common platform for differing interests can be found. These are the main elements of the Lomé Convention:

- opening the European market to products of the partner countries;
- stabilization of their export proceeds for agricultural products and certain minerals;
- enlargement of the European Development Fund.

I suggest that some of the elements of the Lomé Convention could be used also in a wider, in a global context.

Others also ought to give help and set an example according to their means and their capabilities. I am thinking of communist industrial countries, and I am thinking of newly rich oil-producing countries. They must offer the poor Third World countries special conditions for the purchase of oil. The latter especially must give grants, not loans, to improve the situation of the poorest developing countries.

In order to illustrate what I mean, let me point out that in 1972 — before the first oil price explosion — Costa Rica could buy a barrel of oil by exporting 28 kilograms of bananas. Today that barrel of oil costs it 420 kilograms of bananas. There you have in one little equation the yardstick for measuring the ever more difficult situation in the developing countries.

When I went to school—which was some time ago—I learned that there were about 2 billion people living on earth. Today there are well over 4 billion—and we are told that in the year 2000, which is only nineteen years ahead of us and which I hope to see (but not as head of the Federal German Government), the world population will be in the region of 6 billion.

This is a dramatic rate of growth and the most challenging problem of our time. The experts even tell us that once we pass the 6 billion mark 100 million people will be added every year. My little country has only 60 million inhabitants. Most of the 100 million people by which in the near future the world population will grow every year will be added in the poorest countries of the world. And the experts tell us that by the year 2030, that is within fifty-nine years from today, we will reach a number of 10 billion human beings living on earth.

May we hope that the experts, for once, will be proved wrong? May we hope to provide all these masses with food, with shelter, with energy, with jobs, with peace, with liberty, with justice, with dignity?

I very much doubt it. I do not want to speculate further about the growth of mankind or about the load limit of our planet, which the American Academy of Sciences put at about 10 billion people. But I want to emphasize that there is an urgent problem of global proportions which in the last analysis is a family problem for the Family of Man.

The decision how many children—if any—a couple wants to have is a personal decision. It must remain a strictly personal decision. It must never be subject to rulings from outside and it must be respected. Unborn life requires equal respect.

However, the attitude of future mothers and fathers is certainly also dependent on economic and social circumstances. In a great many poor nations, children are seen as welcome additions to a family's labor force. And to many parents they are also an old-age insurance.

The World Bank, in its *Development Report 1980,* points to the link between household poverty and high rates of childbearing—and to the fact that the poor mostly have very limited access to means of birth control.

In view of this situation, we must strive to raise the standard of living in the poorer countries; to reduce the economic motives for very large families; and—at the same time—to teach family planning and make it socially acceptable.

It is in this context that I hope for a change—and I say this very frankly—in the theological attitudes toward contraception. I favor family planning because I fear for human values, for justice, freedom, and dignity in the future. I fear, indeed, for the survival of man if the population growth continues unchecked along the statistical charts and figures that I have given.

Now, ladies and gentlemen, mentioning the World Bank leads me back to the much too flattering remarks of Robert McNamara. You may not, Bob, recall this, but I have come to see you almost every year or every second year in whatever office you have occupied in Washington, D.C., since 1960. I was at that time what they call a "promising young member" of Parliament. Like Bob McNamara, I was then a member of the international defense community. He was a great man; he was secretary of defense of the United States. But I have maintained the habit of visiting Bob McNamara from time to time after he moved to the World Bank, after I had become minister of defense in my little country, and after I had become minister of finance. I have always liked to come to him, to talk to him, to listen to him especially. He is one of the great Americans who not only serve their own nation but the world. And I would like to express my appreciation to Bob McNamara.

Now let me say that in the reception line tonight I met quite a few old American friends, many people whom I have known for twenty years as in the case of Bob McNamara; some for twenty-five or twenty-seven years, and one even thirty years. I would like to take this opportunity to thank all the Americans for the firm cooperation, for the steadiness, for the reliable friendship which they have extended to me, and to other of my countrymen. Without that kind of steady friendship and help it would have been even more difficult, much more difficult for us Germans to get out of the mess which we inherited after the Hitler period. But there is one man here tonight — and I was deeply moved by the words that Ambassador McHenry has said about him — to whom I would like to be permitted to specifically pay tribute. I am talking of a man who again has served his country as a patriot, has served in the world, but also has served the cause of the world and has been welcomed, honored, and respected and loved in Europe and in Germany especially as a great friend. I am thankful to you, Cyrus Vance.

Justice, freedom, and the dignity of man — these are the common values and principles which also form the basis of German-American friendship and solidarity. We are not of one spirit because we are allies — it is the other way round: we are allies because we are of one spirit, because we have the same moral standards. And as it is the spirit which governs our actions, I hope our solidarity will remain steadfast in the future.

We stand at the end of the difficult year 1980 which has marked the beginning of a very difficult decade. The tragic plight of the American hostages in Iran is still not over. The bloody intervention in Afghanistan continues. The war between Iraq and Iran rages on. The conflict between Israel and her neighbors is unresolved. The process of arms limitation is stagnant. The development of the world economy is still fraught with crises.

A world in this state — that is an acid test for the solidarity of the industrial democracies. We must act in unison. We must profit from a division of labor while maintaining our unity of purpose.

I want to assure you Americans that my country will meet to the full its responsibility with you in the Alliance and also worldwide. Our policy will remain predictable, calculable, reliable, and sound. We shall continue to put our faith in America, in the strength, vitality, and dynamic energy of your great nation. If you have the same faith in us, we shall be able to master the future together in peace and in freedom and for the benefit of the world in which we jointly bear responsibility.

9

Speech at the Commencement Ceremony at Harvard University

(June 7, 1979)

Ladies and Gentlemen, and Mr. President,

Thank you very much for your kind and generous words of introduction. Let me tell you that in my country the name Harvard has a clear ring — it tells of a spirit of academic enlightenment embracing all fields of life, including the political sphere. What is being thought and published at Harvard can be certain of the attention of European intellectuals and German intellectuals alike. Thus it is all the more gratifying for a politician today to receive such a high award from Harvard University.

My satisfaction and my gratitude is all the greater knowing that the award is intended, not least, for the democratic and peaceful Germany of today. It seems in my interpretation to be meant for the successful development of a democracy which has now well functioned for thirty years. That democracy had to be built out of the debris of Hitler's Second World War and had to be integrated into the community of Western democracies. For both these tasks your country provided immeasurable inspiration and assistance.

It has not been forgotten at home that a considerable number of scholars who had to flee the Nazi regime in Germany were able to resume their activities here at Harvard.

And after the Second World War, German science, which had either been hampered or even interrupted in its development by Hitler, also received valuable impulses from Harvard. During the last thirty years many German scientists were able to work at this university and take home new ideas, both in their respective fields and for teaching and research in general.

And there are some particularly striking examples of the close link between your university and politics. I would gratefully name three Harvard personalities from which I personally have received political advice on several occasions. I would like to mention the late James B. Conant, also Professor Robert Bowie, and of course Professor Henry Kissinger.

More than thirty years ago, on the 5th of June, 1947, Harvard did become the cradle of a European economic renaissance because at that date the then American Secretary of State George Marshall announced the great aid program for the reconstruction of Europe.

Marshall, it seems to me, was the first statesman to acknowledge the economic and social components of a peace policy when he declared that without the return of normal economic health in the world there could be no political stability and no assured peace.

Yesterday night in Columbia, South Carolina, I had a chance to speak at length on American solidarity vis-à-vis my country, and on German-American cooperation, which I certainly trust will be carried on and developed also by the next generations. Today I would like to concentrate on peace policy, as being conceived from a German point of view.

Peace is the central and prime concern of our German overall policy. It determines our outlook on the world and our attitude toward other countries. At the same time we do not regard peace policy as being merely aimed at the prevention of war. Our notion is rather more comprehensive. And it does include—like George Marshall's interpretation—economic and social factors as well, and also of course the cultural elements.

Nowadays new emerging forces are making themselves felt in world politics. For instance, the People's Republic of China, the largest population in the world, is emerging from its previous isolation, which is an important development in world politics that we welcome, and we welcome also its being assisted by the normalization of China's relations with the United States of America and with other countries.

The emancipation of the Third World in general is a multifaceted force of great complexity that changes the world. The developing countries have become more self-confident. They have learned how to act independently in the world's political arena where they actively stand up for their interests. And at the United Nations their great number has given them a powerful majority.

As their self-confidence grows, the diversity of interests—and I have to add, and the tensions—become clearer which have been hidden behind the makeshift term Third World. This term so far does include rich OPEC countries as well as the poor countries of the Sahel zone in Africa, it does include democracies and military governments alike, conservative, liberal, socialist, and Marxist governments. The political activation of Islam also is creating motion and, at some places, unrest, and not only in Iran.

My conclusion of all this is that all of us are living in an economically interdependent world of more than 150 states, without as yet having enough experience in managing this interdependence. What we need is in the first place partnership for security, and afterward partnerships in cooperation for economic well-being.

History has shown that all countries base their external security largely on their military capabilities. If only one country had to ensure its security, it could do so by attaining military superiority over its neighbors. But a country in such a position of superiority is considered a threat by the other countries. And their feeling of insecurity can have effects which are ultimately no longer controllable by political means. There can be security for both sides simultaneously. And that means the renunciation of military superiority.

In my judgment, equilibrium is the main element underlying security. For many years I have regarded balance of power as an indispensable precondition for peace, and now I find that this conviction more and more has been borne out.

The renunciation of military superiority by the great North Atlantic Alliance to which both you Americans and we Germans do belong, however, does not mean that we are prepared to accept a dangerous inferiority. The decisions of the last few years show that the Atlantic Alliance is ready and in a position to preserve the military balance and also to restore it, where that was necessary. I think one has to agree with the assessment by your Secretary of State Cyrus Vance, made at the thirtieth anniversary of NATO, namely that this alliance is the most successful alliance in history. Not only because the Alliance has prevented a new war, but also because the Alliance, with its renunciation of military superiority, laid the foundation for a policy of equilibrium.

I think that military contributions, yours, of other nations, ours, to that Alliance, in order to enable our common defense, are indeed vital. But like our partners, also we Germans can render them only if and as long as we ensure that there is a balanced political and economic development also.

In saying so I have in mind in particular for us Europeans the importance of the European Community, founded in 1957. A few days ago, a ceremony took place in Athens, Greece, at which the treaty on Greece's accession to the European Community was signed. And the decision to include first Greece, and then afterward Portugal and Spain, was never seriously questioned, despite all the implied and resulting economic, political, financial, and organizational problems. This enlargement of the European Community, which now comprises ten and will soon comprise twelve European nations, is, in my view, a contribution to strengthening and stabilizing democracy on the continent of Europe.

Immediately after the war the goal of European integration, which from the beginning on has received generous and far-sighted support from the Americans, for us Germans had been the signal for a new political start. And we gratefully think back to those Americans who have helped us Germans to

On American television, May 1978.

find our way, among which I would, amending my previous remarks, also like to mention John McCloy and Lucius Clay, and first of all, in terms of history, James F. Byrnes.

Now, in coming back to our Alliance, I wish to state my belief that equilibrium and balance cannot be established once and forever. One has to work on it all the time, and it can be endangered at any moment. It can be endangered by changes. Typical features of change, for instance in the strategic threat to Europe, are the multiple increases in the medium-range missile area, missiles with nuclear warheads targeted against Europe, very mobile and thus invulnerable missiles. Our alliance cannot remain idle in the face of such developments. Its renunciation of superiority does not mean that we are prepared to jeopardize our own security through a position of inferiority.

And it's natural therefore that the Alliance should urge that the Soviet nuclear capability, not covered by SALT so far, should also be subjected to arms control.

The weapons which I'm talking of, often referred to as "grey area weapons," in my view some of them ought to be called more appropriately "Eurostrategic weapons," because they have a strategic destructiveness. These weapons, I hope, can be included, will be included into arms control negotiations. And I hope that SALT III will be a suitable forum for restricting such weapon systems also.

We may here follow up the readiness of General-Secretary Brezhnev, who said that approximate equality and parity will be sufficient to ensure security. And he said that adequate disarmament and arms control measures in the nuclear and conventional fields, which correspond to this principle, are of great importance now, given the Warsaw Pact's repeated assurance of its readiness to negotiate mutual arms limitations also in the Eurostrategic field, and not only in the central strategic field.

We must also make adequate and suitable means available for the Alliance's strategy of flexible response and forestall any developments that might undermine this strategy which continues to be valid. Therefore our Alliance must improve its deterrent and defense capabilities also by modernizing its nuclear forces as well as this is being done by the Soviet Union and her allies.

But I consider it important to emphasize that our Alliance's decision in favor of modernization does not represent an alternative to an arms control policy.

The Alliance knows that defense and arms control measures are not only mutually dependent but they are complementary. It was obvious from the start that the attempt to curb the unrestrained arms race by means of arms control would be very difficult and would take a great deal of time.

It's in keeping with the interests of all mankind that the process of arms control between East and West has made the greatest progress in the field of the most dangerous weapons.

And I should like to insert here a remark on SALT II. And in doing so it's not my intention to interfere with the United States Senate's oncoming decision on ratifying SALT II. But SALT II is of course not only a domestic matter for the American nation. This treaty is a piece of world history. It's also a piece of world security and it's a piece of my country's security. For the present this treaty is the climax of cooperative arms limitation. And the Federal Republic of Germany supports the SALT II treaty, and we hope that it will soon be ratified by Washington and Moscow.

The main aspect of the SALT II treaty is the codification of the intercontinental strategic nuclear balance, or the balance in the central strategic weapons field. And this is a prerequisite for the military and political stabilization of the East-West relationship, and it is also a decisive factor in military and political détente. It's also psychologically a decisive factor.

A failure of SALT II would be a serious setback for détente and a serious setback for ongoing arms control efforts. We would have to expect an even fiercer arms race. A failure of SALT II would also be a wrong signal to the East. It would weaken the political elements there who are in favor of reconciliation and understanding with us in the West.

In Europe no nation would be more seriously affected by the consequences of a failure of SALT II than my own people, the German nation. For in our geopolitical situation we need to be able to trust in two things more than anybody else needs this. On the one hand, trust in the ability of the West to achieve and preserve a stable equilibrium, and secondly, trust in the continuity of détente, on the basis of that equilibrium. The successful conclusion and ratification of SALT II will reinforce this trust. The success of SALT II will encourage the West and the East to find solutions, including arms control measures, for other potentials that are threatening the military balance of power.

I feel sure that the successful conclusion and ratification of SALT II will also create the conditions for progress at the talks on the mutual and balanced reduction of armed forces on the European continent. In the heart of the European continent there is today the highest concentration of arms among all other regions of the globe. We therefore do have a special interest in not only global parity but also in regional arms limitation.

In my opinion there is no alternative, not in the 1980s either, to détente, to the policy of détente, as an instrument of strengthening the security partnership between East and West. And I have chosen this word very considerately — security partnership.

I've always considered our policy of détente to be a very sober policy of interests which can only be successful if its possibilities and its limitations are recognized and observed.

Of course, détente cannot ever eliminate differences in values, it cannot ever eliminate differences in ideals and in political and social systems. We have to live with a paradox. We cannot trust in the communist ideology, we cannot trust in its political aims, but we can and we must endeavor to make use of the interest which also communist leaders clearly do have, namely in preserving peace and, what they clearly have, in the dependability of treaties which they conclude.

By the way, the Conference on Security and Cooperation in Europe, and its Final Act, in Helsinki in 1975, was and remains to be a political success. One of the main results, in my mind, of that negotiation process, which will be continued in Madrid in 1980, has now in the meantime become a matter of course, namely that the Soviet Union has recognized that the United States of America and also Canada must be involved when security and cooperation in Europe is at issue.

Détente between East and West depends considerably on the state of relations between the United States and the Soviet Union. It's therefore important for all of us that the conclusion of SALT II does finally permit the personal meeting between Jimmy Carter and Leonid Brezhnev next week.

I think partnership and security does involve trust and predictability, calculability, it does necessitate transparency. For that reason personal and direct contact between political leaders is indispensable. One has to know the man with whom one has to reckon, whose future actions one has to calculate. It's indispensable.

I have, for quite a few years now, been acquainted with both my friend Jimmy Carter and General-Secretary Brezhnev. My hopes that the summit meeting between them in Vienna next week will be a success is therefore well founded. Their meeting can become an important step toward a partnership for security in the eighties.

Let me say a word about the role of my country within détente. As one state of the divided German nation, placed at the interface between East and West, the Federal Republic of Germany, in my mind, has a specific contribution to make to détente. Because it's only through détente that we Germans can hope to ease the tragic effects on our people resulting from the division of Germany. We therefore have a direct human interest in progress of détente.

Two weeks ago in Germany we celebrated the thirtieth anniversary of our democratic constitution. Neither we nor our partners have any doubts that our thirty-year-old democracy belongs to the family of Western democracies. But neither we nor our partners will forget that thirty years ago the founding of the two German states also entailed the consolidation of the division of Germany for many decades since and many decades to come, probably. Today we are unable to say when and how the German people will be able to fulfill the mandate of our constitution, that is, to achieve in free self-determination the unity and freedom of Germany. But we do know from thirty years of experience that the knowledge of being one nation will remain vivid and will remain important for future generations in both German states.

However, we also know that the idea of the nation cannot be the overriding criterion of our policies. The ultimate goal and the ultimate orientation must be to preserve peace. Only in a state of peace, secured by political and contractual means, will it be possible for Europe to grow together again, from the economic viewpoint, from the cultural, from the human viewpoint. And only after a long period of peace will unity be conceivable.

To leave Europe for a moment and have a glance on other continents of the world, let me state that we are witnessing an alarming increase in military intervention by one country into another, which is the case in Southeast Asia, also in East Africa. We witness the dangers implied in the developments in the southern part of Africa. And let me please insert here that I personally was deeply moved by the way in which you, ladies and gentlemen, this very morning greeted Bishop Desmond Tutu, a black bishop of South Africa. The dangers of the African continent are perhaps highlighted by the fact that the military interventions of Cuba are already part of that continent.

We are against conflicts on one continent being transferred to another continent. Nobody can in the long run plead credibly for détente in Europe, for instance, while at the same time offering the export of weapons and political ideologies as a solution for the problems of the Third World in other continents, but not providing vital development aid. Rather conversely must we try, by uniting our efforts wherever possible, to apply the experience gained from détente and from crisis management also to the solution of the problems in the Third World.

Only recently the whole world was witness to the moving scenes in El Arish which accompanied the first steps in the implementation of the peace treaty between Egypt and Israel. President Sadat's courageous move in November 1977, the positive reply of the Israeli government, plus President Carter's personal commitment, have, for a historical second, led a way out of the vicious circle of force and distrust and hatred. But the ultimate historical significance of this peace treaty will be measured by whether or not this agreement between two states leads to an overall solution which can be accepted by all states and all peoples in that region. This involves, in the first instance, acceptance of the rights of the Palestinians to decide for themselves on their political future.

Let me come back to the commencement speech of George Marshall at Harvard thirty-two years ago. He said: "It is logical that the United States should do whatever it is able to do to assist in the return of normal economic health in the world, without which there can be no political stability and no assured peace." I think he was right. Lasting prosperity can only be achieved or preserved by joint efforts. This necessity of joint efforts has consequences for the relationship between the industrialized and the developing countries. Development assistance is a human and a moral and also an economic obligation. This necessity for joint efforts must also have consequences, for instance, for the relationship between oil-exporting countries and oil-importing countries. In fact, I would go as far as to say that a cooperative management of energy supply and energy demand is becoming an essential element in the preservation of peace worldwide. And it is becoming an essential element thus in world security. A worldwide struggle for the distribution of decreasing energy supplies would inevitably produce serious tension and conflict among a great number of countries. And the poorer developing countries certainly would be the most seriously affected ones.

In this situation the world as a whole cannot ignore any possible source of energy. We cannot ignore solar or geothermal energy, we cannot ignore nuclear energy either.

Nuclear energy already plays an indispensable, albeit complementary role in the world's energy supply. I personally believe that nuclear energy, including the option for fast breeders, must continue to play this role within the foreseeable future, simply to meet the developing countries' demand — it must continue to play its role in the world within the foreseeable future, if only to meet the developing countries' demand for energy resources on favorable economic terms.

For this reason Article IV of the Non-Proliferation Treaty, since more than ten years, states expressly: "All the Parties to the Treaty undertake to facilitate, and have the right to participate in, the fullest possible exchange of equipment, materials and scientific and technological information for the peaceful uses of nuclear energy." And the article makes it the explicit duty of the contracting parties to take into consideration the "needs of the developing areas of the world."

However, especially after the incident at Three Mile Island at Harrisburg, in your country, scientists, engineers, plant operators, also political leaders, must reexamine on an international scale and cooperatively the necessary safety provisions, and one will have to learn from the experiences of the other.

Therefore, I have proposed that this should be done in an international cooperation by the International Atomic Energy Agency in Vienna, and I'm glad to acknowledge the consent of the United States.

Let me conclude by saying, ladies and gentlemen, that the road toward a security partnership, especially a security partnership between East and West, but also between North and South, is a long road, a road paved with obstacles. But we already have embarked upon that road, and we Germans want it to be continued all along, step by step. The mere prevention and the mere absence of war is not the only thing and not everything we want to attain. We want to attain partnership for security between West and East and want from there to advance toward partnership of cooperation.

Just as proper political action must always be guided by moral principles, equitable peace must be the subject and purpose of our political ethics.

With this intention we are in good tradition. We are in tradition with President Roosevelt and Winston Churchill, who, forty years ago, jointly declared their hope in the Atlantic Charter "to see established a peace which will afford to all nations the means of dwelling in safety within their own boundaries, and which will afford assurance that all the men in all the lands may live out their lives in freedom from fear and want."

Our values and ideals are based on the best of what mankind has conceived and combined so far: freedom, tolerance, equity, and justice.

I feel confident that freedom, that the basic rights of the individual person and the principle of the dignity of man are on the march and cannot be stopped.

All of us in the West have the obligation to keep this torch alight and make it be seen throughout the world. This also means that we must critically examine our own positions from time to time.

And let me say this. A partnership of peace in only conceivable without victors. It's a partnership of reason for which there is no alternative.

Harvard, which has managed to reconcile intellect and power, also has, in view of its historical role, an obligation in this respect. It is the illuminating force of the investigating intellect striving for the truth.

10

Continuity and Concentration: Policy Statement Delivered to the Bundestag

(May 17, 1974)

The new government of the Federal Republic of Germany is a continuation of the social-liberal coalition which set out its political intentions in the policy statement of January 18, 1973. That statement applies for the entire legislative term. Today we will take stock.

The change in the chancellorship does not alter the fact that a social-liberal policy in this country continues to be right and necessary. We intend to pursue that course consistently. At a time of growing international problems, we shall concentrate realistically and soberly on essentials, on what needs to be done now, leaving other matters aside.

Continuity and concentration, that is the theme for the new government.

II

The federal government today does not want to speak about its intentions without first addressing the previous chancellor.

We are conscious of what Willy Brandt has achieved for this country. What he has done to win for the Federal Republic both respect and attention has been an outstanding service to our nation and one on which German policy can be based.

We owe him thanks for the creative energy he has demonstrated in bringing this country onto a new course of internal reform.

The reform policy initiated by his government achieved more social progress in just short of half a decade than has ever before been achieved within such a period.

His government's policy toward Eastern Europe and regarding intra-German relations was courageous and successful. As the *New York Times* wrote: "He has helped the world to take a big step toward peace." We are grateful to Willy Brandt. We know that we shall continue to need him and his counsel.

We owe thanks to Walter Scheel, the new federal president. As foreign minister he has stood side by side with Brandt in pursuance of the government's peace policy, and his liberal spirit and warm-hearted nature have added to our friends in the world.

In his new office he will follow in the footsteps of Theodor Heuss, Heinrich Lübke, and Gustav Heinemann. We are sure the Federal Electoral College has made a good choice. Walter Scheel will be a convincing representative of this country, both in its external relations and at home.

We also extend our thanks to the ministers who have left the federal government.

III

The social-liberal coalition has been the motor of progress in the Federal Republic since 1969. This is also true of the past eighteen months. The progress report submitted by the federal government in December 1973 was impressive evidence of this.

To begin with I should like to make an interim survey of the main areas of work in the current legislative term.

Our program of tax reform has been before the Bundestag in package form since the beginning of this year.

- The new legislation on the taxation of external earnings which makes it more difficult for companies to evade taxation has been enacted.
- Also on the statute book is the new property and inheritance tax law. Here we have noticeably eased the burden on those with smaller assets.
- The trade tax allowances will be raised as from January 1, 1975. Thus from then on one in every two traders will no longer pay any tax on trade earnings.
- The debate of the new Revenue Code in the finance committee of the Bundestag is about to be concluded.

Now we have to turn our attention to the nucleus of reform measures in this field: the modification of wage and income tax and linked with it a readjustment of the equalization of family burdens with new children's allowances. Our aim with these new measures is to create a more equitable and, as far as possible, more simple income tax system, which is an elementary right. Once this reform has entered into force (that is, on January 1, 1975) the burden on the taxpayer, and in particular the lower and middle income groups, will be 10 to 12 billion deutsche marks a year less; as a result the incomes of people in these groups will increase accordingly. I shall be coming back to the grave consequences this will have for the public finances and the efficacy of the public budgets.

On February 20, 1974, the federal government adopted the new bill on co-determination. We see in a system of co-determination based on the principle of equal rights and equal representation for workers and shareholders an essential credit item of the coalition in the field of social policy. A society wishing to move forward both economically and socially is inconceivable without co-determination and without the sharing of responsibility that goes with it.

The enactment of the Works' Constitution Act and the Personnel Representation Act has strengthened the position of the individual employee in the factory and in the office. Now it is a question of enabling employees to have a say in company decision making. Through co-determination we want to give employees opportunities and rights to exercise more influence on the shaping of their conditions of work and life. Our purpose is to enable them to bring their own experience and proposals to bear. I am confident that it will be possible to give effect to this important law by the beginning of 1975.

With the enactment of the law to amend the Federal Building Act the federal government has taken a further important step forward in reforming land law. It will ensure that a proportion of the increase in the value of land as a result of public measures can be claimed for the community. The objective of this system is to hold the rise in the price of land, to put a stop to speculation and to make it easier for larger sections of the community to acquire property.

The federal government has taken steps to improve the quality of life and to protect the environment.

- The Federal Emission Control law establishes the basis for the taking of legal action against those responsible for air pollution and excessive noise.
- New legislation on waste effluent, forest and nature conservation, and landscape management, as well as the necessary amendments to the Basic Law, have already been put before Parliament. It is now up to the opposition to show whether they merely pay lip service to environmental protection or whether they are prepared to play a constructive part in putting the necessary measures into practice.
- We shall have to see whether the present organization for coping with these problems is an optimum solution. Moreover, as a result of the energy crisis of recent months some problems have become even more acute or have newly arisen.

It will be the aim of the federal government to ensure that the younger generation can acquire appropriate vocational qualifications. For this purpose it has drawn up the principles for the revision of the Vocational Education Act. In shaping the bill the federal government will listen to the advice and call upon the experience of those directly concerned with vocational education.

We want vocational training to be of equal standards and equal value in all fields. In seeking to achieve this we shall proceed cautiously and, in close cooperation with all concerned, try to find solutions which will meet the justified demands of the young for the kind of training that will provide them with the qualifications they need, and which will at the same time promote the development of the national economy.

The further development of vocational education does not merely mean sending people back to school. Our aim is an appropriate distribution of responsibilities and cooperation among firms and schools and, where necessary, among central training establishments. Speaking on this problem in Hanover on April 25, 1974, Chancellor Willy Brandt said: "No member of the federal government is thinking of doing away with the well-tried dual system of vocational education, in other words the system based on the joint responsibility of government and industry."

The federal government and the states, industry, schools, factories and craftsmen, employers and trade unions, instructors and trainees, must all contribute to the reform of vocational education. We appreciate the great achievements of many instructors and the institutions active in this field in past years. We want to provide not less but more training opportunities for the young in workshops and offices leading to appropriate qualifications.

I cannot list all the measures the social-liberal coalition has either put into effect or launched since the Bundestag elections of 1972 in other important areas of social policy. I will merely mention a few.

We have extended the system of social security and social benefits have been improved.

- In the three years from 1972 and 1974 pensions were increased by 44 percent. Of course, part of that has been eaten up by rising prices, but the fact remains: actual purchasing power after deduction of price increases has risen by 19 percent.
- Considerable improvements have been made not only to pensions but also to war victims' maintenance: apart from the increases in benefits and structural improvements of recent years, the dates for increases of the pensions of war victims have been brought forward stage by stage.
- Improvements to the farmers' social welfare scheme are still being made. In the course of this old-age benefits for farmers will be income related as from January 1, 1975.
- In future, benefits from works' provident funds will not be forfeited, for example, where an employee moves to another firm or where his employer goes bankrupt. This will give additional security to twelve million employees.
- The Third Social Welfare Amendment Act which entered into force on April 1, 1974, has brought significant improvements for older people, those needing care, and the handicapped.

The new Works' Safety Law, which requires firms to employ doctors and safety specialists, as well as the bill for the protection of young workers, are designed to further the humanization of the working environment.

There is no need for me to emphasize the fact that the Works' Constitution Act and the pending Co-determination Act are important instruments for achieving the aim of humanizing the working environment.

The core of the rehabilitation action program, the new law concerning the severely disabled, came into force on May 1, 1974. A bill for the adjustment of rehabilitation benefits is before Parliament.

Health protection is being consistently improved. Since January 1 this year all persons covered by health insurance schemes are entitled to hospital treatment for unlimited durations.

A new federal scale of charges for hospital treatment as well as the law on hospital financing are designed to improve hospital treatment.

The federal government will systematically continue its promotion of basic medical research and research on the combating of disease, especially such widespread diseases as cancer.

We have introduced an up-to-date family policy:

- The new marriage and family legislation is down for final debate in the Bundestag.
- The law on parental care affords children greater protection and extends their rights.

Permit me in this connection to say a few words about the amendment of section 218 of the penal code, a bill which has been a major point at issue in the house and has been debated with due seriousness by all. I should be happy if we continued to work in this spirit and to display the same respect for the opinion of our political opponents.

The decision taken recently has confronted all of us with a severe test of conscience. Proper advice and assistance together with public understanding for women and families in such situations of conflict, as well as respect for the dignity of women and for their sense of responsibility, form part of the effective protection for the embryo.

How seriously we take this matter is shown by the additional advisory and family planning services offered by the health insurance institutions, the benefits available to working mothers who have sick children to take care of, the house-nursing services for families in difficult situations, in fact the overall improvements in our social security system to give not only the individual but also families greater security.

The legislation to protect tenants from wrongful termination of their lease contracts will be incorporated in the Civil Code. In the past two years the new legislation has already provided better and more effective protection for tenants and has at the same time made allowance for the interests of the owners. Since

Taking the oath for the office of chancellor, May 16, 1974.

the introduction of these measures there has been a noticeable drop in the number of eviction actions.

In addition to this protection in law, tenants may increasingly be eligible for financial assistance. Today three times as much is paid out in rent subsidies as in 1969. Nearly one and a half million households now receive such assistance.

The overall educational plan introduced by the states and the federal government in the autumn of 1973 is the framework for the long-term development of the education system as a whole which will have to be filled out with a sober appraisal of what can be achieved. In this connection I wish to quote a passage from the minutes of the meeting of the heads of the federal and state governments on September 20, 1973: "Insofar as the educational targets for this period have financial implications, the scope and the schedule for their implementation will be determined in accordance with the modalities of the medium-term financial planning programme."

The skeleton law on higher education currently before the Bundestag will smooth the way not only for a uniform national organization of the university sphere but will above all create the prerequisites for the long overdue reform of study courses. This law must be given quick passage through Parliament. The states and the federal government bear considerable responsibility in this respect.

The Federal Education Promotion Act has been extended to include large groups of pupils attending specialized vocational schools.

We have improved the law on competition and measures to protect consumers:

- The new Cartel Law will improve the basis for competition.
- The Hire Purchase Act entitles the purchaser to withdraw from his contract within a certain time limit.
- Food legislation is to be tightened to reduce the dangers of harmful substances finding their way into edible goods. The appropriate laws are before Parliament.

The joint program of the federal government and the states for the safeguarding of internal security is designed to enhance the rule of law as exercised in this country, a system which enables us to act resolutely while at the same time respecting the rights of the individual. It costs money but it helps to protect our democratic system.

- The Federal Criminal Investigation Office has in the meantime become a modern crime-fighting organization.
- Compensation for the victims of acts of violence is guaranteed by law.

All the measures I have mentioned represent improvements in the quality of life in this country which every citizen can judge for himself. This interim balance speaks for itself. Yet the opposition maintains that our reform policies have failed. The facts tell a different story and we shall not let these achievements be talked away.

IV

We want our friends and neighbors, our alliance and treaty partners in the world to know that the positions of our foreign and security policy remain unchanged. We shall continue our policy of safeguarding peace and we shall guard and strengthen our country's security. We shall actively contribute toward maintaining the balance of power which is requisite to peace.

We subscribe to the political unification of Europe in partnership with the United States. The irreplaceable basis for this is the European Community. I shall refer to it later on. More urgent than ever is the establishment of a European political union. Together with our partners in the European Community we shall strive to realize this goal.

The Atlantic Alliance remains both the elementary basis of our security and the political framework required for our efforts to promote international détente. We shall continue to work for the political strengthening of the

Alliance and by means of our armed forces render our contribution to collective security as agreed within the Alliance. Our soldiers fulfill this task. We owe them our thanks. International equilibrium and the security of Western Europe will, within the foreseeable future, remain dependent on the United States' military and political presence in Europe. The European-American relationship is governed by identical security interests.

The federal government is determined to support, together with its allies, a policy of arms control and reduction with a view to limiting the threat of power-political and military pressures. In this context it observes not without concern the increasing armament efforts of the Warsaw Pact.

The federal government hopes therefore that the Russian-American efforts to bring about a limitation of nuclear strategic weapons systems (SALT) will be successful, and it continues its own endeavors to help achieve a mutual balanced reduction of forces and arms in Europe (MBFR) with the sincere desire for success.

Resting on the firm foundation of our alliance within the North Atlantic Treaty Organization we foster good relations with the Soviet Union and the countries of the Warsaw Pact.

The federal government considers the Conference on Security and Cooperation in Europe (CSCE) to be important in confidence building. The cooperation practiced by the member countries of the European Community in matters of foreign policy has proved its value at this conference.

It is our aim not only to adopt resolutions but to arrive at practical results so as to give more substance to the policy of détente in Europe.

We are no less inclined to cooperate with those European countries which do not belong to any political or military grouping but are nonetheless interested in the progress of détente and the safeguarding of peace. We shall continue to foster our good and proven relations with these countries whose importance we rate highly.

International developments are showing us that it was right to conclude treaties with our eastern neighbors and thus not to miss the chance of combining our own interests with the process of worldwide détente. The treaties of Moscow and Warsaw and the treaty of Prague which has not yet been ratified are the fruits of our efforts at international détente.

The resultant Quadripartite Agreement on Berlin has placed that city's viability on a secure basis and contributed toward peaceful conditions in central Europe. The federal government for its part will do everything in its power to safeguard Berlin's viability, to strengthen the Berliners' confidence in the future, and to maintain and develop their city's ties with the Federal Republic of Germany.

By its treaty policy, especially by concluding the Treaty on the Basis of Relations between the Federal Republic of Germany and the GDR, the social-liberal coalition has opened up a practicable road for a policy of attaining regulated good-neighborly relations in Germany. Despite all difficulties and setbacks we shall not slacken in our effort to improve mutual relations. We abide by our view that the relations between the Federal Republic of Germany and the GDR are of a special nature.

In the spirit of the policy of détente and in the interest of all Germans we have concluded treaties with the GDR. These treaties do not just consist of letters. Both contracting partners must also observe the spirit of the treaties concluded.

The grave spy case which has deeply upset people in East and West these days is not in keeping with that spirit. We rate it, in all frankness, as seriously straining the relationship between the contracting parties, especially since we for our part are determined fully to honor the treaty in letter and in spirit.

We have an unchanged vital interest in a just and lasting peace settlement in the Middle East. I reaffirm my predecessor's policy. As in the past, we support the peace efforts in that region, and, together with our partners, we want to help in the search for peace.

We shall, moreover, do everything in our power to develop our relations with the Asian countries, our traditional friendship with the Latin American countries and our partnership relations with the African countries. The right to self-determination which we claim for ourselves must apply everywhere.

V

The Federal Republic of Germany will face up to its international responsibilities. By joining the United Nations we completed the process of our reintegration into the family of nations. This step entails obligations because numerous members of that family of nations are in need of help. It is our firm intention to fulfill our obligations. One can count upon us but one should not make excessive demands on us.

Next to the United States, this country is the world's leading trade partner. While the Americans export 4 percent of their gross national product, we export 22. This shows clearly how much this country depends on its foreign trade. We are therefore susceptible to all kinds of disturbances in the world economic system and the safety of our jobs is greatly dependent on the development of world trade. Earnings, the size of investments, the progress of productivity, and hence the standard of living are most strongly influenced by our foreign trade.

We therefore need a stable world economy, free trade, and a properly regulated monetary system. Protectionism is a blind alley. We are therefore in favor of intensified cooperation in the field of monetary policy and consider that the rules for world trade should be developed and strengthened within the framework of GATT. The decisions taken by the Special Session of the United Nations General Assembly on Raw Materials and Development have made it clear that the future world economic system must also be based on a new relationship with the developing countries. We shall take account of this by pursuing an open trade, structural, and monetary policy.

Roughly two-thirds of our imports and exports are being transacted with our EC partners and the former EFTA [European Free Trade Area] countries linked with the EC. For these and general political reasons it is of great political importance to us that the European Community and the elements of common action and economic cooperation which it has already carried into practice should be kept fully efficient. We are aware that our prosperity is also bound up with the European Economic Community and its continued existence.

In many years of hard work, during which Willy Brandt in particular made an untiring effort, it has been possible to give the European Community a new dimension by the accession of additional members. However, the problems which were aggravated by the fact that the accession was delayed so long have not yet been solved.

At the summit conferences held in the Hague in 1969 and in Paris in 1972, the European partner countries set themselves ambitious objectives which continue to be valid for us. Nevertheless, we cannot ignore today that in particular the turbulences upsetting the world monetary system, the massive rise in the prices of raw materials vital to Western Europe, and the inequality of efforts to ensure price stability and the growth of productivity in the EC countries have led to far-reaching disparities within the Community.

We view with deep concern the measures to which some member states have resorted in this situation and which are apt to isolate the European partners from one another. The federal government will therefore have to impress on its partners the need for concrete steps. The Community and especially the Common Market must be maintained. European solidarity must be assured and developed further. My country is prepared to contribute to this in keeping with its productive capacity and stability. Our traditionally friendly relations with France will be helpful in this effort but at the same time will have to prove their value anew.

Under these circumstances which we see without any illusion we must examine, together with our partners in the European Community, how the timetable envisaged so far for economic and monetary union can be met. There can be no doubt about our cooperation.

It must, however, be clear to all concerned: the recovery of economic stability is a task which can and must be achieved by the governments and parliaments chiefly in their own countries. Any assistance by the Community, and that is also by the Federal Republic, can merely be supplementary. Assistance on a partnership basis is, however, only justifiable in one's own country if the recipient country makes resolute efforts of its own to ensure the effectiveness of such aid.

VI

Since the policy statement of January 18, 1973, the world economy has undergone a drastic change. These upheavals originate in the energy and raw material sectors with their excessive price rises in the world market which are beyond our influence. In no time crude oil prices have trebled, all raw material prices are nearly twice as high as they were a year ago, the totality of our import prices has risen by a good 35 percent within twelve months.

In the Federal Republic, on the other hand, the rate of increase in consumer prices has hardly changed since a year ago. It amounts today to 7.1 percent as compared with 7.0 percent twelve months ago. At a time when in other countries prices are rising very much faster and sometimes by leaps and bounds, this is a success which is unequalled in any other country. This is recognized by the majority of the people.

We shall continue our endeavors to keep employment at its present high level. Comparing ourselves internationally with others, we find that we have to guard and develop valuable assets: jobs are safe, wages respectable, we have industrial peace.

The work done by workers and trade unions goes far beyond material considerations. The strength of democracy in this country is due quite largely to the fact that the workers stand loyally for this second German republic. Only as long as this is so democracy will remain stable.

Economic want and mass unemployment once kindled the fire in which the first republic was burned to death. Those in government have to take this as a lesson: it is their duty to realize step by step the kind of social security and justice from which the workers' identification with the state is born.

In 1973, too, real incomes rose by an average of just under 2 percent. In 1974 they will rise as well. In 1975 the reform of the wage tax and children's allowance alone will, for a typical employee's household with two children, increase the net income by approximately 4 percent.

However, the restructuring of the world economy, the explosion of raw material prices (and the reversal of the terms of trade to the detriment of industrial products) set limits to the growth of our real incomes which it is hard to overcome.

Our repeated (and, since the floating of the exchange rate, lasting) upvaluation of the deutsche mark has helped us to master worldwide problems more easily than other countries.

Unbiased observers of the achievements of the Brandt-Scheel government rightly come to the conclusion that, of all other industrialized countries, the Federal Republic at present comes closest to the principal targets of economic policy: (1) a high level of employment, (2) price stability, and (3) economic growth (quotation from the *Handelsblatt* 13 of April 11, 1974). Looking at equally important objectives such as (4) social security and (5) social justice, this conclusion applies all the more.

It is therefore quite logical that a large majority of people, when asked how they see their economic future, answer, "I am well off and I expect things to remain like that in future." Nevertheless, so say some of them, the general, overall economic development is by no means to be judged as favorably as their personal situation. We understand such worries in view of the new and unusual processes that are going on in the world economy. But we have no understanding for the opposition's exploitation of such justified concern for a campaign which is designed to foment fear.

This government will not allow the opposition thus to talk us precisely into the state of affairs which it intends to make people believe. The achievements of our economy and of the government so far make us confident that we shall also be able to meet future challenges.

If we keep to the facts we find that the greater part of our people are economically better off than ever before: The real incomes of employees have in recent years risen more sharply than the incomes from entrepreneurial work. The proportion of employees' incomes in the overall national income rose from 65 to 70 percent between 1969 and 1973. The increase in the number of employees being eliminated, the wage and salary ratio rose from 61 to a good 63 percent between 1969 and 1973. At the same time the proportion of incomes from entrepreneurial work and property decreased from just under 35 percent to 30 percent. In view of the present size of our national income each shift in proportions by only one percentage point means that roughly 8 billion deutsche marks have been transferred from one group to another.

But we must also see the limits. Adequate profits are prerequisite to the necessary investments. Falling investments would do neither our economy nor the individual employee any good. Only a continuous modernization of our national economy will assure and improve our standard of living and the efficiency of the state in the service of its citizens. For that purpose we need adequate investments though not only from private but also from public sources. Without investments there will be no growth. Without growth there will be no safety of jobs, no higher wages, and no social progress.

We shall continue the present course of our economy and financial policy in order to regain step by step greater stability of purchasing power while ensuring a high employment level. This means that:

- Our monetary policy will, on the basis of flexible rates of exchange, and in concert with our partner countries in the European "snake," continue to be oriented to safeguarding the economy as much as possible against external influences. In this process we cannot, however, preclude adjustments in individual branches. Our hard deutsche mark cannot be defended with soft measures.
- While safeguarding our currency against external influences, our monetary and credit policy will ensure an adequate but tight money supply. Our close cooperation with the Bundesbank will be continued.
- The federal government's budgetary policy will, within the framework of the 1974 draft budget presented to this house, counteract exorbitant employment risk in specific regions and branches.

We intend to keep the inevitable strain caused by the necessary policy to ensure stability as small as possible. For this reason we have, for instance, resumed and expanded our program for the promotion of the industrial middle classes. For the same reason the federal government, in concert with the Länder and municipalities, is carrying out a special program with additional infrastructure investments and public procurements in the amount of approximately 900 million deutsche marks in areas with special structural problems.

In its future efforts to ensure stability the federal government will not discharge the social groups of their responsibility. This goes for management and labor alike. A sense of responsibility for the whole is a decisive prerequisite for the autonomy in negotiating wage rates which we defend.

We are faced with an opposition in the Bundestag and Bundesrat which demands a lowering of taxes and at the same time an increase in budget expenditures. This is suggesting to pressure groups that they can make claims although the opposition knows that such claims can never be fulfilled. The efficiency of the state is thus called into question, which is not to be justified.

During the remaining legislative term the chief concern of financial policy will be to accomplish the urgent public tasks and to give consistent support to the policy for stability. To put it clearly: in the performance of this task the chancellor will be on the side of the minister of finance.

VII

Though international comparison shows our economic situation to be good, we cannot afford to overlook the fact that world economic developments demand from us a new consciousness of what is possible.

The tasks of the state have increased. This means that the need is more than ever acute to complement the expectations directed at the state with the necessary responsible awareness of the capacity of the state to fulfill such expectations. The realization of the reform of taxation and children's allowances will place a heavy burden on public expenditure, setting narrow limits in 1975 to the state's capacity for action in other fields. This applies to the municipalities and towns, the Länder and the federal government. It is impossible to reduce next year by 10 to 12 billion deutsche marks the burden on the taxpayer and still spend that same amount elsewhere.

We must, therefore, in determining public expenditure for the year 1975, ward off all excessive demands. This applies to all fields, including the civil service. This we owe to the taxpayers.

In this connection a word on the development of the federal capital of Bonn. It is necessary, even if only to prevent undesirable developments, to make plans for the future. For many years there were none. However, all concerned should know that our financial situation admits of no excessively high expenditures, especially not in the near future.

A severe standard must also be applied to any extra demands levied by the parliaments at the finance ministers both of the federal government and of the Länder.

The federal government will fully exploit all the constitutional and political means at its disposal to commit the federal government, the Länder, and the local authorities to an austere expenditure policy. When in 1975 the tax reform, bringing with it cuts in taxation worth billions of marks, enters into force, we shall — at least as things appear today — not be able to afford high rates of growth in public expenditure.

The easing of the burden on the taxpayers as a result of the tax and children's allowances reform will call for solidarity on the part of all central, regional, and local subdivisions and authorities in order to ensure that the losses in revenue are borne jointly in accordance with the revision clause agreed by the heads of the federal and Länder governments to the financial equalization arrangements.

The Bundestag and the Bundesrat in particular have it in their power, by abandoning legislation and initiatives entailing considerable expenditure, to avoid an increase in the value-added tax. For this would be the only way to close gaps in revenue of this magnitude. It is not the intention of the federal government to increase the value-added tax.

I will not deny here that the federal government, in having had to accept the Bundesrat's proposals on the equalization of children's allowances, has, on this point, put itself entirely at the mercy of the Länder. We are thus dependent on the perspicacity of the Bundesrat. If we fail to reach a reasonable agreement on the apportionment of revenue (financial equalization), we would be forced — that is already clear — to reduce the federal budget, a measure which we believe is neither politically, in substance, nor economically justified.

We are therefore counting on the common sense of the Länder majority to reach an agreement on the apportionment of revenue from the turnover tax, which corresponds to the revision clause agreed on earlier by the heads of government and also, by and large, leads to a distribution among the central, regional, and local authorities of the losses of revenue ensuing from the tax reform similar to that which would result if the so-called law to ease the effects of inflation supported by the Länder majority were to enter into force.

We exclude the curtailment of benefits and services which our citizens enjoy as legal rights. However, the federal government will act with consistency where limitation of expenditure is necessary and justified.

Under the Federal Education Promotion Law, for example, expenditure by the federal government alone will double from 1972 to 1975, an increase of almost 1 billion deutsche marks. We therefore consider it appropriate that a part of the funds to promote students' education should be placed on a loans basis. I welcome the acceptance on May 10, 1974, by all the Länder in the Bundesrat of the federal government's loans concept.

It is encouraging to see that, in so doing, they distanced themselves from the very popular but irresponsible proposals of the opposition in the Bundestag calling for measures, over and above the increases planned by the federal government, which would cost almost an extra 500 million deutsche marks annually.

With the twenty-eighth amendment to the Equalization of Burdens Law introduced by the federal government and at present being considered in the parliamentary committees, and possibly with some minor changes connected with our history, the federal government considers that the complex of legislation dealing with the consequences of the war (in particular compensation to prisoners of war, the equalization of burdens, restitution, and the law on Article 131 of the Basic Law) has now been concluded. It has cost the Federal Republic to date 220 billion deutsche marks and in the future, under present law, a further 174 billion deutsche marks.

Beyond this the federal government can see no possibility of further improvements. The federal government knows that a fully satisfactory settlement of compensation cannot be achieved; this would exceed the financial capacity of our nation. Priority must now be given to tasks before us; they will benefit us all, including those who have suffered loss or injury.

The federal government is engaged in serious efforts to draw up a law on the accumulation of capital by employees and is determined to carry the project through. The basic principles of the law have already been agreed on by the cabinet. The work of drafting the bill has shown that in this relatively unexplored territory there are great legal and technical problems. For example, no satisfactory solution has yet been found to the question of how to determine the value of shares not quoted on the stock exchange. These and other difficult questions must be thoroughly studied.

The federal government will therefore continue its work of drafting this bill. For this purpose it will set up an interministerial body which will be attached to the federal minister of finance and will have the aim of ensuring the passage of the law through Parliament in time to enter into force on January 1, 1978. This means that the bill will be introduced in Parliament in this legislative term.

The federal government is also resolved to introduce the tax credit method within the framework of the corporation tax reform; the surcharge will be replaced by an increased rate of corporation tax. It is envisaged that the bill become law on January 1, 1977.

Here, too, we have learned from experience; neither the ministries nor the finance committee have been able, despite long hours of work, to cope with the overall tax reform program begun in 1969 in the time then envisaged.

Parliament's legislative capacity is limited. We have therefore set different dates for the entry into force of the various elements. However, the reform as a whole, in its substantial aspects, retains its unity. (Land tax January 1, 1974; inheritance and property tax January 1, 1974; income tax January 1, 1975; corporation tax January 1, 1977; accumulation of capital January 1, 1978.)

In the policy statement of January 18, 1973, the preparation of a tax on land value increments was announced. The progress of the work indicates that it will not be possible to complete it in the present legislative term.

VIII

Progress in our country is the fruit not only of social policy but also of the continued modernization of our economy. In this context the energy crisis, the shortage of raw materials, and the shift in the terms of trade have introduced new factors. We are thus faced with new tasks which we will lose no time in tackling. Industry, science, and the state must act together to overcome the problems.

The federal government accords energy policy a high priority in its work. The energy program of summer 1973 put forward for the first time a concept for the safeguarding of our energy supplies in the long term. This foresight proved of considerable value during the energy crisis at the end of last year.

One of the central features of this program is the regrouping of German petroleum companies into a single enterprise capable of holding its own on the international level. We have made good progress in this direction: In 1973 the federal government became a majority shareholder of Gelsenberg and during this legislative term will undertake a merger between VEBA [a state-owned energy company] and Gelsenberg [a petroleum company] within the VEBA combine.

The federal government intends to take further steps to reduce in the long term the share of oil in our total energy supplies and to promote more intensively other energy supplies such as natural gas, nuclear energy, and hard coal and lignite.

In the light of recent developments domestic coal mining has gained new importance. Its position has been consolidated. This will also be reflected in carrying forward the energy program, as planned for this year. It is, however, obvious that it is impossible for the federal government to finance an expanded energy policy alone.

When building new power stations due consideration must be given to the justified demands of environmental protection without causing unnecessary delays.

In the longer term energy research is the indispensable key to the improvement and safeguarding of our country's energy supplies. On January 9, 1974, the federal government adopted, in addition to its other measures, a program for non-nuclear energy research. We are also already engaged in the intensive promotion of nuclear energy. The fourth nuclear program was adopted by the cabinet on December 5, 1973.

However, these important decisions for future developments in the field of energy must not blind us to the fact that our energy supplies may be threatened with disruptions in the immediate future. We shall make provision both on the public and private level to counteract these dangers, but we cannot entirely exclude them.

In the sphere of agricultural and food policy we shall continue resolutely with the successful policy of the social-liberal coalition. Our goal remains—also in the interest of the consumers—to maintain an efficient agriculture which is an equal and integral part of a modern economy. Those working in agriculture must therefore, as hitherto, share in the general rise in the standard of living. With this in view the federal government will also devote special attention to price-cost trends in agriculture.

The reorientation of the agricultural structural policy in the shape of the individual farms promotion program has proved its worth. We shall also work toward a still closer link with regional policy.

The ability to function of the common agricultural market has, especially recently, been impaired by measures of various kinds. In view of the importance of the common agricultural policy for European progress, and also for German agriculture, we shall endeavor to restore the ability to function of the common agricultural market. One aspect of this must be establishment of fair terms of competition for German agriculture. The federal government therefore expects quick decisions from the Commission and Council of Ministers of the European Community in the interest of agricultural producers and their markets.

Today agricultural policy is a policy for everyone who works in the country or seeks rest and recreation there; that is, it is an integral part of our social policy.

The self-employed in commerce, crafts, trades, and in the professions, the small and medium-sized enterprises remain indispensable elements of an economy-oriented competitive efficiency. Without viable small and medium-sized enterprises competition is in the long run not possible. For this reason we shall support them in their desire to hold their own.

A final remark on competition, the guiding principle of our market economy. Competition calls forth the will to achievement. Competition has created in our country the foundations for social and economic progress. Embedded in the framework created by the state, the market economy solves the economic tasks better than other comparable systems. However, the market economy is at no point perfect. Rather, it must be constantly developed. In this context the federal government will continue also in the future to strengthen and promote the forces of competition.

We reject freezes on prices and wages, nor do we believe that tying wages to a cost-of-living index is an appropriate instrument for a policy to regain stability. All countries which have tried this have registered higher price increases than ours.

IX

We are pledged to the Basic Law for the Federal Republic of Germany which in a few days' time will be twenty-five years old. All of us in this freely elected Parliament are agreed that this constitution has come through the test exceptionally well. The federal government therefore advocates that this proven constitutional framework should be kept intact, the mandate it embodies be carried out, and our democratic state based on the rule of law developed into a likewise democratic social state.

Our democratic state concerns everyone. It lives on the responsible commitment of the individual citizen who helps to do the thinking and helps to take the decisions. The people are not only there on election day. Only if they devote themselves to the state, the champion and guardian of the rights and freedoms of all, will the state have the energy to assert the liberties and rights of the individual for the benefit of all against sectional interests.

The federal government also expects that the statutory framework established to preserve our liberal legal system is respected by all social and political groupings. We are determined to preserve and defend freedom and the system of laws created for that purpose. The judicial authorities, the police, and other institutions for the upkeep of internal security can be sure of the firm support of the federal government in carrying out their responsibilities in keeping with the rule of law.

Upon taking the oath the federal chancellor and federal ministers have reaffirmed that they will uphold and defend the Basic Law and the laws of the federation. The fundamental concept of this oath pledges all democrats.

Opponents of the liberal democratic basic order do not belong in the public service. Freedom must also be defended against its enemies on the basis of the rule of law. For the sake of legislative uniformity, the federal government will cooperate with the Länder to bring about the early enactment of the legislative measures it has proposed.

An essential element of our political system is, and remains, the federative structure embodied in the Basic Law. Federalism only survives on the basis of close cooperation. The federal government is ready for such cooperation. Nor should the Bundesrat evade its responsibility. It is a constitutional organ of the federation and together with the Bundestag and the federal government is directly responsible for the federation. We know that the Länder with opposition-led governments have twenty-one votes as against twenty because the four votes of Land Berlin do not count. But no matter who commands a majority in the Bundesrat, they should not succumb to the temptation to make this constitutional organ of the federation a countergovernment.

We pledge ourselves to an open society which leaves room for a multiplicity of views and social groups. The government cannot do everything alone. It needs the forces generated in a free society and cannot forego the active self-help of its citizens. It knows and appreciates the great services performed by the charitable and independent welfare organizations.

As regards our relationship with the churches, what we said in the policy statement of January 18, 1973, still holds true:

> "We do not regard the churches as just one group out of many in our pluralistic society and therefore do not want to meet their representatives

as agents of mere group interests. On the contrary, we think that their necessary spiritual impact will be all the stronger as they free themselves from traditional social or party ties. We want partnership with them on the basis of distinct freedom."

X

In this policy statement I have drawn up an interim balance sheet on which we shall base our work. It is at the same time a balance sheet of achievements which we need not be ashamed of:

- Our economic situation is good.
- The people enjoy social security in freedom.
- Internal and external peace has been consolidated.
- This country is respected and has friends in the world.

Thus the present government stands on firm ground. Our coalition is oriented to the continuity of social-liberal policy.

The formation of a cabinet is always a new beginning, but it need not necessarily be an incision in the life of the nation. The social-liberal coalition began in 1969; it is being continued. No government starts from scratch; each builds on the work of previous governments. No government can work miracles, but it must do everything in its power to achieve what is possible. In this respect we are making a new approach in that we are concentrating our energies on what is essential today.

Theodor Heuss said: "Democracy is government with a deadline." In two and a half years' time the social-liberal coalition will be facing the decision of the people. Until then there is a lot to be done.

11

The State of the Nation: Statement Delivered to the Bundestag

(May 17, 1979)

Mr. President, Ladies and Gentlemen:

I wish to begin with the subject of intra-German relations during the past year and then go on to speak about the situation now reached in the two parts of Germany after thirty years and finally report on the prospects for the future.

1. THE CURRENT SITUATION IN RESPECT TO RELATIONS BETWEEN THE TWO GERMAN STATES

In the last Report on the State of the Nation in the spring of last year, I summed up the position by declaring that on the whole, despite the occasional setbacks, the federal government took a positive view of the development of relations between the Federal Republic of Germany and the German Democratic Republic (GDR). At the time, I added the observation that Federal Chancellor Brandt and the present federal chancellor as well as others since 1969 have reiterated the call to be prepared for setbacks and not to be disconcerted by them. That also applies without reservations to the pattern of events since last spring and since our last report.

In the course of 1978, about another 12 thousand people came to the Federal Republic from the GDR—including over 8 thousand who left the GDR with the permission of the public authorities. We regard this as a notable result of our humanitarian efforts.

For a number of years, there has been no change in the volume of tourist traffic. Compared with last year, the large number of journeys by West Germans and West Berliners to East Berlin and to the GDR remained at the same high level. A total of 8 million journeys from West to East was recorded. On the other hand, only 1.5 million GDR citizens came on a visit to the Federal

Republic, and most of them were old-age pensioners. In addition, 50 thousand journeys were undertaken for urgent compassionate reasons. This category of visitors recorded an increase for the first time in years (by nearly 20 percent). We welcome this!

It is, however, deplorable to note that travel opportunities for GDR citizens other than old-age pensioners are still extremely limited. Innumerable people who wish to travel are denied this right, even though there can be no doubt about their intention of returning and even though any problems with regard to foreign currency which might exist could certainly be resolved.

All other East European governments place more confidence in the loyalty of their citizens and display more understanding for their natural desire to travel. The federal government continues to attach great importance to the improvement of travel opportunities.

The vital traffic links between Berlin and the area of the Federal Republic were further improved in 1978. Pursuant to last year's agreements, a start will be made in a few days' time on the construction of the autobahn between Berlin and Hamburg and the repairing of the Teltow Canal. At the same time, urgent repairs will be carried out on the transit waterways. Further traffic improvements are scheduled for negotiation in 1980.

For the first time, the transit lump sum which we have to pay has been fixed on a long-term basis, i.e., for a period of ten years. All these improvements cost a great deal of money. Nevertheless, we decided in favor of these projects because on the one hand they enhance Berlin's viability and economic strength and thus also the political and psychological situation of the city, and on the other because these projects contribute additional elements of stability to the continuing unstable relations between the two states by virtue of their order of magnitude and their long-term nature.

In the course of the traffic negotiations, we finally found a way to resolve the problems which in past years have aggravated the transfer from the GDR to the Federal Republic of assets belonging to older persons or to young indigent men and women. To this end, the GDR has made DM 200 million available.

At the end of November 1978, the Border Protocol was signed in Bonn. Its subject matter is the marking of the borders between the two German states. It contains in the form of an annex a set of documents on border issues designed to resolve practical problems pertaining to the course of the frontier. These documents—prepared as they were with great care—represent the outcome of many years of work by the border commission. Clearly, the border commission could not settle the fundamental problems and hardship caused by the frontier. Nor, indeed, could that have been its purpose.

For that reason, it is all the more important that the agreed arrangements will furnish a wider measure of security for people along the border and in effect render their situation more bearable. It is not by chance that there has been a marked decline in serious incidents in recent years. We regard the work carried out by the border commission—and it is to be continued—as a significant contribution toward easing tensions.

We must, however, add one qualification. The border commission has been unable to reach unanimous agreement on the course of the Elbe border, and a few other small sections of the border. Nevertheless, both sides agree that, despite their difference of opinion on the legal position, difficulties and conflicts must be avoided also in the Elbe region.

Economic relations between the two German states did not develop last year as much as the federal government had hoped in the joint interest of the two countries. Although the total volume of intra-German trade runs at the high level of nearly DM 9,000 million, this represents an increase of only 1 percent in 1978 compared with the previous year. Deliveries from the GDR even declined.

I do not wish to dramatize the situation. However, we must make the point that both sides will have to strive hard in order to increase trade in line with overall economic growth. This includes not only the creating of a suitable framework, but also the application of political will to promoting trade. That will is present in the case of the federal government. We proceed on the assumption that the GDR is also interested in a steady and balanced advancement of economic relations.

The recent restrictions on working facilities for Western journalists in the GDR and the expulsion of another television correspondent are seen by the federal government as a serious setback to its endeavors to achieve correct and good-neighborly intrastate relations with the GDR. Such measures strike at the basic principles inherent in the freedom of the press, about which East and West entertain deep-seated differences of opinion and which were naturally not eliminated at Helsinki.

Matters taken by us for granted and virtually forming part of the free interplay between forces are deemed by the GDR government to constitute an undermining of the foundations of the state and its ideology. Although we cannot resolve this fundamental ideological conflict today, we do demand that concrete contractual obligations should be observed. This includes the obligations deriving from the Final Act of the CSCE. We also attach great importance to a similar attitude on the part of the East European states, including the Soviet Union.

But we must also bear in mind for political, humanitarian, and other reasons that the free journalism which forms an indispensable component of our system is not the sole factor determining relations between the two states. We feel it would be neither sensible nor admissible to take penal action, for example against GDR journalists accredited to Bonn. They can continue quite freely to report on the alleged "exploitation of the working class" in the Federal Republic.

We wish to continue steadfastly along our chosen path, for the policy we initiated ten years ago has undoubtedly helped to ease life for people on both sides and for the two states. This trend is continuing and will continue as it accords with the interests of Germans on both sides and with those of Europe, too.

With that in mind, we, at any rate, shall continue our endeavors to increase contacts between Germans, to mitigate political differences and expand cooperation between the two German states wherever that is possible.

And now a few words about Berlin. During my talks with General-Secretary Brezhnev last May, I gained the impression that the Soviet leaders take a more realistic view of the situation in Berlin today and, like ourselves, see its importance for détente in Europe and for German-Soviet relations. In point of fact, the political situation in the city has calmed down since the middle of last year. The friction with the Eastern side has diminished.

We, too, have striven for reason and moderation to prevail. Our Berlin policy does not consist in carrying out demonstrative tests of European détente in Berlin. On the contrary, we ensure that Berlin also benefits in full from the fruits and results of détente. We have made good progress along this path.

In less than a month from now, on June 10, Berlin will take part in the elections to the European Parliament. Unlike the procedure in the area of the Federal Republic, however, the Berlin deputies will not be directly elected, but appointed by their House of Representatives. This not only takes into account the quadripartite status of Berlin, but also guarantees that the city remains included within developments in the European Community as far as that is compatible with the rights and responsibilities of the Three Powers. This has also applied since the conclusion of the treaties establishing the European Communities. Hence, there is no justification for speaking of an infringement of the Quadripartite Agreement on Berlin. The federal government is in complete agreement with the Three Powers on this point.

True, we do not expect the Soviet Union and its allies to abandon their legal position on the question. Nevertheless, it is our hope that a pragmatic attitude will prevail and that this will respect the fact that West Berlin belongs to the European Community while the rights and responsibilities of the Three Powers are being observed. By the same token, we and the rest of the Western world do not question East Berlin's membership of the Eastern economic grouping, Comecon.

Ladies and gentlemen, the last few months have seen a spate of suspicions designed to cast doubt on the stance adopted by the federal government or the coalition on the question of German unity. No one with a knowledge of our postwar history will be surprised to see some of our leading Social Democrats accused of a "sell-out of German interests" or a "betrayal of Germany" or calumniated in similar fashion. Such malicious campaigns cannot fail to sow uncertainty not only among us, but also among our neighbors in the East and West.

I call upon the opposition to clarify among themselves what charge they really wish to make. On the one hand, they allege that Social Democrats ostensibly want to quit NATO because of German unity. Yet during the same period—spring 1979—they asserted that the very same Social Democrats allegedly no longer wanted to see Germany united. Both allegations are false and moreover the two charges obviously mutually exclude each other. In effect, one should really append a piece of advice for them, namely to observe the elementary rules of logic in their arguments about foreign policy. It only remains for me to add that such charges leveled against one's internal political opponent can gravely impair German interests.

For the sake of clarity and for the record, I would like to repeat two short observations. The Federal Republic of Germany is, and will remain, a member of the European Community and of the Atlantic Alliance and one which takes its duties and responsibilities seriously. Similarly, the GDR will be equally unwilling to quit its economic and military alliances and indeed it probably would not be able to do so in any case. This situation has not changed.

We see no discrepancy between our place in the Western communities and the aims set out in the Preamble to the Basic Law, which reads: "The entire German people are called upon to achieve in free self-determination the unity and freedom of Germany." This aim of achieving the unity of Germany is not an attempt at restoration intended to revive submerged periods of history or conditions or philosophies.

As Federal President Scheel noted last year in his speech on June 17, the unity of Germany is a European goal in peace which remains inseparable from the idea of peace, nonviolence, and mutual respect between nations. As the federal president also made clear in his very moving address, the unity of Germany is the consummation of our free democracy.

2. THIRTY YEARS OF THE FEDERAL REPUBLIC OF GERMANY

When we celebrate the thirtieth anniversary of our Basic Law coming into force, that is undoubtedly a good date for us to remember. Yet 1949 was also the year in which the division of Germany became consolidated for a long period of time. Hence, this anniversary is also a painful date for all Germans.

And then of course 1979 also reminds us of 1939, the year when war broke out. That makes it a date which brings home to us the realization that there would have been no division of Germany without the war.

When we in the democratic parties set out thirty years ago to build up this state of ours from the debris, the first thing which we had to do was to come to terms with the burden of the past. Many people in Germany faced up to the facts of history, and those of our most recent history in particular, from the very beginning. But we should not and must not fail to point out that not everybody did so.

On the other hand, there was the declaration made in Treysa by the Protestant Church of Germany as early as 1945 — a declaration which owned up to the mistakes of the past. There was also Theodor Heuss's great speech in November 1952 when he inaugurated the commemorative monument in Bergen-Belsen. Let us recall, too, the arguments about Alain Resnais's film *Night and Fog* or the unusual success of *Anne Frank's Diary*, with over 400,000 copies being sold in Germany at the time. But then there also was neo-Nazism: the Socialist Reich Party, later banned by the Federal Constitutional Court; then the DRP and later the NPD [two right-wing parties]. There was also the daubing of swastikas on walls and the desecration of Jewish cemeteries.

Among a large part of our nation — and this is something which still has not yet been fully overcome — there existed conflicting feelings on the German Resistance and on the 20th of July. Then there were the arguments about the film director Veit Harlan, who had made the inflammatory motion picture *Jew Süss* — arguments which took Erich Lüth, the pioneer of *Peace with Israel*, as far as the Federal Constitutional Court. There were also the attempts to offset reparations against the losses suffered. Mention may be made, too, of something which irritated the young generation in particular: dubious appointments to high-ranking governmental positions.

These all represent stages in our attempt — encumbered as it was with weakness, mistakes, doubts, anxieties, repressions, and guilt feelings — to come to terms with the past and to learn from it. No doubt, we made too late a start on many things such as the concentration-camp trials. Yet we made a very serious attempt at the beginning and from the beginning to take this course of action. The attempt has not yet been finished, it has not been consummated.

When the "Holocaust" serial was being shown on television, we found ourselves confronted with our National Socialist past in a manner which we had hitherto not attempted. Although we had tried to understand our past in rational terms, we had largely shut it out from our emotions.

Why had this been so? Perhaps it was our apprehension about exposing ourselves to this shock. But it may also have been the case that a feeling of shame prevented us from giving expression to our sorrow. Our sorrow for the suffering of the persecuted cannot be separated from our sorrow at German guilt. Perhaps there was a danger of this pity for the victims turning into self-pity. Was it right for us not to be self-conscious, could we simply give way to our feelings of pity? At all events, it was a good thing that we were shocked by the television film "Holocaust," young and old alike. The younger generation asked the older ones: Was it like that? And many of the old people could but nod their assent.

This experience has certainly not overcome the gap between the wartime and postwar generation. But it has nevertheless helped to bridge it or to establish lines of communication. The younger generation can now see more clearly why any threat to freedom and democracy assumes such huge proportions for us older people. For the youth of the country, that all belongs to past history: in their minds, it lies as far back as Bismarck or Napoleon. It is a long way off—simply a chapter of history for which they bear no responsibility. Perhaps they now have a much better understanding of our concern for freedom; yet only in a few cases do they share our concern.

Be that as it may, Germany's past will also catch up with the young generation. In fact, it is already catching up with them. The debate on the limitation of the prosecution of murder, which we are at present conducting in the Bundestag, also furnishes an example or rather another example of the seriousness with which the democrats and their parties face up to the past. It is a debate which we are conducting in the knowledge that the whole world is closely following it.

The world noted how some of the accused were acquitted in the Maidanek trial. Especially in Israel and Poland, this caused astonishment and in some cases indignation. The inner conflict besetting each one of us in the limitation debate becomes particularly manifest in the case of this example. We understand the reactions of the concentration-camp survivors and particularly those of the relatives of murdered men and women. There must be punishment for wrongdoing! But such punishment can only be handed down with the means and within the framework of the law. We owe that not only to ourselves and to our constitutional system, but also to the murdered people themselves.

Ours is not a judicial system which sympathizes with or protects murderers; ours is a judicial system bound by law and statute. However terrible the guilt he may have taken upon himself, every person in this country is entitled to a fair trial. Hence, the mandate set out in the Basic Law about achieving freedom and the rule of law in Germany is directed in the first instance toward ourselves.

The thirty years that the Federal Republic of Germany has been in existence are not only thirty years in the life of a state which has functioned fairly well during this period, a state which advanced from the debris to become economically one of the strongest countries in the world, a state which has acquired stature and respect in the world during this time. The thirty years of the Federal Republic for us signify above all thirty years of democracy and thirty years of civic freedom based on the rule of law and social security.

I am pleased to say how happy I am about this steadfastness of our democracy, for at no time during our German history have there ever been thirty years of democracy. The Weimar Republic lasted for less than half of that time. If one adds the years of the Weimar Republic to those of the Hitler dictatorship, they still do not add up to thirty years.

If we of the older generation who have worked for the Federal Republic from the very first day during these thirty years stop to think for a moment, we shall realize with a certain amount of surprise that our state already has a history of its own. In my view, it is the best German history. This part of our history has found worthy representatives in the persons of the three deceased federal presidents: Heuss, Lübke, and Heinemann.

Following the Weimar Republic, the Hitler dictatorship, and the misery of the war and postwar years, it would not have been unnatural for us to be faint-hearted and anxious about whether we would succeed in becoming a real, free German democracy. Admittedly, there were misgivings about whether the West German constituent state ought to be a fully fledged state and if we should allow it to become one. Would we not in fact be sanctioning the division of the nation in this way? We all hoped that the Federal Republic of Germany was only a provisional arrangement and we wished this to be so. But we had no doubts about the fact that it was to be a democratic state.

By then, the most important political forces had lined up. There was a profusion of parties. Apart from the four which are now represented in the Bundestag, they have all gradually disappeared from the scene. The four parties or three parliamentary groups have all undergone fairly fundamental processes of change and maturity during the thirty years and these have altered their appearance, their programs, and probably their self-image, too. We have all developed.

Back in 1949, we hardly had any time to look far ahead into the future. As I seem to recall, we were too busy to be fainthearted. There was simply too much to do: the rebuilding of the destroyed cities, the integration of over 10 million refugees, the equalization of burdens (to compensate those who had suffered from the war and the currency reform), the reuniting of families, the expansion of the economy—each of them an immense task in its own right.

The reconstruction of our country was marked by a political decision in favor of a free-market economy. This decision had been taken before the Basic Law entered into force. It was a controversial issue. Today, we are still arguing about whether and to what extent this decision must be corrected or amplified in sociopolitical terms in order to bring about the social federal state pursuant to the mandate contained in the constitution (Article 20 of the Basic Law).

There is no denying the fact that the free-market system has been crowned with success. Both in net and real terms, wages have risen more than threefold during these thirty years. Pensions have increased even more sharply in real terms. With figures like these, we can trace the path leading from misery and poverty to affluence. The choice of a free-market system thirty years ago has proved to be the right answer to the task of reintegrating our country into the world economy. The adjustment to demand on world markets has been extremely successful.

By the same token, economic advancement has helped us to build up a social security system which, in our view, ranks among our country's most significant political achievements.

In all of this, we received crucial aid from outside at the beginning. We recall the CARE parcels, the air-lift operation, and the Marshall Plan which laid the foundations for the reconstruction work which we then carried out ourselves. We gained friends: in America, in France, in England, and then gradually throughout the Western world. George Marshall, Lucius Clay, Jean Monnet, Robert Schuman, Victor Gollancz — once you start enumerating, you can remember more and more names. In those days, it was not exactly easy for a European or an American to be a friend of Germany. We have a great deal of reason to be grateful when we cast our minds back to the beginnings of our state.

At that time, we began to clear away the mountain of guilt bequeathed by Hitler as best we could with the available material resources. We enacted indemnification laws: we paid compensation to the State of Israel where the Jews had finally found a homeland; we paid compensation to Nazi persecutees in many nations of the world.

But all this took place within the shadow of the cold war. In a certain sense, the cold war marked the birth of our state. The foundation of both the Federal Republic as well as the GDR took place in a period when tension between East and West escalated into the cold war. We Germans did not invent the cold war, but its front lines ran right through the middle of our country.

The cold war tore Europe asunder and it tore Germany asunder, thus separating us from important parts of our history. The fertile cultures of Eastern Europe faded from our view; "Europe" often became synonymous with Western Europe with the concomitant impact of current threats, the traumatic experience made at the end of the war, and perhaps also the residue of former deep-seated prejudices against Eastern Europe. Many people repressed their knowledge of the fact that the German invasion had cost the Soviet Union 20 million casualties and Poland 6 million.

The observation of the repression by our East European neighbors produced an aftereffect which lingered for a long period of time. The people in Eastern Europe noted that we Germans apparently evinced understanding in every direction except theirs. Was not this repression of guilt perhaps guilt in itself? At a later point of time, Willy Brandt did what was necessary in this field over and beyond politics in his unique gesture in Warsaw.

Yet have we all mastered and overcome this problem? Many men and women in our country have taken great pains in their attempt to convey to us the spirit, the culture, and the history of the people of Eastern Europe. We owe them our gratitude. But how great is the respect for the culture of the Poles or that of the Czechs? Is it comparable with the respect for the cultures of our Western neighbors? Goethe welcomed Adam Mickiewicz as an esteemed visitor to his home. That was one of the great encounters in the annals of German and Slavonic culture. Goethe also stood sponsor to the foundation of the National Museum in Prague, because he grasped the European significance of Czech culture.

What do we know about all these things? Do we know that many great Russian writers have made brilliant translations into their mother tongue of the masterpieces of our literature?

We want German unity and we know that it will not be obtainable without the approval of the East European peoples. Moreover, we assure them time and again that we aspire to German unity only within a European peace order based on mutual esteem and respect. If we wish to achieve this European peace order, however, it will be necessary for us to extend our own mental and historic concept of Europe toward the East. It must include Pushkin and Petöfi every bit as much as Shakespeare and Dante or Boris Pasternak and Ernest Hemingway, as well as Jan Sobieski and Prince Eugène.

Is it not so that we tend to neglect the Russian language or Slavonic languages in general in our schools? Can we really afford to do this in view of the greatness of Russian literature and the political significance of the Soviet Union? Ought we not to examine the content of our school curricula to ascertain how much they help our youth to understand the people of Eastern Europe?

Ladies and gentlemen, the thirty years of existence of the Federal Republic of Germany have also signified thirty years of internal peace. This internal peace has grown on the basis of our constitution, the Basic Law. Internal peace does not mean that there are no disputes. There always will be disputes. Internal peace means that we resolve and settle our disputes peacefully and pursuant to appropriate procedures which we have agreed upon with each other. Our constitution has gradually educated all of us to accept this peaceful and agreed-upon procedure for resolving conflicts. Excessive respect for public authorities and undue servility are now beating a retreat.

The Weimar Republic also practiced democratic forms of life. However, there were too few democrats. Today, our democracy is sustained by the overwhelming majority of citizens and social groups. This constitutes the great positive turning point in German history. Like the Weimar Constitution, our Basic Law merely provided an opportunity. As Gustav Heinemann once observed, the Basic Law was an offer. Yet we grasped the opportunity and we accepted the offer—all of us did!

The Basic Law ought to stand at the heart of our political education, whether it be at schools, at universities, or in adult education. We want a critical youth. But the criticism voiced by our young people ought to rest on a knowledge of the rights which our constitution guarantees every citizen and of the duties which it demands of him. Much remains to be done in this respect.

Thirty years ago, it was by no means certain that all social groups would adapt to democracy. In the wide-ranging speech which he delivered at the end of the Parliamentary Council's negotiations, Theodor Heuss referred to the relationship between the state and the church as one of the central problems

The Chancellor and Mrs. Schmidt with Pope John Paul II, Germany, November 1980.

facing the Federal Republic of Germany. At the time, he may well have been right.

Today, we can see that there is a measure of mutual respect between state and church and of freedom for churches such as has hardly ever existed before in German history. Yet how much distress and suffering, how much embitterment this distorted relationship between state and church—distorted from both sides—has generated in the course of our history: starting with the dispute about the investiture, continuing with the wars of the Reformation, the Thirty Years' War, and Bismarck's Kulturkampf. We could add numerous other interludes which spring to mind during such a retrospective survey.

The broadly successful self-integration of the churches within our democratic society and the religious tolerance which we thereby attained constitute great and new events in this chapter of German history—events of conciliatory momentum which imbue many democrats and Christians with gratitude. This high degree of self-integration has enabled the churches to render a constructive contribution toward resolving the difficult questions involved.

Democratization clearly implies the introduction of democratic methods in politics and in numerous spheres of society. Above all, however, it means that citizens, social groups, and institutions become democratic. In this sense of the word, the self-integration of the churches furnishes an outstanding example of the successful democratization of our society. I consider that to be one of the most important cultural and political events of the last thirty years.

If we speak of the democratization of our society and of internal peace, we must also refer to our trade unions. In my talks with our partners abroad, they often say: "It's easy for you with trade unions like yours." Naturally, it is quite wrong to think that things are easy for me. Nevertheless, I consider it to be my duty in this survey of the last thirty years to point out that the state, society, and economy have owed much to the trade unions over these thirty years.

If asked what has enabled the trade unions to achieve what they have done, I would judge it a mistake to ascribe their success solely to the chosen organizational form of unitary unions. Another factor has been the succession of distinguished figures, beginning with Böckler and continuing through Brenner and Rosenberg down to the present day, who have headed the trade-union movement.

But another decisive point is that the cleverness, experience, prudence, moderation, and responsibility with which the leaders are endowed can only prevail in a major democratic organization if they evoke a positive response from the members. On this account, we may safely credit the millions of German trade unionists with a major role in the attainment of our thirty years of internal peace.

Indeed, German trade unionists were democrats long before democracy came to Germany. And thus it was quite natural in 1949 for this democratic state to become their state. From the very beginning, they became closely linked with the democratic state: they fought for it and felt responsible for it—including the period of the first twenty years when the Christian Democrats formed the government.

The fact that moderation, which calls for a high degree of democratic self-confidence, proved in effect to be most advantageous for the members of trade unions, i.e., for the workers, and the fact that our trade unions have achieved exemplary real wages, working conditions, and legal safeguards together with genuine social benefits—these seem to me to be a fair remuneration for their proven sense of democratic responsibility.

Most entrepreneurs in our country have known for a long time that social progress for employees does not engender the ruin of their firms; on the contrary, it forms the safest foundation for joint future success in business.

We are quite rightly gratified at the relatively small scale of strikes here compared with other countries. That furnishes a widely manifest mark of the extent of our social peace. But the fact that lock-outs take place relatively often here compared with other countries should give us food for thought. There are neither strikes nor lock-outs in the other part of Germany: all conflicts there are decided from above and the workers and citizens have to adjust or to obey.

The entry into force of our Co-Management Law formed a milestone in our social and legal history. It has given us one of the most progressive economic systems in the whole world, whether East or West. I am firmly convinced that this co-determination will become one of the pillars of our future society. It is quite clear that there can be no thought of this being achieved in the GDR.

Right up to the present time, our people have retained a certain measure of the original feeling of solidarity from the time immediately after the war, that is to say thirty years ago, even though this is often unfortunately suppressed in our consciousness by loud protestations. But we ought to retain this solidarity during the next thirty years. We shall be needing it. The problems ahead of us will be different, but they will not be smaller than those in the past.

As I said, the problems will be different. Together with the GDR and other Central European countries, the Federal Republic is one of the states with the lowest birthrates in the world. I am unable to regard this as a tragedy. In geographical terms, we are a small country. We are also one of the most densely populated countries, nearly three times as densely populated as France. But are overcrowded recreational areas around our cities, overcrowded roads, and over-crowded classes really something that we should strive after? Furthermore, the new population trend will furnish us with an opportunity to devote more atten-tion to the education and upbringing of our children.

But there are many questions as to the stability of the accord between the generations. How are the dwindling numbers of young and able-bodied per-sons to support the many old men and women? As far as future population trends can be estimated in very rough terms—and that means until the last decade of this century at the latest since anything beyond that is highly speculative—there is no reason in my view for viewing the situation too dramatically. Up to the end of this century and the beginning of the next one, the age structure of the population will be even more favorable than it was in the middle of the present decade.

As a whole, the changes lie within that margin of fluctuation which a modern state possessing an adaptable social system and flexible economy is capable of handling. Nevertheless, such problems have to be recognized in good time and taken into consideration in many of our plans and a great many different decisions.

There are some people who make the emancipation of women responsible for the reduction in the birthrate. Some of them find the declining birthrate a welcome argument in order to restrain the positive developments made towards an equal standing for women in society. We shall face up to this argument. The decision on equal rights for women ought no longer to be a matter for debate. The decision was already taken in the Basic Law: "Men and women shall have equal rights." It may also be noted that the GDR is probably somewhat ahead of us in the realization of this principle.

How has the emancipation of women hitherto taken place? Many women aspire to gainful employment and they are perfectly entitled to do so. This has decisively changed the world of women whereas men's life hardly altered as a result. Although this kind of emancipation was, historically speaking, in any case unavoidable, it would in the long run overtax both sexes.

The emancipating of women will only prove successful if the traditional world of men also changes—a move which calls for a shift in the conscious approach adopted by all sides and one, moreover, which in my view will last for many generations.

The important thing in this issue, too, is to be realistic and step by step to expand the available scope for enabling men and women to achieve a new self-image which accords with the provisions of our Basic Law. Instead of setting out to reverse the degree of equality so far attained for women, we ought for instance to try—and this brings me back to the democratic issue again—to create a social environment which is more congenial to children.

It would certainly be an exaggeration to claim that we Germans dislike children. Yet if there is a swing and a chute on a new housing estate but also a firm injunction to keep off the grass, or if we remember how as boys we used to steal apples from other people's gardens but find that either the gardens or the apples are beyond reach today so that the boys go shoplifting or steal a bicycle and land in the juvenile court—then in that case we must seriously consider whether in fact we grown-ups have created enough recreational facilities. I do not mean youth clubs, however necessary they may be, nor do I mean any organized or administered facilities. But I recall how as a child, fifty or fifty-five years ago, I could play in the staircase or the cellar and the attic or in the backyard. There was a factory nearby with a forecourt where we could play and there was the harbor—a world for grown-ups and children alike. There were few playgrounds for children, hardly any reserved areas for children. There are many more of these things nowadays. In those days, there was no world in which a youth welfare office and academically trained pedagogues had arranged everything for the children. Today, the question is whether so much importance really attaches to keeping off the grass. And I only mention that as one example of many.

My concern here and now does not involve our organizational or governmental ideas for the next thirty years but simply the need for us to realize that we must open up our adult world more than hitherto to children and young people, too.

Perhaps it could even be arranged for Bonn's new government district, which is engaging the energies of a number of men and women here in our Parliament, to be designed in such a way as to permit a few children to play games without being chased away by overzealous adults.

A great many complaints are voiced today about the growing volume of juvenile delinquency, juvenile alcoholism, religious sects for young people, rising suicide rates, and the mounting violence at schools—all of them phenomena which have sprung up during the last thirty years (and not only in this country). To put it briefly, there is more and more talk of youth problems. But youth problems are really adult problems, too.

We shall not master these problems if we simply send children and adolescents to court or put them into reform schools or institutions for alcoholics and drug addicts or send them to the psychiatrist. In reality, it will not change much. In reality, we must probably change some of our own attitudes.

The everyday reality of life as lived by young people in the GDR and in our country is different. It is very different as regards politics. The young generation here have not experienced the horrors of servitude or, of course, the horrors of war in particular. They have had the good fortune not to have to yearn for freedom as they yearn for happiness. Hence, it does not prove easy, either, to experience freedom as happiness. But that is precisely what we wanted. We wanted to make sure that our young people did not have to worry about their freedom. Now they have grown accustomed to freedom. Let us thank God for that.

Perhaps I may add an observation and return to a passage in my New Year's address in which I adopted a very optimistic attitude to the same topic. I quoted from a letter written by St. Augustine. Although correct in substance, it was shortened to save time and on this account misunderstood. What I really intended to point out with my quotation from St. Augustine, and this is certainly correct: the generational problem always repeats itself over the centuries and even the millennia and the older generation must always try in this situation to exercise self-control.

Safeguarding the substance of freedom which many young people today may take for granted and regard as something quite ordinary and everyday or perhaps even as a little boring or a matter which is not really noticed at all — that is not the central problem of our modern youth's political philosophy. They are more concerned about what use to put that freedom to. Hence, they do not so much question democracy as pose questions (both serious ones as well as some foolish ones) to democracy and also about what it can achieve.

In my view, we do not provide any useful answers to these questions by the sometimes exaggerated and often absurdly polemic domestic polarization of third-rate problems or imaginary problems which we witness more often than not, for example here in Parliament or in the media.

There can be no objections to controversial polarization when it involves great and decisive matters. In that case, polarization is necessary in a democracy; it cannot be avoided. But those who magnify marginal issues such as whether or not a partition window should be constructed and make fundamental issues out of them, and those who regularly charge their political adversaries with a breach of the constitution on every conceivable occasion, must put the question to themselves as to what impression politics of that kind are bound to produce among young citizens.

Is it not unfortunately true that, for the younger generation, politics largely

consist of the inevitable squabbles about people and appointments—
sometimes misnamed "strategic discussions"—and often of tactical feints as, for
instance, when satellite parties are to be created by a process of splitting or expanding "in order to make full use of the reservoir of voters" (as this operation
is called) or when majorities are to be put together? What is the fundamental
substance of all these pseudopolitics for the rising generation? What does their
real subject matter consist of?

Irrespective of their political stance, these rising generations do not accept
the view that the issue is one of "freedom or socialism." These people know
other states quite well, including those governed by social democrats or by
socialists. They know that the freedom existing in the Free State of Bavaria or in
Filbinger's Baden-Wurttemberg—both with conservative governments—is by
no means greater than in Norway or in Denmark or Austria.

Many young persons have mentally disassociated themselves from our
state—and they are not always the worst young people—and are trying to
develop alternative forms of corporate life outside our general political and
social patterns. Others attempt to flee from an anonymous bureaucracy and a
civilization which is destroying the natural environment by building up a
small community in which everyone shows consideration for the others and
assigns due importance to them.

However imperfect and transient such experiments may be and however little
those concerned may bear in mind that it is the very society upon which they
turn their backs that enables them in the first place to practice their own exclusive form of life, the fact nevertheless remains that the efforts undertaken by
these young men and women pose a question which one cannot prematurely
assume to have already been answered—the question as to the humaneness of
our democratic form of life. There is, for example, the question as to whether
the new tower blocks of apartments really express what the Basic Law meant by
the "dignity of man."

In the Ruhr district, for example, the miners are fighting to retain their old
workers' housing estates. Why is this? One reason is because the kitchen and
living-room windows face the street with the window-sill at chest level for
passers-by, thus enabling those inside simply to lean out of the window and
shake hands with their friends as they walk down the street. They can talk with
them and look into their faces. Between the houses, there is a bit of lawn.
Perhaps it is rather threadbare and brown in places, but there are children playing on it and their mother can keep an eye on them. Another reason is because
the people there talk to each other and help each other and take their recreation
together. Thus, I am not sure whether the anonymity which we have attained
by all these tower blocks of apartments really is a benefit in the long run.

The housing estates of miners that I was just speaking of mostly date back to
the old days when our country was not yet democratic. Democrats must ask
themselves if they cannot develop more congenial types of housing estates. Our

present-day town planners and architects have not yet achieved a sufficiently profound understanding of our emotional needs. This probably applies to the GDR even more so; it is not a specifically German problem, but in fact a problem in both parts of Germany. It will become a problem in the next thirty years if we do not realize that it exists.

But perhaps it is quite right to recall that the term "social"—such as it occurs in the Basic Law and such as it is used in the name of my party and in the name of other parties—has so far mainly been taken to mean the protection of our citizens against material indigence in old age, against illness, unemployment, or disablement. We have succeeded in providing that protection. We can rely on a network of social services which can support everyone. We feel that we can rightly be proud of this and we shall continue to work toward improving it and making it even more efficient and secure.

But "social" means more than that. We must bear in mind after the passage of thirty years that "social" really pertains to the links between man and his fellow men, to a spirit of humanity or to corporate life. That is something which the state cannot decree. But it can help to ensure that the advance of science and technology does not destroy the opportunities for contacts between man and man. The state can encourage such developments which extend the opportunities for social intercourse.

Scientific and technical progress has increased our life expectancy and made our existence easier and more comfortable. It has opened up fresh vistas. We can travel wherever we like and telephone each other. Television brings entertainment and information into our living rooms while our refrigerators make sure that our butter does not turn rancid. These are all advantages and nobody would like to forgo them.

Things were different thirty years ago. For that reason, it is foolish to condemn in blanket terms the march of scientific and technical progress. Moreover, such condemnation does not solve any problems. But we must also see the negative sides; for there is a price to be paid for every advantage. Let us take a few examples. The more frequently we travel, the shallower our impressions; the more we telephone, the fewer letters we write; the more television we see, the less we talk or listen to each other.

Scientific and technical advances may serve our freedom and humanity if we put them to use in a controlled and critical manner. They may also cause damage if they are consumed mechanically. This presents our highly industrialized society with one of its principal educational tasks for the coming decades. For instance, we are faced with the decision as to whether we should introduce cable television and, if so, on what conditions. Technically speaking, it would be a wonderful thing. There would be no more trouble with the aerial. Furthermore, it would be technically feasible to receive twenty-five or thirty different programs for twenty-four hours a day.

But is that the progress to which we have aspired and to which we should be aspiring? That is something which we shall have to carefully consider. This is not a question which can be left solely for the electronics firms and telecommunications engineers to decide: it is a social and political issue whose resolution will exercise a great influence on social relations between people.

Perhaps I may add that our publicly owned radio system has proved to be very satisfactory during these last thirty years. We consider it to be just as regrettable as it is disquieting when certain politicians—some for politically transparent reasons and others for personal considerations—wish to set this comparatively rational and successful system at risk. The plans for a private radio system can impair the substance of our democratic way of life and must therefore reckon with our resistance.

Data technology and microelectronics will continue to change society in general and our working world in particular. As long as they free people from mechanical chores and tedious activities, they will be welcome and indeed they must be utilized. But what we want is, as it were, a computer designed for human beings and not human beings designed to suit a computer.

Clearly, these dangers loom larger in communist-governed countries than they do here. Nevertheless, they exist for us, too.

We are one of the leading countries in the world from the scientific, technical, and economic standpoints. That is why it depends to a considerable extent on us ourselves which direction science and technology take. We can even help to determine the definition of what should constitute progress. Any progress which minimizes, neglects, or represses its own inherent risks and any progress which destroys human links and social considerations represents a danger. But if we recognize and consider these risks and draw the correct conclusions from our misgivings and if we devote it to the service of man, then it is something which we ought to aspire to.

At this point, we may well be confronted with criticism of the federal government's decision in favor of a limited development of nuclear energy. I had occasion at the beginning of last week personally to explain the reasons for this decision once again. I need not repeat them today and, indeed, it would not be convenient in this context. There are sound arguments against nuclear energy; equally, however, there are sound and good arguments in favor of nuclear energy. We have given careful consideration to all of them. Our decision was taken pursuant to the best of our knowledge and belief. I feel bound to add the following: It is not only the opponents of nuclear energy who are moved by their conscience—the others are, too!

The nuclear energy problem will not be the last problem which we encounter in the course of our scientific and technical advancement. For the same reason, we shall also be faced by a growing number of other problems. These are the issues inherent in present-day social policy. They are the problems besetting the East as well as the West, the GDR every bit as much as the Federal Republic of Germany.

We shall have to apply not only thought but also determination and energy if we are to direct progress along a human avenue of approach. We must take care lest we build up a future world which, albeit superbly efficient, provides an ever-dwindling range of opportunities and possibilities for friendly and happy human intercourse.

If we do manage to succeed, it will perhaps make it easier for us to integrate the many children of foreign workers as well as the latter themselves into our society. That is a decision which we shall have to take in the near future, ladies and gentlemen. Perhaps it will then prove easier for us to meet our obligations vis-à-vis the developing countries.

The Basic Law furnished an opportunity to espouse democracy and we seized that opportunity. Democracy furnishes an opportunity to practice humanity and we must avail ourselves of it.

3. THIRTY YEARS OF HISTORY IN THE GDR

The other German state, the German Democratic Republic, can also look back upon three decades of existence this year. Everyone in Europe and throughout the world is aware of the fact that the German Democratic Republic is a German state.

We are the last ones to overlook that it is a German state. Even if we wished to do so, we could not overlook it because the division of Germany and above all the responsibility for Berlin are present to our minds—and indeed urgently present to our minds. Hence, it would be a good thing to remain conscious of the fact that the GDR is German, that Germans live there and that everything happening there forms part of the present history of the German people.

The Germans living in the present day—the present generation—are undergoing a unique experience. I do not mean the experience of living side by side in different German states. We Germans have been aware of this for centuries of our history. No, what I mean is the experience that the division of a state is accompanied by the development of a far-reaching divergence in social, political, and sometimes cultural matters.

When the GDR was founded in 1949, it lay in the throes of the "antifascist revolution"—as they termed it. This phase saw the creation of the socioeconomic and political conditions which appeared necessary to the then leaders in order to build up a socialist, Soviet-type society involving, for example, the overthrow of the bourgeoisie, the assumption of political power by the Communist Party, and to a large extent the dismantlement of the newly reemerging trade unions. At its second party conference in July 1952, the SED [Socialist Unity Party] laid down that the "fundamental objective of the GDR" was "to build up socialism."

Thus, even before Soviet policy on Germany abandoned its options and strategies for Germany as a whole in the mid-1950s in favor of strengthening and consolidating the GDR as a state, a sweeping transformation of all aspects of public and private life had already been initiated in the GDR. Over there, it was called a "uniform revolutionary process."

In other words, the SED (or at least the SED leadership) had from the beginning considered its primary aim to be the erection of a socialist state and a Marxist-Leninist type of social order on the territory of what is now the GDR. This led in no small measure to the bitter events of June 17.

Today, about a decade since it promulgated its second constitution of 1968, the GDR refuses to acknowledge that there ever was a German question or a German nation. It does so even though it still referred to itself in the constitution of 1968 as a "socialist state of the German nation" and undertook to "overcome the division forced upon the German nation by imperialism." Following another change in the constitution in 1974, the GDR now designates itself a "socialist state of workers and peasants." Its citizens are not allowed to call themselves Germans by citizenship although by nationality. According to the official version, the socialist German nation is being developed in the GDR while the bourgeois nation continues to exist in the Federal Republic.

Clearly, these kinds of change and falsification do not form part of the conscious approach adopted by Germans in the GDR: on the contrary, they reflect the shallow political opportunism of the leadership. The last word on the nation has by no means yet been spoken in the GDR and it will not be spoken all that quickly, either.

Ladies and gentlemen, there is nevertheless no denying the fact that a sovereign state has come into being there and that we could not impose our will upon it even if we wanted to. This other state also ranks among the leading industrial countries of the world. Its industrial production has more than doubled during the last two decades.

Because of its economic achievements, the GDR occupies a top position in Comecon. It is the leading state among the members of Comecon in regard to economic efficiency and standard of living. Many citizens of the GDR—and not only communists—are proud of this. I believe they have every right to be proud of it, since that economic upswing was a great deal more difficult for the GDR than for us. The starting conditions were worse: factories had been dismantled and supplies were being taken from current production. Political factors which prevented inclusion within the Marshall Plan and which led to separation from Western Germany necessitated a complete restructuring of industrial relations and economic relations in general. At the beginning, there was no heavy industry.

When one takes all this into consideration and sees the achievements which have nevertheless been realized, one must bear in mind on the one hand that they are German achievements and on the other that these achievements and events represent the outcome of another policy—a communist policy which also produced results which would be intolerable for us, which demands of people great sacrifices in personal and civic freedom, which enjoins people to lead a life subject to restrictions and constraints which none of us living under our free and democratic system would tolerate. The leaders of the GDR government expect all those who are allowed to make pronouncements in public to give their uncomplaining approval of everything. It is quite obvious that there are many constraints on intellectual independence and intellectual freedom there.

4. THE FUTURE OF THE NATION

I have the impression that the leaders in the GDR are in fact fully aware that their view of a special nation which differs from the Germans in the Federal Republic and indeed sets itself off from us by virtue of a special national awareness was unrealistic and remains so.

Today, the impression is often put about in the GDR that it has preserved or resuscitated the good elements of German history whereas the negative ones are to be found on our side. That is a misrepresentation of history.

Yet it is certainly a good thing if we in the two parts of Germany take a critical look at the national history of the Germans, for neither here nor in the GDR do people want to speak and write about the nation as Treitschke did 100 years ago. Moreover, the television serial produced in the GDR on Scharnhorst is probably not above criticism as far as historic reality is concerned. At any rate, I consider it a good idea that we shall soon be seeing it on our TV screens, too.

Fundamentally, it is no bad thing that the history of Prussia and Germany is now being studied and discussed afresh in the two German states and, as I say this, I also recall Sebastian Haffner's book on Prussia. Nonetheless, we shall not be able to join in if the GDR wishes, as it were, to monopolize Prussian reformers such as Gneisenau, Stein, and Hardenberg, while we are blamed for the authoritarian nature of the Prussian state. That is mere buffoonery and farce!

For a long time now, many people in the GDR — and among the leadership in particular — have misunderstood our adherence to the concept of the nation. The ideologists in favor of detachment suspect it to be a policy of what they call "revisionism." They sense an attempt to deprive the GDR of its constitutional status. That is nonsense. We have long since recognized the existence of the second German state.

But we would be failing in our duty if we behaved as though the concept of a single nation were to be abandoned by the German people or by us. That will not happen! And it did not happen to the Polish nation, either, even though it was partitioned for a long, long time.

At all events, I feel sure that the existence of one single nation will remain an important matter for future generations in both German states, irrespective of how the two states develop internally.

A review of the past thirty years or a look forward at the next thirty years reveal much that is different and opposite both in regard to the past and future, but also much that is common and mutual. On one point at least, the Germans in the two states agree politically — and this even includes the politicians: We all share the wish, which became particularly manifest in Erfurt and Kassel nine years ago, that no war will ever originate again on German soil.

The Germans in the two parts of the nation want peace also and even precisely because of the existence of a division into two differing forms of state and society. Moreover, we want to make the consequences of the division more bearable by pursuing a policy of cooperation and good-neighborly relations. But, in effect, only the two German states can do this, and they can only do it jointly. The Federal Republic of Germany is willing to play its part.

The question of what becomes of the German nation is not only a matter for the Germans, but also for our neighbors in Europe, our partners in the economic communities and in the alliances to which the two German states belong.

The peoples and the governments on this continent and throughout the world know that one can speak of "the Germans" even though they live in two states. Sometimes, the image of Germany abroad draws less distinction between the Federal Republic and the GDR, less distinction than we do — we who are confronted with the harsh facts of the division of the nation and its consequences every day. Perhaps it is even comforting to see that many foreigners in the world regard our nation with eyes in which — for them, for our neighbors, and for our partners — the German nation has not forfeited its independence and its identity even after the span of a whole generation.

By the same token, it must also be realized that we Germans are not regarded by other peoples with the same calmness as other nations. The very thought of a state comprising 75 million Germans emerging in the heart of Europe worries many of our neighbors and partners, even though this worry is not expressed loudly.

We must therefore accept the fact that we Germans and the developments in both German states and the relations between the two states are scrutinized abroad very consciously and attentively and sometimes very critically.

We must not overlook the fact that in the eyes of the others the division of Germany forms a part and element of the European equilibrium which safeguards peace in Europe. Our neighbors and partners know that very well and they say so. We can only reckon with their understanding for our national issues if we approach these circumspectly and carefully and realistically: in other words, if we approach them with thoughtful regard for the interests of all our neighbors.

On several occasions I have stressed in the Bundestag that the question as to the unity of the nation must not thrust aside peace as our foremost priority. Nor must we create the impression that we wish to pursue a policy on Germany which may lose sight of the requirements of European peace. Given our geopolitical situation and our recent history, we Germans cannot afford to be politically schizophrenic, for example by promoting a realistic peace policy on the one hand while simultaneously conducting an illusory debate on reunification.

Allow me, by way of exception, to quote one of my own observations and one which I still stand by. Ten years ago, I wrote the following words: "A willingness to accept reality is necessary if our will to preserve peace is to be valid."

These thirty years of existence for the Federal Republic of Germany and for the German Democratic Republic have been thirty years of external peace for all Germans — despite the cold war, despite the highly dangerous crises in many of the earlier stages, and despite the many individual and family tragedies.

Our peace policy rests on the firm anchorage which we found in the West: in the European Communities and the Allantic Alliance in particular, in the close links with France, in the friendly partnership with the USA, Great Britain, and others.

We have in fact made peace in Europe more secure by our policy of concluding treaties, our policy of nonviolence and cooperation. We try hard and resolutely to attain good-neighborly relations with our Eastern neighbors — and with the other German state, too.

Our relationship with the East European states and the Eastern world power, the Soviet Union, is different from our relationship with our Western partners, since we belong to different political and social systems and pursue different philosophies. For all that, I would also speak of partnership in the direction of the East, namely treaty partnership and in particular security partnership.

The Eastern treaties created contractual links and these are continuing to grow despite all the setbacks. The Quadripartite Agreement and the Basic Treaty created the political preconditions for the Helsinki Conference. Relations between the two German states and the situation of Berlin — all this has since become embedded in Europe's policy of détente. This has benefited the Berliners, the Germans in the GDR, the Germans here, and all the peoples of Europe.

Beyond the contractual relations, it has also become possible to conduct a political dialogue with East Europe — which alone creates in politics that degree of mutual predictability and mutual trust upon which a growing measure of cooperation can be built.

A major part of détente policy and the East-West dialogue is today made up of the efforts directed toward limiting and reducing arms potential. We are pleased that the USA and the Soviet Union were able to conclude the SALT agreement, which also lies in our interest. We Germans hold a special interest in a reduction of the high concentration of troops and war material on German and Central European territory and on the establishment of a European balance of forces at a lower level. For this reason, all states in East and West can count on our commitment to disarmament and arms control.

The most recent developments in the European Community such as the European Monetary System, the first direct elections to the European Parliament, or the enlargement of the Community to include Greece in two weeks' time and then later Portugal and Spain are in line with our own goals. For the interlocking of the Federal Republic of Germany into a growing democratic community of Europe helps us to counter any suspicion of presumed or feared German preponderance.

The historic lesson and experience which we have learned in these past thirty years, i.e., that the nation must not be the supreme criterion for all policy, forms the requisite precondition for a circumspect German policy of reaching an understanding with East Europe and also with the GDR. It not only serves peace, but also prevents any violation of the awareness of the enduring identity of the nation taking place under the mask of transient political realities.

Those who realistically tackle the problems attendant upon the division of Germany know that the realization of German unity and of a joint roof for all Germans is only conceivable if East and West really free themselves from their cramped and militarily supercharged polarization and if they relax the tension existing between them and indeed are able themselves to relax because they can rely on the dependable peaceableness of the partners on the other side.

There is still a long and vast journey ahead of us before we reach that point. That is why we do not yet know whether or when, in what form, and by what stages German unity can be attained. But we do know that both German states, embedded in differing communities and alliances, will have to recognize and carry out their part of the task and their part of the responsibility for peace in Europe today, tomorrow, and the day after.

Thus, we have reason to ask: What can the Germans in the two German states do today and tomorrow in order to make peace in Europe a more reliable factor for the future? Despite all the distinctness of existing criticism, I think the answer to this must include the fact that we ought mutually to recognize the contribution which the Germans in both German states have rendered toward the reconstruction of Europe in thirty years. In other words, we should mutually recognize the achievements to date.

Each side ought to promote and support the general process of cooperation on détente in Europe by its own cooperation, for instance, on disarmament and arms limitation.

Our colleague Herr Barzel recently pointed out in an essay that everywhere in the world those people who gathered their decisive political experience prior to the era of the European dictatorships and the Second World War had already reached old age and retired from leading positions in the state. That was the generation of Schumacher, Adenauer, de Gasperi, and all the others.

During the approaching decade of the 1980s, we also shall see the departure of the war generation from the political arena everywhere in the world. We should be asking what we can do to make sure that the lessons learned from the bitter war are not forgotten.

The time has come for us to complain less about our common losses and instead to think and talk about what both sides can do to promote a peaceful future for Europe. After all, there can only be one peace and that is the peace which is common to East and West. There can only be a joint peace.

Only in a politically and contractually organized peace can Europe once again grow together in terms of its economy, its culture, and its people. Unity is conceivable only after a prolonged period of peace.

12

Statement Delivered to the Bundestag

(November 24, 1980)

1. On October 5 the Social Democratic Party of Germany and the Free Democratic Party were again given the mandate by the citizens of this country, with an increased majority, to continue the social-liberal coalition and its political course: the course of peace, security, and good neighborliness, both in its external relations and in our own country.

2. The federal government, like the previous one, is the government of all citizens. The election campaign is over. I welcome the appeals made by the senior member of Parliament upon opening the new session, and by the president of the Bundestag, as the first steps toward normal parliamentary work.

3. Our friends and neighbors all over the world have welcomed the continuity of our policy. President Giscard d'Estaing said: "I attach the greatest value to the continuation of Franco-German cooperation that we have developed together with the federal chancellor over the past six years. This cooperation is an irreplaceable contribution to Europe's progress and stability." With this sentence, President Giscard has expressed the heartfelt feelings of millions of Germans and Frenchmen.

COURAGE TO FACE THE FUTURE

4. Both coalition parties and their parliamentary groups together stand for freedom and social justice.

5. The years ahead will be difficult: on the international scene, as regards the world economy, and consequently in our own country as well. We therefore have to understand the manifold and complex interrelationships of this world, and there must be resolute joint action focused on the major tasks. We are not an object of history. We are capable of action—and we have a will to take action. Depending on the political decisions we take, our country may look completely different in ten or twenty years' time.

6. We shall tackle our problems with courage, and the courage to face the future is justified:

- because we can bank on the hard work, on the intelligence and the sense of responsibility of the Germans, who after 1945 worked hard to build this country, literally with their hands;
- because we know from experience what we achieved in the seventies, both in economic and social terms, in spite of the two oil price explosions and the world recession. We can count on our adaptability and on our will to work hard;
- because we have developed over the decades a body politic which is exemplary in the social field. Social peace in our country rests on a solid basis;
- and finally because we have learned what partnership means and that we can rely on our friends in the world.

7. The young people of this country are willing to commit themselves to a better future. We are pleased to note that in the election for the Bundestag young people who were having their first chance to go to the polls were particularly numerous among those who voted for the social-liberal coalition. I consider this to be a commitment. This, too, is one of the reasons why we have the courage to face the future.

8. A government policy statement cannot serve to describe all the problems and the probable solutions. It can only present the basic outlines. The agreements between the two coalition partners are in some respects more detailed. But the most important thing is that we have in recent years further developed our ability to work together toward common achievements.

PEACE THROUGH SECURITY AND COOPERATION

9. With our foreign policy we aim to help safeguard world peace. We must do justice to our increased share of responsibility. But at the same time we must not overestimate the German role in world affairs, nor let others do so, so that expectations are not aroused which we cannot meet.

Our foreign policy is clear and calculable. With it we have won the trust of others. In the eighties the security and prosperity of our country will depend on that policy and the effective representation of our interests. The basic lines of our foreign policy are as follows:

First: Without equilibrium there is no dependable peace in the world. We can feel secure because the Atlantic Alliance maintains the equilibrium to which we have contributed by placing our whole political and military weight on the Western side of the scales.

Second: Equilibrium is a necessary if insufficient condition for peace. Peace therefore has to be safeguarded by a policy of arms limitation and cooperation as well. "Military security and a policy of détente" (Harmel Report, December 1967) have been the two main elements of the Alliance's security policy concept for over ten years. We shall continue the policy of cooperation with our Eastern neighbors in the interest of peaceful development in Europe and of the future of the whole German nation.

Third: The European Community remains the indispensable basis for peace and freedom and for social and economic progress. It also helps to preserve the equilibrium.

Fourth: With our policy of partnership among equals we will help secure the economic, political, and cultural independence of the Third World countries in the long term.

MAINTAINING OUR DEFENSE CAPABILITY
WHILE BEING WILLING TO SEEK AGREEMENT

10. Only within the Atlantic Alliance can the Federal Republic of Germany find its security. Only with that security are we capable of pursuing, in cooperation with our partners, a successful policy of détente, arms limitation, and cooperation with countries with different social systems.

11. Partnership with the United States of America remains the core of the Atlantic Alliance. It is a reflection of common vital interests. This partnership is also based on common value concepts which were first developed by the French, formulated by the founding fathers of the United States over 200 years ago, and which have been the fiber of German democracy since 1848 at the latest. Over the past thirty-five years, a friendship which in the meantime has taken deep roots has developed between Germans and Americans through constant and fruitful contacts.

12. This was again fully confirmed in the talks which Federal Minister Genscher and I had in Washington last week with President Carter and President-elect Reagan. Having fallen in the period of transition from the present to the new administration, our visit came at the right time. In the light of my intensive discussions with President Giscard d'Estaing and Prime Minister Thatcher, I was able to meet the future president and his advisers in full knowledge of the views of our principal European partners. These were meetings with many old acquaintances and many good friends. We were impressed by the warmth of the reception we were given and I am grateful to have had this opportunity for an exchange of views with the president-elect and his associates.

13. Together with our partners in the Alliance we are making efforts in the arms control negotiations with the East to achieve a stable military balance at the lowest possible level in order to halt the arms race and reduce the burden of military expenditure. Mankind could arm itself to death if the arms race were not stopped. That is why the negotiations between the superpowers on the limitation of strategic arms are of central importance. We strongly advocate the continuation of the SALT process. After my discussion with President-elect Reagan, I am pleased to be able to report to the Bundestag that he is thinking along the same lines.

14. We welcome the commencement of talks on October 17 between the United States and the Soviet Union on medium-range nuclear weapons. Our Alliance created the basis for these talks with its twofold decision of December 12, 1979. We adhere to both elements of that decision:

- The West, in view of the dangerously increasing Soviet superiority in the field of Eurostrategic weapons, must modernize and strengthen its own capability in Europe.
- But — and this is just as important — we want mutual limitations in this field.

15. In the Vienna negotiations on mutual and balanced force reductions in Central Europe, we, together with our partners in the Alliance, are aiming for an early interim agreement.

16. We abide by the process that was initiated by the Conference on Security and Cooperation in Europe and the adoption of the Final Act of Helsinki. At the present follow-up conference in Madrid, the federal foreign minister made it clear that it is especially in difficult times that the Final Act — in all its parts — must serve as a yardstick to all participating states for their actions. We aim to build on this basis. Détente cannot be a one-way street. In this process the observance of the Declaration of Principles and the easing of restrictions for the benefit of the people are to us Germans of equal importance. We support the French proposal for a conference on disarmament in Europe which is to agree on confidence-building measures applying to the whole continent of Europe. We are also in favor of a European energy conference.

17. With our Federal Armed Forces which, thanks to our conscription system, thanks to well-trained reservists, can in a state of tension be considerably strengthened, we are making our contribution to collective defense. Our volunteers, conscripts, and regulars, with their attitude to democracy and the rule of law, and their willingness to serve their country, determine the quality of our defense contribution. With their military service they are helping to maintain the equilibrium and hence peace. They are making sacrifices for the community.

18. In the course of the past twenty-five years the Federal Armed Forces have found a firm and acknowledged place in our society. It is therefore incomprehensible and alarming to many members of the armed forces — and I myself am very concerned too — when criticism and derision of their pledge to serve their country make it more difficult for them to carry out their duty. The

Federal Armed Forces have been shaped by a democratic, not by a militaristic tradition.

Tradition must not conflict with the basic values of our society. And it does not, for that matter. But we want that tradition to be a link between the armed forces and the citizens. The manifestations of tradition should be abreast of the times and we are therefore willing to discuss the forms of such manifestations. But the debate on this matter must not be used as a vehicle for attacks on the Federal Armed Forces and the Alliance.

19. We look after our servicemen and see to their social security. We aim to strengthen the position of their elected spokesmen. We aim to increase servicemen's pay. We are conscious of the problems connected with the age structure of regular soldiers and the reduced promotion chances ensuing therefrom.

20. A thorough modernization program over the past ten years has increased the efficiency of the Federal Armed Forces. We have well-trained armed forces with sophisticated equipment and a high degree of readiness, forces which are considered exemplary in NATO. A particularly large proportion of our defense budget is earmarked for investment purposes because we have a conscripted army. Our defense expenditure over the last ten years has increased at an average of just under 3 percent a year in real terms. We have committed ourselves to try and maintain this rate of increase. We shall meet our commitment.

21. Civil defense is part of overall defense. Many thousands of volunteers are rendering an important service.

22. Security and stability in Europe are increasingly affected by crises in the Third World. It is all the more important that we should coordinate our efforts within the Alliance and help to ensure that the instruments available to the United Nations for crisis management are used to the full.

EUROPEAN COMMUNITY

23. Maintaining and developing the European Community continue to be central tasks of our policy, which never loses sight of the goal of European union. In the past four years, we in the Community have:

- directly elected the European Parliament for the first time;
- created the European Monetary System (EMS);
- resolved the internal crisis due to the British contribution to the budget;
- combated protectionist tendencies and substantially developed the Community's foreign relations, particularly in the North-South relationship;
- negotiated the accession of Greece and finally set in motion negotiations with Portugal and Spain.

24. One of the accomplishments of the EC is European Political Cooperation, i.e., cooperation in the field of foreign affairs. In making their growing contribution to overcoming political crises in the world, the governments can now build on ten years of experience in intensive policy coordination and joint diplomacy. On the whole the European Community has made good progress!

25. On the other hand, it is also faced with substantial problems. In European agricultural policy, the federal government will, in view of increasing structural surpluses, make vigorous efforts to ensure that the principles of market economy are realized more fully than has so far been the case. This means a cautious price policy which must be primarily directed toward reestablishing market equilibrium. It means surplus production must be reduced by including producers in the financing of surpluses, and it means the agricultural intervention mechanisms must finally be relaxed in order to regain an equilibrium in the markets. The federal government does not regard more stringent restrictions on imports or aggressive promotion of exports to be suitable solutions to the problems of surpluses of the European Community.

26. As for financing, the payment of value-added taxes to the EC must remain at a level which does not exceed 1 percent of the assessment basis. All member states are in agreement on this. The French president and the British prime minister recently confirmed this expressly once more. Thus the increase in agricultural expenditures must be markedly less than the increase in the EC's own revenues in the future.

POLICY ON GERMANY AND BERLIN

27. When the social-liberal coalition eleven years ago initiated its policy of a contractually regulated way of living side-by-side of the two German states, there could not be any doubt that this course would involve difficulties, burdens, and setbacks. The federal government has never allowed these to sway it from its course. Even in difficult times, we have adhered steadfastly and tenaciously to our goals.

28. Our long-term efforts to improve the situation of the Germans who are suffering from the division of Germany has put many things in motion: millions of people have made journeys, relatives make telephone calls to each other, families have been reunited. Roads to Berlin are being built. Trade has shown a vigorous development—to name a few examples. All in all, we have been able to keep the Germans from drifting apart from each other.

This policy is and remains an integral part of the general policy of reconciliation between West and East. We regret that the GDR, only a few weeks before the Madrid CSCE follow-up meeting, has detracted from humanitarian improvements which had been reached so far, by taking measures such as the increase in the minimum daily amount of currency to be exchanged. This is a severe setback for all Germans.

The federal government will not resign itself to this. It will maintain its goal of easing the lot of the German people through improvement of our relations with the GDR. There is really no other way. For the future, too, we offer

With Erich Honecker, chairman of the Council of State of the German Democratic Republic, Belgrade, May 1980.

cooperation and development of our relations with the GDR. We have no intention of answering acts of delimitation by reacting in kind: this would only deepen the gap between Germans and Germans still more!

29. We stake our will to cooperation against this delimitation. I appeal to all Germans to summon the perseverance and patience we need to overcome the present, particularly difficult stretch of the road.

30. Both German states have a common responsibility and common tasks. These cannot be shirked by the leadership of the GDR either. The chairman of the Council of State, Erich Honecker, and I were able to speak for all Germans when we said that no war must ever originate again on German soil. Normalization of cooperation and active securing of peace in Europe must include both German states.

We are aware of the basic differences in the political goals of the two German states. We want to work toward a peace in Europe in which the German people are able to exercise free self-determination. The GDR leadership has set itself a different goal. We want to keep alive the consciousness of the unity of the German nation. The GDR leadership does not want this.

We realize that the existing political and ideological differences cannot be overcome by practical cooperation. And they must not be obscured. These differences inevitably lead to varying legal interpretations of basic questions which cannot be reconciled; this was true at the time when the Basic Treaty was concluded and it is still true today. Nor can we reconcile ourselves to mines and self-triggering shooting devices along the border.

31. But the substantial progress made in the past years has also shown that these differences need not stand in the way of practical cooperation to the benefit of both sides. I welcome the fact that trade between the two German states has increased in the past four years by 50 percent to approximately 11 billion deutsche marks. The continual development of economic and traffic relations, which we desire, must naturally remain in harmony with the development of relations as a whole. We are in favor of intensifying cultural relations with the GDR. The GDR leadership should recognize that it harms not only us but also itself when it refuses to allow its artists to make guest appearances over here. Initial talks on specific environmental questions must develop into practical negotiations.

32. The work of our journalists in the GDR is being restricted once more. I regret such setbacks. Objective reporting from the GDR is in the interest of both sides. This means that our journalists' working opportunities must not be restricted but rather improved.

33. The federal government continues to be interested in careful discussion of its policy on Germany here in the Bundestag and its committees. It is prepared to receive suggestions. In this regard there can be no doubt as to the basic direction of its policy on Germany.

34. We are all thinking of the lot of all Germans. We take an interest in what the Germans in the GDR are thinking. We do not want to patronize the

GDR. We are continuing to strive for a dialogue with the leadership of the German Democratic Republic. In view of the situation which has now developed, we will have to take into consideration the total context of our relations.

35. We are committed, in the political, human, and economic areas, to the city of Berlin and its citizens. Thanks to the efforts of the Berlin Senate, of entrepreneurs and labor, also of the Bundestag and the federal government, Berlin has fully caught up with our economic development. In Berlin, the consciousness of local capabilities has clearly assumed priority over calls for help from outside; this is borne out by the Berlin Senate's latest economic report. I am impressed by the vitality and diversity of the intellectual life of the city, its theaters and concerts, its literature and its museums.

36. We will continue to work together with the Three Powers for the benefit of Berlin, who guarantee the security and freedom of the city on the basis of their rights and responsibilities. The federal government acts on the assumption of strict observance and full application of the Quadripartite Agreement. This is in the interest of all those involved—especially when the world political situation is difficult.

37. We aso want to continue to assist the areas along the border with the GDR.

EASTERN EUROPE

38. The *Ostpolitik* of the social-liberal coalition has become an essential element of West-East relations in the whole of Europe. Not only do we want to make full use of the scope provided by the treaties and agreements, we also want to develop it further.

39. Our relationship to the Soviet Union is marked by the willingness for long-term cooperation. I recall the statements on the occasion of my meetings with General-Secretary Brezhnev here in Bonn two years ago and in Moscow last summer. These also express the Soviet Union's interest in cooperation between the two German states. Precisely in difficult times, the federal government does not want to allow the dialogue with the Soviet Union to be interrupted.

40. However, we must also note "that, as a result of the events in Afghanistan, détente has become more difficult and more uncertain." These are the words of the Franco-German declaration of February 5, 1980. It also states "that détente would not survive another blow of the same kind." We therefore condemn, along with the overwhelming majority of the international community, the continuing armed intervention by the Soviet Union in Afghanistan and call for the unconditional and total withdrawal of foreign troops from Afghanistan.

41. On the basis of our treaties we want to continue our cooperation with Poland. It should be possible, as in the past, to solve the humanitarian problems. We are following the development in Poland with attention and concern. We are not interfering. But when we attempt to help the Polish leadership, at its request, in overcoming its present economic crisis, we refuse to allow anyone to accuse us of interference.

UNITED NATIONS AND THE THIRD WORLD

42. The federal government seeks cooperation with the countries of the Third World in a spirit of partnership and on the basis of equality. We reject any striving for domination in the Third World. We advocate the development of regional structures promoting stability and cooperation.

43. We welcome the fact that China has opened its doors to peaceful international cooperation. We intend to develop our relations with the People's Republic.

44. We shall render our contribution to the North-South dialogue for which the so-called Brandt Commission has made important suggestions.

45. In the past two years we have almost doubled our development assistance. In 1981 it is likely to increase at twice the rate of the overall budget. Of all donor countries we are at present, together with France, second only to the USA. We intend in particular to promote the development of new sources of energy, to contribute to the development of a new independent food supply basis in the developing countries, and to keep our market open for products from the developing countries with which we transact one full quarter of our external trade.

46. I intend to take part in the talks of heads of government on North-South problems scheduled to take place in Mexico in June 1981. At that meeting I shall, above all, plead for two challenges to be met, which might otherwise lead to human and political disasters:

First: More than 4 billion people live in the world today. Their number increases every year by 60 to 80 million, that is as many as the total number of people living in Germany. In twenty years the world population will be 6 billion and in another thirty years perhaps 10 billion. It is hard to imagine how all these people will be able to find sufficient food and accommodation, work, and a life worthy of human dignity. This is a realization from which conclusions have to be drawn—today, and not only in ten or twenty years when it may be too late.

Second: The oil price explosion has pushed up the oil bills of developing countries which amounted to 8 billion dollars in 1973 to almost 70 billion dollars in 1980. Some countries, in our neighborhood Turkey for example, have to spend more than half of their total export earnings on urgently needed oil imports. The entire volume of development assistance provided this year by all Western industrialized countries is not sufficient to cover as much as the 1979-80 increase of the developing countries' oil bills.

Think of what this order of magnitude means. Here all countries must help. Also the communist industrialized countries and above all the OPEC states by providing direct investments and grants.

47. The United Nations is the most important forum of the dialogue between North and South. This is another aspect which makes the United Nations an ever more important field of activity for our foreign policy. I have just had a valuable exchange of views with Secretary General Waldheim in New York in which I confirmed this opinion and found once again how highly our contributions to cooperation in that world organization are valued.

48. We take an active part in the efforts being made for a peaceful settlement of conflicts:

- Together with our EC partners we want to help in the search for a comprehensive, just, and lasting peace settlement in the Near East on the basis of the Venice Declaration.
- We support the demand for the release of the American hostages in Tehran.
- In the war between Iran and Iraq we support the efforts of the Islamic states and the United Nations to bring about a cease-fire.
- We reject the racial policy pursued by the South African Republic. We promote peaceful change and seek dialogue with all political forces in the south of the African continent, including the liberation movements.
- Together with them, we resolutely continue our efforts to achieve internationally recognized independence for Namibia by peaceful means.
- Here I should also like to appeal once again to the government of the Republic of Korea to grant freedom to the democratic politician Kim Dae Jong.

49. In the United Nations and the Council of Europe we have launched an initiative for the worldwide abolition of the death penalty, and another initiative in the United Nations for international cooperation to avert new flows of refugees.

50. We are working for a worldwide agreement on the renunciation of force as a peace-keeping instrument. In the United Nations we advocate the disclosure of arms supplies. We are making the concrete proposal that two registers be set up with the United Nations, one for recording the per capita expenditures of states for their arms build-up and for development aid and another one for listing worldwide arms exports and imports.

TASKS TO BE ACCOMPLISHED IN OUR OWN COUNTRY

51. Compared with the hunger, the acts of violence, the destitution in many regions of the world, the problems facing us in our own country appear to be somewhat trivial. In those regions it is a matter of life and death. Here, it is a matter of incomes and livings. But yet, our country requires creative and formative power and ability. Even for the sole purpose of preserving the measure of prosperity, of social peace, of liberty which we have achieved we need the courage to make corrections and gradual improvements. Reform, adjustment, and modernization continue to be necessary.

LESS OIL!

52. To become less dependent on oil — that is a crucial economic and technological task of ours. Without secure energy supply there will be no economic and social stability, no growth, no efficiency, either internally or externally. The second oil price explosion, which began in 1978, has left unmistakable traces on our national economy. We see rising costs and rising prices, a current account deficit, a rising level of unemployment. The higher oil bill deprives the people of a real income in the region of 30 billion deutsche marks a year. This loss of purchasing power cannot be amended by domestic means.

The war in the Gulf region has drastically illuminated the worldwide risks inherent in the supply of energy. True, we have full tanks for the coming winter, and we have numerous sources of supply. But high oil and natural gas prices, and supply risks owing to international political circumstances, will be marking the eighties throughout.

53. Since 1973 the federal governments have consistently adjusted themselves to this situation. The aims of our policy are and remain to get away from oil, to use energy more economically and rationally, to give priority to domestic coal, to proceed to a limited development of nuclear energy, to develop and introduce renewable energies. This policy has proved effective: Our supplies have always been sufficient, the proportion of oil in the energy consumption, which was still as much as 55 percent in 1973, is falling below 50 percent this year for the first time. Only 7 percent of our electricity still comes from oil-fired power stations, which is a result of our electricity-from-coal policy.

Incidentally, we shall introduce legislation in the Bundestag whereby oil will be completely ruled out for use in power stations. In the long term we are also aiming at lowering the proportion of gas burned in power stations. Otherwise, the federal government will continue its present energy policy which will as far as possible be based on market economy principles. Next year the third forward projection of the energy program will be put before Parliament.

54. It is obvious today that our coal policy in recent years and throughout the last one and a half decades has been right and justified — obvious even to those who did not agree. The financial assistance provided by the federal government and the Länder with coal mines as well as the electricity-from-coal legislation have decisively improved our security of electricity supply. But the subsidizing of coal, too, has its limits in terms of public finance. The coal and steel industries must expect the present subsidies for coking coal to be cut down.

55. Early this year the federal government adopted a coal processing program. The large-scale industrial conversion of coal requires considerable effort in the field of research and development so as to achieve the necessary economic efficiency and control the sizable environmental problems which may emerge. Industry and government are thus faced with huge financial tasks.

56. There exists broad international consensus about the need for peaceful use of nuclear energy. The federal government considers that the further development of nuclear energy is justifiable on safety grounds and—in the foreseeable future, i.e., for the next few decades—necessary on energy policy grounds. It therefore supports the limited development of nuclear energy— naturally with priority being given to safety.

This presupposes that the proper handling and management of waste are ensured. These continue to be governed by the decision on the management of waste from nuclear power plants taken by the heads of the federal and Länder governments in September 1979 and by the revised principles on waste management of February 1980. The federal government will, together with the Länder, examine in what way the procedures for the licensing of power stations can be expedited without detriment to safety and legal protection.

57. The federal government refuses to pursue the development of nuclear energy "without ifs and buts." One cannot simply force nuclear energy down people's throats; its development necessitates a broad democratic consensus. The federal government considers the report by the Enquete Commission of the Federal Parliament as an important contribution toward making the public debate more businesslike and objective.

58. The federal government expects further contributions in terms of "soft energy," if I may put it that way: from solar installations, from heat pumps, from new inventions altogether. We shall continue to encourage and promote such developments.

59. We also trust that industry, energy supply companies, the Länder, and the local authorities will join in a cooperative effort, so that off-heat will be better exploited, so that we do not have to consider the introduction of an off-heat levy, and so that better use is made of long-distance heat supply. We shall also examine ways of making additional economies by appropriately structured electricity rates.

(After covering the subjects of job creation, unions and workers' participation, opportunities through structural change, training schemes for boys and girls, social security, environmental protection, housing in urban and rural areas, integration of foreigners, federal government and Länder, budget economies, education and training, marriage and family, opportunities for women, solidarity of the young, media, sport, the law and internal security, and the state and the churches, the chancellor concluded as follows.)

135. The eighties have begun with a variety of international crises. We sense that peace is fragile. We sense also fear and uncertainty. The world has grown more complicated than many people had realized. For this reason, too, there can be no simple, let alone final, answers to political issues. In politics it must not merely be a question of achieving quantitative success—either for the in-dividual, the various groups, or the people as a whole. Rather it must also be a question of giving qualitative substance to the basic rights for the individual, of ensuring spiritual, human, and moral progress. All this, however, cannot be assessed by quantitative standards.

And it also has to be appreciated that most people need recognition of the efforts they pursue in a sense of responsibility and solidarity. And difficult times do call for greater solidarity. Many of the solutions of yesterday do not always suit the purposes of today. We therefore need the courage to proceed in a spirit of renewal. But we also have reason to be confident, to have courage, and to enjoy life.

136. We may all derive pride and confidence from the overall development and consolidation of our democracy. State and social institutions have stood the test. They have the backing of the people—that is not to be found everywhere, not in all countries.

137. Young people are looking for human values. The great majority of them are willing to commit themselves. They will also take on responsibilities if they can recognize and understand them. We must help in making them understandable. I appeal to the young people: Criticize the state, but also give it your loyalty, your solidarity. This is your state, this is your country, this is your future.

138. If in difficult times, notwithstanding highly divergent approaches and positions, we are all

- receptive to new ideas;
- if we look for fair solutions;
- if we act in solidarity;
- if we apply all our energies to the search for peace;

then every one of us can face the future with courage.

13

The Challenging Decade Ahead: Speech at the SPD Party Convention

(December 4, 1979)

THE CHALLENGES OF THE EIGHTIES

The eighties will be full of challenges and dangers, but they will also be full of opportunities and hopes. Hopes, because there are also paths that lead out of danger. If we miss them the outcome could be fatal, but we have the capacity to think ahead, to pose the right questions. We also have the courage to give the necessary answers, and we shall mark those paths and we shall follow them. It will not be a decade for those who take the wrong road but it may be our own hour of success if we steer a clear course.

We face the challenge of safeguarding peace both internally and externally in the eighties, of securing more justice. Without peace, without justice, there can be no human progress.

We face the challenge of translating technological developments, the amazing achievements of industry, into human progress. Progress without the human element is pointless and dangerous at that.

We face the challenge of defending freedom, especially against those to whom "freedom" appears to be nothing more than a stick with which to beat one's enemy; those who abuse freedom are not fit to have it.

ANSWERS TO THE CHALLENGES

I see our answers to the challenges of the eighties in terms of five main concepts. First, those who want to live in security tomorrow must shape the future

Excerpts from a talk delivered by Chancellor Schmidt in Berlin on the occasion of the Social Democratic Party's convention.

today. We need farsightedness in order to perceive the problems of tomorrow, power of judgment and courage to resolve them. This also means that today in Berlin we have to set the course for security in the eighties as well.

Second, we live in an unsafe, an unstable world. We must therefore link together the political stability of our country and our economic dynamism so that we, together with the other nations, will be able to consolidate and secure more justice in the world. This also implies a specific commitment to help the people in the Third World living in terrible poverty.

Third, we do not live in order to manage our affairs, we manage our affairs in order to live. But in future we shall have to manage things better than we have in the past. This means, for instance, conserving energy. It also means that not everything technically or economically possible must be made a reality for that reason alone. Fourth, we want change and renewal without losing that which has proved to be of value. We want to develop the nation's intellectual forces without any kind of tutelage and on a secure economic basis. This also implies an unequivocal commitment to the young generation and an unequivocal rebuff to anyone aiming to reduce social security and intellectual and cultural freedom. Fifth, those who want to be good neighbors tomorrow must accept and cultivate the diversity of Europe's history and culture, and with Europe the culture of our own nation. In other words, Europe's humanity, Europe's capacity for enlightenment and rationality. They must continue Europe's liberal traditions and respect people who hold views that differ from their own.

In recent years we have made considerable progress in this direction. We can stand comparison with other industrial countries. In the last ten years we have undertaken a large-scale restructuring of our industry to make it less harmful to the environment, and to conserve energy. We shall ensure that the main consideration will be prevention and that problems will be tackled not individually but in relation to one another.

POPULATION EXPLOSION

We Germans cannot have prosperity alone; peace and prosperity for ourselves presuppose more and more cooperation with others, especially with the nations in the southern hemisphere. The world political landscape is undergoing a transformation. We shall help in this process as we have done up to now. We want to help the nations of the Third World develop as steadily as possible. But this does not mean that we shall condone corruption, dictatorship, and oppression. When I was a schoolboy the world population stood at 2 billion. Now it exceeds 4 billion, and soon afterwards it could be 8 or 10 billion. It is beyond my powers of imagination to think that in fifty years' time we shall have to provide enough energy and food for 10 billion people. This is one of the most urgent problems attending the evolution of the world. One must ask whether something should not be done to check this population explosion. Do we have the right to do so? This is not only a social and economic but also a grave moral question.

Up to now nearly everyone has evaded this issue — the churches too and we ourselves. One cannot constantly harp on the exhaustibility of all goods and stand by and allow mankind to go on developing in this way.

ENERGY PROBLEMS OF THE DEVELOPING COUNTRIES

In making decisions on energy policy today one cannot ignore the population explosion in the Third World. The developing countries have been much harder hit by the oil crisis than we were. In 1972 they had to pay 4 billion dollars for their oil imports. In 1980 it will be 40 billion.

Allow me to make a comparison to show what 40 billion dollars means to the developing countries. All the official development aid provided by the industrial countries together this year amounts to only 20 billion dollars. But the developing countries have to spend a large proportion of their own export earnings on oil. Turkey, for instance, spends more than 80 percent of all she earns

With Hans-Dietrich Genscher, German foreign minister and leader of the Free Democratic Party (FDP), July 1980.

on exports—four-fifths of her earnings simply to pay for the vital commodity, oil. Brazil has to spend 50 percent of her earnings. And that money is wanted for the fight against hunger, against unemployment, money that is also needed to develop the country's economy. Three-quarters of the energy requirements of the developing countries have to be met by oil. In our case it is just under half. If poverty and unemployment in the developing countries is to be combated, an increasing proportion of the ever scarcer world oil reserves will have to be reserved for them and, I hope, at prices they will be able to pay.

WORLD ENERGY CONFERENCE

The exacerbation of the oil crisis this year and the events in Iran have demonstrated to us that energy supply is the life artery of all nations. Nobody knows what is going to happen on the oil markets or in the Middle East. We therefore strongly urge the resumption of the energy dialogue between the producing and the consumer countries, and we support the proposal by Lopez Portillo for a world energy conference, and we also want a European energy conference. At last week's meeting of the European Council in Dublin, I appealed urgently for a common energy policy within the European Community. We need more clarity in the oil markets and in the conduct of the multinational corporations. With this in mind, we decided at the last international economic summit in Tokyo, at my suggestion, to introduce a system of registering international oil transactions and stated our intention to secure better information on the profits of oil companies. And we shall continue to ensure that this is actually done.

GERMAN ENERGY POLICY

Our away-from-oil policy is showing initial signs of success. Whereas our gross national product has risen by 15 percent in real terms over the past five years, our oil consumption in 1970 was only marginally higher than in 1973. And was even less in the intervening years. But we can by no means afford to be satisfied with this result. True, the price mechanism will continue to make people economize and also to cause oil to be replaced by other sources of energy, in all branches. But this process will take a very long time, which is why we shall not be able to renounce regulatory measures. For instance, the use of oil for generating electric energy will rely as far as possible on the understanding and sense of responsibility of the people.

The Federal Republic of Germany will always remain an energy importing country. We shall only be able to reduce our dependence on imports if we resort to all available sources of energy, both today and tomorrow, and if we do not exclude any one of them from the outset or on principle. In this context, we have given priority to local coal since as early as 1973. Even if we succeeded in raising our coal production substantially in the next few years, we must not overlook the fact that if there should be a world energy crisis we shall not be able to determine the use of our national coal by ourselves.

A quarter of a century ago we committed ourselves in the treaty establishing the European Coal and Steel Community to supply coal to all members of the European Community in the event of a crisis. Some members, such as Italy, have no coal at all, neither has Denmark. And some have allowed their pits to be flooded. We have committed ourselves to the EC, and decisions could be taken by the European Commission in Brussels even without our agreement. This is one of several reasons why one has to be very cautious as regards the many optimistic forecasts one reads about Germany's energy consumption and supplies.

A world oil crisis would lead to a gas and coal crisis. As a precaution we have kept large stocks of coal, but in such a situation we would not be able to keep them for ourselves. In the long term, the threat to the atmosphere and the climate will come not only from lignite but also from oil and gas combustion. So far these risks have not been clearly distinguished from one another. Scientists have, moreover, established that the carbon content of the atmosphere is constantly increasing. There is still disagreement about the effects on the climate. One cannot foresee the outcome, but there is a risk, a risk that one day, perhaps several decades hence, we shall therefore have to cut down on the combustion of fossilized sources of energy, thus including coal.

DEVELOPMENT OF ALTERNATIVE SOURCES OF ENERGY

Because coal entails these risks, we are striving at considerable cost to develop clean, alternative, inexhaustible sources of energy, such as solar energy, and heat from the earth with the aid of thermal pumps. But we have to realize that we shall not be in a position to draw on such alternative sources on a large scale before the end of this century, with the exception of the thermal pumps — they will be a big "hit" in the next few years. These taken together are the compelling reasons why, for the next few decades at least, we cannot dispense with the limited expansion and limited use of nuclear energy.

NUCLEAR ENERGY

I know that nuclear energy has made many people anxious and this has to be taken very seriously. Hence our motto will continue to be: safety first. Compared with other countries, we have achieved very high safety standards. And through my initiative we have also achieved international cooperation in the matter of reactor safety.

Everywhere, oil substitution leads to an increase in electricity consumption and this can very quickly produce supply bottlenecks. For all these reasons, France, for instance, is already in the process of building an additional thirty-three nuclear power stations to be completed by 1985.

This is causing many people in the Saar and in Rhineland Palatinate much concern: thirty-three nuclear power stations. France will then produce 50 percent of its electricity from nuclear energy—six years from today. The Eastern bloc plans to expand its nuclear energy production from 33,000 megawatts to 140,000 megawatts within ten years.

In Dublin a few days go, the president of the European Commission, Mr. Jenkins, said that the Commission saw no possibility at all in overcoming the threats to their energy resources and the economic dangers of the future without considerable exploitation of nuclear energy. I cannot imagine that all these governments in East and West are wrong and that we alone are so much wiser with regard to energy and have so much bigger reserves than others.

BALANCE IN EUROPE

Stable as we may seem, we still live with risks, including the risk of inadequately safeguarded peace. That is why peace is the most important task of our foreign policy. A policy for peace demands constant efforts to maintain the balance in Europe, a balance of the powers that affects Europe.

This includes the need for our Alliance and our country to retain their defense capability. It includes determination and a will for compromise in our attempts to ease political tensions in the conflicts of interests around the world. It includes above all the development of systems of international arms control and limitation. A policy of détente and defense capability both together form the common policy of the Alliance.

POLICY OF DÉTENTE

It is thanks to the policy of détente that Central Europe is no longer the critical point of conflict, that millions of people in the West who visit the East have helped to preserve the national substance of our people, that Berlin is not a source of recurring crises. And the Berliners in both parts of the city, with whom I have a warm friendship, know this and they appreciate it.

Détente and cooperation with the East are the best policy we can pursue for Berlin. Those who would harm détente are also harming the Berliners.

The Quadripartite Agreement negotiated in close cooperation with the first social-liberal coalition has proved to be a sound basis.

If our foreign policy is to be successful it must be calculable, it must be constant, and it must have continuity. Other governments, other nations—in East and West—must see that we can be relied upon. They must be able to feel safe, that they have nothing to fear from us. That is why the integration of our country in the Atlantic Alliance and the European Community is a pillar of social democratic peace policy. Only on this foundation can the balance of forces be preserved, can a successful détente policy be pursued.

To us, indeed to the entire European Community, the Americans are not only irreplaceable partners, they are also our friends. We know the anxiety for hostages from our own experience, which is why we share the feelings of our American friends and President Carter. A great nation is bitterly and anxiously waiting for the release of their fellow countrymen in Iran. We respect the right of the Iranian people to determine their future themselves, but together with our friends in the United States, together with the other governments of the world, with the United Nations Security Council, we must insist that all nations of the world respect international law and that the hostages be set free.

CONTRIBUTION WITHIN NATO

We shall continue in the eighties to make our appropriate contribution within NATO to the collective defense of the West, to its defensive capability. But our responsibility at the same time demands fresh efforts to achieve arms control and disarmament. The task of limiting armaments, both nuclear and other, in a verifiable process, and of reducing them systematically while maintaining the balance, can only be accomplished step by step. This can only be achieved in lengthy, laborious negotiations. And it can only be achieved if all members are loyal to the Alliance.

I am firmly convinced that the leadership of the Soviet Union and of the other members of the Warsaw Pact want peace. I have no doubt about it. We for our part expect them to assume that the Western Alliance and we in this country have the same will for peace. We know that this subjective will for peace must also be backed by military and political balance. Equal balance and "equal security" for both sides are prerequisites for the success of détente and arms control policy.

PARITY AND DISARMAMENT

Parity and disarmament: The SALT II agreement has established the principle of self-restraint on the basis of parity in the ICBMs of both superpowers. I have stood up for this principle in many ways throughout the world, both through diplomatic channels and in public statements. This parity concerning intercontinental missiles means that there no longer exists a U.S. overhang—nor may it be reestablished—with which formerly the U.S. deficit in LRTNF [long-range tactical nuclear forces], which was quite considerable even then, could be offset.

It would have been logical in terms of a balance of strategic arms if the Soviet Union had exercised self-restraint with regard to its LRTNF. But in actual fact it has for the past two years been introducing the most modern missiles in this category, the SS-20s. In terms of quality, they are far superior to earlier Soviet systems. They carry three nuclear warheads, each aimed at a different target. They are of long range and great accuracy. They are reloadable, mobile, and therefore practically invulnerable. In May 1978, I had an opportunity to explain my concern about this development to Mr. Brezhnev, and this summer to Mr. Kosygin and Mr. Gromyko. Mr. Brezhnev stated in general terms that he was willing to enter into negotiations on this issue as well. And in his speech in East Berlin in October he came out in favor of specific negotiations in this field.

The United States of America is also ready to negotiate. We can but warmly welcome this readiness to negotiate on both sides, which we have played a considerable role in bringing about.

The Western Alliance could not, however, overlook the fact that the Soviet Union has continued to build up its lead in LRTNF, which even previously was quite considerable. Every week it adds another SS-20 with three warheads — 50 a year — and 30 new Backfire bombers a year — well over 100 nuclear warheads in all.

In view of this situation, the United States of America and the Atlantic Alliance want to give themselves the possibility of counteracting the growing imbalance in this field. This will be done in two days. Next week the Alliance will be addressing a specific offer of negotiations to the Soviet leadership. The purpose of the SALT III negotiations will be to establish a balance by mutual limitations on LRTNF as well. But as I said, it will be a twofold decision because the Western Alliance will at the same time decide to modernize its own TNF (tactical nuclear forces). This means that when the decision has been taken the first modern systems will be deployed at the earliest six years after the introduction of the Soviet SS-20, in other words not before 1983. It would be ideal if prior to that the negotiations were to produce results which would make it possible to dispense with the deployment of these more modern TNF in the European NATO states.

But this ideal situation would also mean that the Soviet Union for its part would not only stop deploying SS-20s but also take out of commission those already deployed.

But even a less comprehensive or ideal result could help considerably to stabilize the balance and thus afford further opportunities for expanding the policy of cooperation between East and West. Only in the course of the next few years, can we, must we, assess how far the results of the negotiations justify or require the nondeployment of such systems. That will have to be decided after the negotiations have been completed or have made considerable headway. The Federal Republic of Germany, being a non-nuclear country, will not be a party to the negotiations, will have a crucial interest in the decision to be taken within the Alliance as to how far actual deployment can be dispensed with.

Let me add that we are not precursors in the Alliance, nor do we want to be. We do not want to nor can we play a special, or as I once said a singular, role in the Alliance. Nor will we allow ourselves to be pushed into such a special role. But we do stand up within the Alliance for our own security interests. That is why we have helped to ensure that the two parts of the NATO decision I have just outlined will be inseparably linked together. Now we are being told with such an unusual amount of propaganda that if the West takes that decision next week the Soviet Union will no longer be prepared to negotiate. Such propaganda is of no use, and I will give you my reasons why.

First, I can see that the Soviet leadership wants to use this debate in an attempt to test our own loyalty to the Alliance. Here we cannot yield because our solidarity in the Alliance with the United States and the other members is the very essence of our security, and of the security of Berlin.

Second, without those two parts of the NATO decision there can be no negotiations as the United States would have nothing to offer that could induce the Soviet Union to renounce something it has had for a long time, and that not only in the form of a decision but also in the form of actually existing missiles and aircraft.

Third, the superpower Soviet Union will not in the long run want to evade negotiations on mutual arms limitation. I say this although I am sure that today even or tomorrow I shall be hearing protests and denials from the East. Yet I repeat: In the long run the Soviet Union will not want to evade mutual arms limitation talks. Everybody in East and West knows that we Germans have a vital interest in developing and extending détente, the security partnership between East and West, mutual arms limitation, and cooperation with the East. But all this will only be possible on the basis of a balance of forces; an imbalance would be bound to lead to the loss of security and cooperation. This, at any rate, is how for the last twenty years I have thought and written, spoken and acted, for the Social Democratic Party.

Everybody knows too that it was not our fault that the two superpowers did not include the TNF in the limitations under the SALT II agreement. This omission will have to be made up for in SALT III.

Everybody should know that no one can separate us from our American friends in the approach to SALT III. No one should attempt to make the Federal Republic of Germany a lever with which to break asunder the Western Alliance. Negotiations can only be successful if the Western capacity for action remains.

THE MBFR NEGOTIATIONS IN VIENNA

And now a word about the MBFR negotiations in Vienna. On many points the positions of the two sides have moved closer together. Now it is important to reach an interim result, a first reduction step, which can then be a basis for further negotiations and agreement on a second step. We have put forward a concrete proposal on this question for discussion within the Alliance and I hope that it will be adopted by the NATO Ministerial Conference next week so that it can be tabled in Vienna before Christmas. We hope that this important initiative will give fresh impulse to the MBFR negotiations in Vienna.

The Soviet Union's announcement that it will withdraw 20,000 troops and 1,000 tanks from the area of reductions back to the Soviet Union was an important signal of Soviet willingness. That withdrawal does not resolve the problem of balance, whether in terms of personnel strength or in terms of tanks, but it is a welcome step in the right direction.

The West is at present deliberating on the proposal for the unilateral withdrawal of 1,000 U.S. nuclear warheads from Europe. This proposed unilateral action, like the announcement of the Soviet withdrawal, is oriented to the main elements of the positions which both sides have adopted in the MBFR negotiations. The Western withdrawal of 1,000 nuclear warheads would at the same time make it clear that the decisions to be taken by NATO next week will on no account lead to an increase but rather a reduction in nuclear warheads. This would be an appropriate response to the unilateral withdrawal of tanks and troops by the Soviet Union. Generally speaking, I expect that there will be a new period of intensive efforts to stabilize the balance in Europe. They will occupy most of the eighties and affect security during that decade. I know that the East, too, wants to continue this partnership, this policy of cooperation with us. I base my knowledge on in-depth talks with the leaders of the Soviet Union and the other countries of the Warsaw Pact.

Partnership on security as well as cooperation is in the interest of the nations of Eastern Europe. They are also in the interest of the nations of Western Europe. And they are in the vital interest of the divided German nation and the divided city of Berlin. No other nation in Europe must, on account of its geographical position, be on peaceful terms with more neighbors than the German nation. Never again should war start from German territory. From the lessons of recent German history, but for that very reason with deep inner conviction, I support cooperation with Soviet Russia, with the Polish People's Republic, with our other Eastern neighbors, and of course with the German Democratic Republic. It is therefore appropriate that I shall be visiting Mr. Brezhnev in Moscow next spring and that Herr Genscher will be meeting Mr. Gromyko there later. And of course the heads of government of the two German states will have to speak to one another. Herr Honecker and I agreed several days ago to meet for a working session in the first few months of the New Year.

It is not the one who is most vociferous or the most frequent in his use of the word "reunification" who helps the cause of German unity. Most credit goes to those who achieve progress in Eastern Europe and between the nations of Western Europe and Eastern Europe and between the Germans. Only when progress is made in the promotion of this understanding can we hope one day to live again under the same roof.

THE EUROPEAN COMMUNITY

Be that as it may, we remain firmly anchored in the European Community. We have helped to enlarge it: Denmark, Britain, Ireland, soon Greece, and then the Iberian states that have freed themselves from dictatorship. This determination has proved worthwhile. We are growing together. The increasing coordination of foreign policy has for some time enabled Europe to speak with one voice on many issues. The first occasion was in Helsinki four years ago. Naturally, there are crises as well, as for instance on account of the unreasonable economic burden Britain is having to carry. A few days ago in Dublin we said we would be willing to add over DM 600 million to the Federal Republic's annual burden. I hope a solution will be found, but this will call for compromise on all sides. Any other attitude would be but damaging to all nine.

I also see the first directly elected parliament—which will be a source of many tensions—as a major step on the long road toward the democratization of the Community. But there is one point I will stress again: I regard the reform of the system of agricultural expenditure and the creation of a common energy policy as priority tasks for the European Community.

The progress achieved so far in the development of the Community would hardly have been possible without ever closer bilateral cooperation between the member states. This applies especially to Franco-German relations. They have reached a level of intensity and diversity which is unprecedented in Franco-German history. I am particularly grateful for the very close cooperation I have established with President Giscard d'Estaing. I deem it a great honor and am proud of it.

But in occupying ourselves with the further development of the European Community we must not lose sight of the fact that East and West have to reflect on their long-standing mutual cultural inspiration. This embraces not only the classical ages of Rome and Byzantium, not only Oxford and Prague and the Sorbonne; it also embraces Cluny as well as Zagorsk, Bergen or Novgorod, Czestochowa, as well as Aachen or Weimar. The big industrial centers are likewise manifestations of our common culture, those of Lancashire, the Ruhr, and the Donets Basin. One must constantly bear this in mind. It is all one common culture. We have a common destiny. Kant was right when he said: "Peace is not a natural state among men, it has to be nurtured." This is just as true today as it was 200 years ago. That is why a policy for peace is the most important task for the eighties.

14

Political Action Aimed at Fostering Understanding: Speech to the Congress on "Kant in Our Time"

(March 12, 1981)

I have often said in parliamentary debates that the federal chancellor should not see himself in the role of the nation's philosopher doing the people's thinking for them. And today I would add that neither would I feel happy in the shoes of the statesman about whom Socrates said: "At any rate I am wiser than he. Neither he nor I knows much, but he thinks he does. . . . I, too, know nothing but at least I don't imagine myself to know something."

On my occasional excursions into the realm of philosophy my main purpose has been to illustrate the fundamental values and basic convictions which have guided my life in politics. And here today I shall try to show by way of example that my basic convictions definitely have something to do with Kant. But then we will also become aware of the difficulties and the limits which present themselves to the politician who subscribes to Kant's ethical principles.

Kant cannot of course tell us how we should deal with the problems of unemployment; whether and how we should integrate foreign workers; whether and how we should provide more housing; whether and how we can secure our energy supply by acceptable means; or how we can or should maintain the international balance of power (this latter question, incidentally, being a subject to which he devoted a great deal of time later in life).

Kant has nothing to say about any of these problems. Nonetheless as a politician I have received considerable guidance from his works. On no account will I

The Congress on philosophy and politics entitled "Kant in Our Time" was organized by the Friedrich Ebert Foundation in Bonn.

177

try to pass myself off as an authority on Kant. I will merely speak from my own experience.

Right up to this day Kant has influenced my thinking. I have always been fascinated by his ideal of an unconditional devotion to duty not adulterated by self-interest or opportunism. The German philosopher Karl Joel once said that Kant bore Prussian discipline within himself.

On Perpetual Peace, a treatise which Kant wrote late in life and which I read for the first time soon after my return home after the war, left a deep impression on me, particularly his dispassionate rejection of illusionism and fancy and his proposal that they be replaced by specific international steps for maintaining peace. And he did mean "steps." Kant speaks of perpetual peace as a task which can only be accomplished step by step.

My references to Kant in this connection are concerned for the most part with *On Perpetual Peace,* and *On the Concept of a General Evolution with Cosmopolitan Intent,* both of which were written after his great philosophical works.

Three things in Kant are particularly important to me. One is his ethics of mankind, which start from the assumption that all men have fundamental freedoms. Another is the duty to seek and maintain peace and to develop the community of nations as a principal moral and not only as a political norm. The third and most important of all is the close connection between the principle of moral duty and the principle of reason, or, as one might say today, "critical ratio."

I had already become aware of the significance of moral duty from reading Marcus Aurelius's *Reflections Upon Myself,* which I happened to come across as a young man at the beginning of the war.

CONSEQUENCES OF A POLICY DEVOID OF REASON

If I understand it correctly, duty and responsible action meant to Kant acting in conformity with what mankind has in common, that which therefore enables people to understand one another over and above all the differences between them, that is to say in conformity with human reason. I was very much impressed by this conception upon my return from war service because, like many millions of people, I had had firsthand experience of the devastating consequences of a policy without reason, a policy of madness.

Kant's practical philosophy culminates in the categorical imperative (in one of several versions): "Act only on that maxim through which you can at the same time will that it should become a universal law." To me this simply means that the political leader wishing to act responsibly should take into account the consequences of his actions for others, for only in this way can he find out whether the maxims governing his actions really are fit to become "universal legislation"—as Kant says in another version. Obviously, this moral principle should also serve as a guide for our political morality.

Today, incidentally, one might also interpret the categorical imperative along the lines of the German-American philosopher Hans Jonas. One could say: "Let your actions endanger neither the future of man nor the future of nature." I would not say yet that that is also my interpretation. I merely want to suggest that today, 200 years later, some of these imperatives can be updated, indeed may have to be.

Kant's imperative requires the politician not to be an opportunist but conscientiously to acquaint himself with all interests affected by and all consequences of his decisions, and to weigh them up conscientiously.

Let us take, for instance, the current discussion on the export of arms. Here a number of different interests overlap in an extremely complicated manner and they all have to be considered in relation to one another. There are our own interests, the interest of others, and our own interest in foreign interests. And with all possible alternatives we have to weigh up the pros and cons of the consequences of our conduct. Since they are hard to assess it is not easy to weigh them up against one another! And should anyone say that here we have to make a choice between oil and our morals then he has not given the matter enough thought. The crux of the matter, as with many other political problems, is the very fact that both differing and even conflicting assessments and solutions can undoubtedly be morally justifed.

And while I am on this subject, let me say that I know of governments that encourage the export of arms in order to reduce unemployment, and there is hardly anyone who would not say that it is morally right to reduce unemployment. The situation as good as never arises where one political view of a specific political issue could claim to be the only one to be consistent with "morality." As for the Federal Republic's basic position on the export of arms, the main result of the current discussion will probably be that we shall adhere to our restrictive practice. And in our case the export of arms will not be seen as a means of improving our employment situation.

THE MAJORITY DECIDES—WHETHER RIGHT OR WRONG

For governments to show a proper sense of responsibility they must take a very broad view of the interests that are affected. Many of our decisions will affect future generations as well. Take for instance the legislation introduced by the social-liberal coalition over the past eleven or twelve years in the field of environmental protection. In 1970 we launched a program of immediate action to counter the dangers of pollution. If these measures had been delayed the damage would probably have been beyond repair.

But our environmental policies also have to make allowance for the jobs of

the present generation. And when all things have been taken into consideration a decision has to be made, with everything depending on the judgment—or misjudgment—of the majority. That is how things are in a
democracy. The majority has its way even when they are not right. That is one
of the blemishes of democracy which cannot be removed. And in many cases
the consequences do not become visible until very much later. And perhaps
then there will be no one there who has to answer for those decisions, because
he is either no longer in office or no longer alive.

Another example is energy. No one in the federal government believes that
we could rid ourselves of our problems simply by staking everything on nuclear
energy. But neither is there anyone in the federal government who believes that
the other sources of energy are without risk. All of them entail either ecological,
political, economic, or social risks, or perhaps several of them at once. And it is
impossible to make absolutely safe predictions with regard to such risks. Since
this is not possible the risks have to be spread as widely as possible so as to
minimize the overall risk. This explains why we strongly encourage energy conservation; why, on the other hand, we give preference to the coal we have used
up to now and whose risks we therefore know (risks, by the way, that are often
underestimated). And that is why we are also in favor of promoting and using
new types of energy, including, to a limited extent, nuclear energy. Or, to put
it differently, we are against the unlimited use of nuclear energy because we
would make ourselves too dependent on this source of energy and the risks at-
taching to it which we cannot fully calculate. The answer, therefore, is to spread
the risk.

The kinds of considerations that govern our energy policy definitely lie
within the area marked out by the categorical imperative. All the same one can
arrive at different results and quarrel passionately. And it is clear to me that
other arguments with regard to energy policy may also fall completely within
the framework of the categorical imperative. Our decision is the result of a sensible weighing up of the consequences and the risks involved. But I would not
for a moment argue that those who are totally in favor of nuclear energy are
therefore acting immorally, nor, by the same token, would I say that anyone
who rejects nuclear energy absolutely is acting immorally. To the exponents of
both these extreme standpoints I would always merely say: your calculation of
the consequences and the possible risks is irrational. I would not be able to go
further than that, although I would naturally have to explain why I think their
calculations are irrational.

THE POLITICIAN'S DECISION

I wish to repeat in this connection that the politician is responsible not only
for his good intentions but above all for the consequences of his actions or

omissions. I learned this, incidentally, from Marcus Aurelius when I was 19 years old. In other words, he has to answer for the desirable just as much as for the undesirable consequences. He is just as responsible for the results he hopes to achieve, if they actually materialize, as for the side effects which he did not want but which nonetheless happen, and they can be extremely complex and most unpleasant.

In the extreme case, decisions that the politician has to take may be a matter of life and death. I have been in such a distressing situation myself. In October 1977, following the murder of Hans Martin Schleyer and the rescue of the hostages in Mogadishu, I said in Parliament: "The man who knows that he will carry the burden of failure and guilt either way despite all his efforts and no matter what action he takes will know himself that he has done everything and it has been right. He will not attempt to blame the failure on others because he knows that they too find themselves in the same inevitable predicament. But he will be able to say: We have decided this or that, we have refrained from doing this or that, we have done this or that for this or that reason. All this we have to answer for." And by the way, during those weeks when the hostages were held captive there was no political theory, no politological theory, and no moral theory that would have been of any help to us.

The politician is not justified simply by the fact that he pursues the morally right aims. That is at best a part of his justification. His political actions must be preceded by a critical analysis of the situation and the various implications. If they are not then his actions have no moral justification whatsoever. Any mistakes he makes in his assessment of the situation or in his rational choice of the means he resorts to in order to achieve a morally justified aim can have very tragic consequences. They can be just as terrible as the consequences of false moral principles. Both can disqualify the politician.

In this respect I am following very closely the line of thought of Max Weber. This I have always done because from the very time when I studied his works I felt this to be true. I found confirmation in his works. He said: "A politician who acts on behalf of others should by no means fall back upon his fundamental convictions or their underlying ethics. Indeed—and here I quote from his famous essay on *Politics as a Profession* written in 1919—"he has to answer for the consequences of his actions." And he wrote in parenthesis: for the "foreseeable" consequences of his actions. I would prefer to delete the word "foreseeable," although life is of course more pleasant for the politician if he is told that he must only answer for the foreseeable consequences. In reality he must also answer for the consequences he could not foresee!

I once said that politics without a moral foundation are unscrupulous and tend to be criminal. Kant wrote in his treatise *On Perpetual Peace:* "Thus true politics cannot take any step without previously having paid homage to morality." Today I would reverse that and say the pursuit of moral political objectives without the "sense of judgment" as understood by Max Weber might possibly have destructive consequences.

THAT WHICH IS PRAGMATICALLY AND MORALLY RIGHT

I myself have often said with regard to this interplay of purposive reason and moral objectives in politics—and professional philosophers have taken offense because the word "pragmatic" is used here perhaps in a different sense than they were accustomed to—that politics is pragmatic action to achieve moral purposes or moral aims. With this I want to make it clear that pragmatic action—which I can claim to be my own approach in spite of all its imperfections—has nothing to do with the aimless kind of muddling through one is accused of from time to time. On the contrary, a policy which pursues ethical aims or purposes based on practical reason and uses means the effects of which are commensurate with the situation, and whose side effects have been carefully calculated and found to hold little risk, is the very opposite to unprincipled opportunism or irresponsibly letting things drift. Or to phrase it differently, an illusory policy, one which forgoes rational calculation, may for that very reason and in spite of the "theory" used to justify it be immoral, even if the purposes are presented as moral purposes.

Although Kant for the most part does not use the concept of what is pragmatically right in contrast to what is morally right, there are times when he does. In *On Perpetual Peace* he links the word "pragmatic" with the notion of reason which is capable of translating fundamental political ideas into practice in conformity with the moral principle.

It appears to me that to think pragmatically and to act pragmatically is therefore a moral duty incumbent upon every politician who not only wants to talk about moral principles but really wants to give them effect by his actions. And there is a difference between a politician who merely theorizes and one who acts and has to answer for what he does.

Let me illustrate this with the example of the CDU/CSU opposition in the Bundestag. For twelve, or strictly speaking thirty years, they have made hard going of their policies with regard to the two parts of Germany. Somehow they cannot get beyond declamatory appeals. For decades they have with a clear conscience espoused the cause of German unity with many, many words. But during that long period the Berlin wall was erected and ever more links between Germans here and in the GDR have been severed. Then the social-liberal coalition government came to power and in the past twelve years we have halted this trend and entered into negotiations with the GDR government. This long and difficult process has led to tangible improvements between the people in both parts of the country.

WORKING TO PRESERVE THE IDENTITY OF THE NATION

Both coalition and opposition uphold the unity of the nation and insist that the nation as a whole must be preserved. But the means which the CDU/CSU have used in pursuit of this goal have always seemed to me illusory. Conversely, many members of the opposition feel that our pragmatic steps to develop economic and political relations between the two German states, our pragmatic compromise between diverging interests, are without principle. And they are even more convinced of this seeing that, even when faced with setbacks, we have not allowed ourselves to be discouraged.

I still believe that we should develop cooperation wherever possible, that there should be more human contacts, more economic and cultural exchanges. That is the only basis for political efforts to preserve the identity of the nation. I am not by any means implying that the opposition's approach to intra-German relations is immoral, but I do think that they lack a sense of judgment as regards the consequences.

In my last policy statement and then again in my New Year address I said that times would get more difficult, that all over the world there would be less and less scope for political action, especially on economic and financial matters. And I said that this requires us to take a calm and sober view of the situation, to assess it critically and rationally. Some of the proven remedies of the past are no longer suitable in these changed circumstances. In the years ahead when there will be less scope for action we shall have to demonstrate our political flair and flexibility. It will be a matter of finding new ways and means of securing social justice and social reforms even when the growth rates we have known in the past fail to materialize.

To Kant social justice was not a political demand. In this respect he was wholly a man of this time. He pleaded for equality before the law, not equality of opportunity.

Let me give you an example of what I mean by showing political flair and flexibility. Over the past ten years our industrial production has been very good and this has enabled us to ensure steady increases in the social services provided by the state, such as in the case of family allowances, and all have benefited. But in view of the restricted financial scope one must ask whether we shall be able to carry on in this way. Perhaps it will be necessary to distribute our financial resources more selectively in favor of those who are most in need of assistance. In hard times those who are better off should be more willing to help those who are less fortunate.

It is well to remember in this connection that the various reforms that are desirable and feasible must not necessarily lead to higher costs, that they can in fact help us economize. This applies for instance to densely populated areas where the reform of land law might again make it easier for people to build houses. Or let us consider the integration of foreign workers, and especially their children. If we take the right steps now we shall in the long term save not only considerable budget expenditure but heavy social costs as well.

But the fact that times have become more difficult throughout Europe, in North America, all over the world in fact, with the exception of the OPEC countries, is no reason to feel despondent. The strength of the Western democracies lies precisely in their openness, in their ability to learn, in their ability to adapt to new situations and new problems.

ATMOSPHERE OF DEMOCRACY

Kant could not conceive of such a democratic process. He could not have been a democrat in our sense of the world, still less a Social Democrat. But there is one thing wich Kant perceived very clearly late in life, that conflict can be conducive to progress. And it is true that the strength of democracy, especially its ability to learn and to adapt, only comes to bear in a climate that permits of discussion, indeed of conflict.

In recent weeks lively discussions have been taking place within my party on domestic and foreign policy issues. The media have tended to view the differences of opinion that have emerged as out and out strife between different party factions. And the opposition and the media close to them have for pretty obvious reasons even gone so far as to say that this discord threatens to limit the government's scope for action. I will not comment on the way some of these disputes have been conducted, though I have not been at all happy about them, but I would like to stress that the Social Democrats have always been known for their passionate debates on major issues. And that is how it will remain in the future. "Internal struggles give a party its strength and vitality. The clearest sign of a party's weakness is the blunting, the neutralization, of the marked differences." These words were written by Ferdinand Lassalle to Karl Marx as long ago as 1852.

Our political system would be in a bad way if disputes and conflicts were to be condemned. Those who take such a negative view of arguments over convictions and policies fail to appreciate the positive influence of conflicts on the nation's cultural and political progress. Where would the labor movement be today if it had not always got to grips with its situation in ever-recurring conflicts and had not fought for its rights and for reforms? Where would the Federal Republic be today among the nations of the world if the social-liberal coalition had not abandoned the Hallstein Doctrine and pushed ahead with its *Ostpolitik* in the face of massive opposition and in conflict with itself and with others?

At the present time the Social Democrats are leading the discussion on major issues of the future, such as security and energy, on behalf of many others in the country. And I hope that those citizens who may be irritated by this at the moment will come to appreciate that this discussion was necessary. But I will add quite frankly that too much conflict in a democracy is bad and that there is no need to smash the furniture unnecessarily.

But the opposite is also true. If parties are afraid of conflict, if they are too preoccupied with thoughts of harmony, or indeed if they long for one pattern of meaning created by the state and binding on all, this could imperil the political life of the nation, the substance of our democracy. Such an attitude would be well behind the enlightening philosophy of Immanuel Kant. The older Kant, in his *Concept of a General Evolution with Cosmopolitan Intent*, sees the positive effects of conflict and deems it necessary for social progress. Indeed he had no choice but to acknowledge the value of conflict because he considered the individual's reason to be limited. And neither of these two points can be said to be dated, even 200 years later!

LIMITS OF ENLIGHTENMENT

If I understand Kant correctly, the individual's reason is not absolute, or to put it roughly in the words of Adolf Arndt, reason belongs to the "penultimate domain." It must not exceed its limits. It would be going beyond those limits if it wanted to proclaim as a binding truth a comprehensive ideology or doctrine of redemption, or even only a concept embracing the meaning of life. Kant and Lessing are in my view the most outstanding philosophers of the *Aufklärung* in Germany. Both set out to make a critical analysis of the claims of reason, but not to raise them to too high a dogmatic level.

Conservative critics who say that the enlightened political system installs reason as a new dogma in place of the old dogmas are mistaken. Enlightenment can only extend as far as religious beliefs, principles, and values can be rationally discussed.

Kant accepted that values and interests could be assessed in different ways. Unlike Hegel and in total contrast to Marx, he did not perceive in this any "alienation" of man which had to be overcome.

The freedom which Kant demanded for the individual was of course directed against the demands of the absolutist state of his time. But the diversity and divergence of interests linked with the freedom of the individual are today still the roots of conflict in our society.

From the conservative perspective, the body politic should be based on harmony. Harmony, indeed unity, is the very foundation. But party quarrels, pay disputes, the coexistence of, the clashes between the various factions, that is suspect. Conflict, according to the strict conservative model of social relations, does not really fit into any legitimate category. Ludwig Erhard's concept of an "integrated society," for instance, was based on that idea of harmonious relations. But to me it was no more plausible than Othmar Spann's corporate state.

Apart from the fact that the conditions at the time were not suitable, there were also important reasons of principle why the concept of an integrated society could not materialize. It is impossible to conceive a democratic industrial society without its inherent diversity and its conflicts of interests and views. And any attempt to give that society a uniform stamp is bound to come to grief in the light of this reality.

But because the concept of a harmonious society makes no allowance for conflicts, and because individuals or groups who question that harmony are considered troublesome people who do not belong, outsiders with whom there is no need to argue because it is sufficient for the state to "show them the flag" since the state has to provide their intellectual leadership, this can in reality lead to the disintegration of society! If we think too much in terms of friend-foe relationships, in other words if we are not sufficiently prepared, if we do not have enough ability to settle conflicts by peaceful means, if we are not prepared and if we do not have sufficient ability to reach a consensus, this means that we are not prepared and not able to compromise.

POLITICAL SELF-CORRECTION

During the budget debate in the Christian Democrat parliament, Richard von Weizsäcker rather superfluously tried to assess how my chancellorship would be rated in history. I will gladly let future generations decide on that, but there is one point I want to be clear about. I at any rate do not want that period, in spite of the growing difficulties, to be considered as one in which there was less plurality and less discussion.

Those who have different political views, and this applies in particular to young people, must not be forced into the wings of the political stage, however irrelevant their views may seem to the majority.

When they came to power twelve years ago the Social Democrats stopped a current of thought which dominated the sixties to the effect that the state should prescribe what was good for society. But in my opinion the common weal has to be reshaped ever anew as conditions change. And to a democrat in a democratic society this can only be achieved through the confrontation of different opinions and interests. Democracy is a process, not a state.

One basic requirement of that process is that decisions that have been taken should also be reviewed. And it follows from this that if those decisions have proved wrong adjustments have to be made. For instance, we improved the 1972 bill concerning people with extremist views seeking admission to the public service. Unfortunately, self-correction is somewhat rare in politics—and also in the field of science.

When the then federal chancellor and the then heads of government of the federal states took that decision about extremists in 1972 their aim was to standardize procedures for the screening and appointment of people wishing to enter the public service. This aim was not achieved. Instead the authorities overdid things with the result that young people in particular became afraid. This fear spread far beyond those who had a genuine reason to be afraid of the monitoring procedure.

Consequently, the federal states governed by a social-liberal coalition, and the federal government, decided seven years later that applicants should no longer be automatically asked whether they support the state and the democratic system because "cost and benefit" were completely out of proportion. But even with such an adjustment there are some aftereffects. As a result of that decision of 1972, for instance, people sometimes still come up against restrictions, even in their private life. There is the case of the married couple who were refused permission to adopt a girl on the ground that the husband was a member of the German Communist Party. And I consider it just as questionable when a minister-president of one of the federal states proclaims in Parliament that conscientious objectors in his state may not be in charge of youth hostels. One does not have to ponder long to realize which federal state it was and which minister-president.

YOUTH PROTEST

But there must be no discrimination against young or old when they exercise one of their basic rights. Moreover, a democratic society, with different religious beliefs, different outlooks on life, and different interests, cannot exist without tolerance and without each member of the society's respecting the dignity of the others. This was appreciated quite early on in the older Western democracies, but in Germany the fundamental significance of tolerance for such a society based on respect for human dignity was not fully appreciated until after the perversions of the Third Reich. And the dictate of tolerance has still not established itself as firmly as one would like in our country to ensure a stable, well-functioning democratic society. This also applies, incidentally, to some of the trends among the young generation, the protest demonstrations taking place almost every day, not only in our country but in the big cities of many European countries.

There are many reasons for this protest. The motives are usually hidden; in most cases in fact those involved are aware of them. Many of these young people, having grown up in times of economic prosperity and with no material worries, have not too rosy a vision of the future.

They see themselves with gloomier prospects of prosperity although they say society should not think in terms of affluence. The house squatters, for instance, are in some cases in serious circumstances, but others are lodging a

symbolic protest against bureaucracy, against injustice, against urban development plans which they feel are inhumane; they are protesting against the
authorities, against the state as such. This is no doubt partly due to their disap-
pointment at the fallibility of what is supposed to be a perfect democratic
system of government. And the protest against nuclear energy is a conglomera-
tion of the innate fears of many people and the aggressions of small groups who
want to challenge the state or others.

We cannot and will not tolerate violence, but we would be deceiving
ourselves if we felt that we could lastingly preserve the stability of our society by
forcing large groups of young people onto the fringes of society or by leaving
them alone with their problems. And a civil spirit is not a virtue or charac-
teristic that lasts for ever. It must grow anew in every generation; it has to be
taught and given fresh strength. I do not think that measures such as the im-
position of stricter penalties for demonstrators, which tend to make criminals of
a minority, are a suitable way to arouse that civil spirit.

LACK OF CIVIL COURAGE

To be able to tackle these problems one has to explore the causes. We older
ones must seek a dialogue, controversial though it may be, with young people,
and we must take them seriously in spite of their sometimes provocative attitude and the fact that they are at times hard to understand. And in such a
dialogue firmness is also called for. Where necessary we must say no, and
likewise where necessary we must say yes. One could almost say that what is
really causing some young people to be aggressive is the lack of civil courage on
the part of adults. But adults should on no account try to give their cowardice
the appearance of tolerance, for tolerance is not just letting young people do as
they please or neglecting them. It is rather showing respect for the legitimate
values, the legitimate views, of others so long as they respect the rights of
others. Tolerance, I repeat, is a fundamental principle of a democratic society
based on respect for human dignity. Yet it must not be overrated. Tolerance
cannot be a substitute for the peaceful settlement of conflicts, for majority decisions, for compromise and arbitration.

With Kant the state was the authority for settling conflicts. Its purpose was to
establish procedures for social conflicts and to transform them into a productive
function for society as a whole.

As I see the role of the state today, that would be too simple. Moreover, the
state would not only be optimistically overrated and overstrained, it would be
dangerously powerful. The state should not want to settle certain conflicts
itself, such as conflicts over pay claims or, on a different level, religious conflicts, or conflicts in marriage or, again on a different level, aesthetic conflicts,
whether in literature or the fine arts. But in other respects I can go along with
Kant, for instance when he says that the state should protect the nation against

dangers from outside and create and maintain the conditions in which the people can think and act on their own responsibility.

And I definitely agree with his unequivocal reservation as regards government interference with the ideological, the spiritual, foundations of society. If the state were to do the people's thinking for them that would be at odds with the Kantian principle that every man should think for himself. If the state did assume this role the next step could well be tutelage.

Peter Glötz recently wrote that many people, and he meant in particular young people, are now finding the search for their own identity, for their own way of life, too much of a strain. That appears to be true, but I would warn people not to let the government deprive them of the chance to make that strenuous effort to find their own identity, or to expect the government to relieve others of the chance. If they did there would be a twofold danger: the individual would not only be deprived of the chance to search; it would not even be possible to find his identity to give to him.

That is not to say that a federal chancellor, a politician, or a government should keep out of conflicts of thought and opinion. However, I must say that it would be out of character for a Hamburger loftily to present his remarks on fundamental attitudes under the definition of "intellectual leadership." Some of you will recall what I have said on previous occasions on the subject of fundamental values. I shall not dwell on that here but I should like to make one or two points to show the distinction from Kant.

I said earlier on that in Kant's concept of fundamental values the term "justice" means only formal equality in law, not social equality of opportunity. With solidarity he goes even further with his qualification. To him it is morally but not politically binding. In his view the state should keep out of social affairs apart from a few exceptional cases: he specifically mentions the financing of homes for orphans and waifs. To put it rather simply, Kant was a liberal, not a social liberal. His attitude is quite understandable considering his direct opposition to the late absolutist paternalism of the state which invoked the "well considered" interests of its subjects to justify its massive encroachments upon the individual's liberties.

And Kant, like many liberals today still, overrated the opportunities for those worse off and in need of protection to acquire material and nonmaterial self-sufficiency through their own efforts. In this respect the philosophers of socialism and of the labor movement have taken the Kantian concept of solidarity a lot further. To the Königsberg philosopher the problems of the proletariat were still a long way off.

JUSTICE AND SOCIAL PEACE

To Social Democrats today it is clear that a democracy confined to government decisions is bound to suffer from its incompleteness because it excludes areas which are of central importance to the individual and to the larger part of the community, principally employment and the economy. We say that political democracy should be made complete by the addition of social democracy because it is only in such a modern industrial society that there can be lasting justice and social peace.

For this reason the Social Democrats have always considered it the duty of the state to create the conditions which will enable the individual to have real freedom and make for real equality of opportunity. And in our practical application of these principles we have meanwhile advanced far beyond Kant, Marx, Lassalle, Bebel, Bismarck, and beyond Beveridge and Adenauer. We have created a network of social security which is highly differentiated both in its ability to react to the needs of its people and in its efficiency. In fact it is such a sensitive fabric that in difficult situations we have to handle it with great care. And it is all the time necessary to adjust undesirable trends and prevent abuse.

Perhaps I may at this point make a highly political remark. This social security network on the one hand and our unified trade-union system — only Scandinavia and Austria have similar systems — the works councils, the Works Constitution Act, and our system of industrial democracy on the other are important foundations of social peace in our country. They are the main reason for the enormous social and political stability of the Federal Republic of Germany over the past 30 years. Of course, all this should today be seen within the concept of the categorical imperative, now over 200 years old. But then, 200 years ago, no one foresaw that. Nor was it understood like that at the time. In a historical context as well, our social stability has not been developed from Kantian ethics.

Indeed, I am going to disappoint all those who want to misconstrue what I say, those who would imply that the federal chancellor regards the principles of Kantian ethics as the only ones binding upon the state or, in his capacity as deputy chairman of the party, as the only ones binding upon the Social Democratic Party. Anyone misunderstanding the Kantian impetus of the *Aufklärung* in this way would himself be in urgent need of enlightenment.

The Basic Law contains norms — basic rights and constitutional principles — of substantive moral values. They are not complete, nor do they relate to a perfectly clear, fully developed image of man — nor would that be thinkable in a free society. But those basic rights and those constitutional principles do derive from fundamental knowledge of the nature of man, and they represent an attempt to cope with the good and the bad experiences of the Germans with themselves, and of people with other people.

These basic rights embodied in our constitution — and incidentally, as the SPD's Godesberg Program says, the fundamental values of social democracy — are accessible to people who draw the norms for the things they should do, whether they be of a formal or of a substantive nature, from different ideological, philosophical, and religious attachments and sources. But what makes Kant so up-to-date is the fact that he presents modes of thought and maxims which can make people with different ideologies capable of engaging in a process of understanding on common political action for ethical purposes.

PEACE HAS TO BE "MADE"

I began with a reference to Kant's treatise *On Perpetual Peace* and I should like to take that point up again in conclusion. To Kant the maintenance of peace was not solely a dictate of politics, of justice, but a moral duty absolute. And he makes a realistic assessment of the persistence of conflicts between states. To him peace policy does not consist merely of protestations of the will for peace, and least of all of hope for an age of international fraternization. He pleads for the controlled handling of conflicts between states and for continuous efforts to settle them in the interests of all.

In debates on peace policy in recent years, but particularly over the past twelve months, I have frequently invoked Kant because he says that peace among men is not a natural state, that on the contrary it has to be "made."

Incidentally, he also introduced the idea of balance between states, saying that it was necessary for man to discover "a law of balance" among the states. And he wanted such a balance to help create "a cosmopolitan state of public security" between mutually independent states.

In the natural sciences the state of balance can usually be measured. In psychology, in ethics, in politics, and in military strategy, balance is a sometimes indispensable auxiliary notion but in many instances it cannot be exactly defined or measured.

Philosophy and morality cannot provide us with any unequivocal standards for judging what was necessary in 1949, when the North Atlantic Alliance was established, to ensure balance between East and West; what was necessary in 1962 at the time of the Cuba crisis to preserve the balance between East and West; and what is necessary in the eighties to keep the military balance stable; standards for answering such urgent and important questions. On the contrary, we have to resort to reason, which weighs up the pros and cons.

BALANCE BRINGS SECURITY

And here I must say once again that even where the information available to both sides concurs — and it is extremely difficult to ensure this with regard to the political and the strategic aspects — it is possible to arrive at widely differing results and widely differing political consequences. Nevertheless these different results of our thought processes and political consequences may each have their moral justification. This is because in a specific case it is not simple, indeed it is terribly difficult, to determine how, for instance, a balance between the Soviet Union and the United States of America should look.

I should like in this context to mention the two elements which today govern German policy for equilibrium in the field of security. The one is that the Federal Republic of Germany belongs to the West. Only our membership in the Western Alliance can preserve the balance in Europe. This is the very nucleus of our security. We cannot be neutral. The other is that we do need an approximate balance of military forces between East and West. Only then will all concerned have the same security. And only on this basis can peace be safeguarded.

An approximate balance of military forces should not be established merely by both sides building up their armaments because that would be an unstable system and lead to a disastrous arms race. Greater security will come from stabilizing the balance of military forces by means of negotiated arms limitations. If mankind is not to arm itself to death, this is the only answer.

This explains why, for instance, NATO's decision to modernize Eurostrategic weapon systems had to be of a twofold nature. The object was not only to build up the Western—or to be more precise the American—armaments and thus to close the gap, but at the same time to offer the Soviet Union negotiations leading to a treaty on the mutual restriction of such weapons. The federal government is doing all it can to make this indispensable element of the dual decision a success. However, peace policy cannot be confined to the preservation of military balance. Balance is a necessary condition for peace but not a sufficient one. It must be complemented by a peaceful disposition, the will to show restraint toward others, the will to speak to one another and also to listen when the other speaks. And it must be complemented by the will to understand the interests of the other side and to respect those interests. It must be complemented by the will and the ability for compromise, and the will for cooperation.

NO PREOCCUPATION WITH ENEMY IMAGES

We Germans cannot prevent a cooling of East-West relations from time to time. But when they cool we in particular must take care not to abandon our political reason through any preoccupation with enemy images. It is precisely when conflicting positions become hardened that the dialogue with the other side should be maintained.

This recognition of the independence of the other, his security requirements and his interests, precludes any interference with his domestic affairs. Kant himself says this in the fifth preliminary article in *On Perpetual Peace* with the words: "No state should intervene with force in the constitution and government of another state." This idea, and Kant was surely not the first to develop it, is today a natural and important element of international law, of the United Nations Charter, and of the Final Act of the CSCE signed at Helsinki.

Just as important for peace in Kant's view is a continuous process of economic integration. Economic integration for the sake of peace was also the motive of the social-liberal coalition in developing closer trade relations with the Soviet Union and with Eastern Europe.

Finally, the essential basis for any cooperation between states, but also for agreements on arms limitation and disarmament, for instance, is mutual trust. Agreements will then help to promote the growth of that confidence. There is no need for me to give examples of the extent to which mutual confidence among states and peoples is impaired and obstructed. It is necessary for us Germans in particular, in whose name confidence between peoples has been horribly shattered in this century, to work ever anew to create political confidence.

In this process we must realize that in the struggle between East and West prejudice and resentment are not confined to one side—and there is fear on both sides.

International agreements for the building of confidence can create a climate in which fears can be eliminated and in which each side can obtain a differentiated picture of the other. Confidence building also means perceiving the many different elements of the other side's motives, appreciating not only its external but also its domestic situation, and also taking its loyalties seriously.

DUTIES OF THE POLITICIAN

It will therefore be of special significance if the CSCE follow-up meeting in Madrid decides to hold a conference on disarmament in Europe with a mandate to elaborate confidence-building measures in the military sphere for the whole of Europe. And the fact that President Brezhnev stated a few days ago that such measures would be applicable to the entire European area of the Soviet Union means a considerable step forward. This undoubtedly improves the prospects for a successful conference.

I hope I have been able to show clearly that the great Prussian Immanuel Kant has left us politicians something to think about, some ideas which were conditioned by his time and others which are still valid, although one cannot say that he has left ready-made instructions for our political actions. Professional philosophers may feel a little irritated by the fact that I have made no mention at all of much of what they consider to be of fundamental importance in Kant. But to me it was important to establish a relationship between the categorical imperative and the active politician.

- He has the duty to think ahead and make a critical assessment of all possible consequences.
- He has the duty to weigh up all interests against one another.

- He has the duty to bear in mind the morality not only of his aims but also of the means.
- In a democracy he must go to the tremendous trouble of making his reasons clear to others and of convincing them, because after all he needs the majority on his side.
- He must answer for the desirable and the undesirable consequences of his actions.
- He must do everything aware not only of his own fallibility but of the fallibility of all democratic decisions.
- And consequently he has the duty to make a considered and correct assessment of every step taken on a long road.

These maxims for political action are perhaps incomplete. Kant was important to me in adducing them, but so too were Karl Marx, Max Weber, and Marcus Aurelius, who is perhaps not taken so seriously by most, a philosopher whose self-discipline in acquiring a sense of duty and composure has particularly impressed me. Yet I must add that the idea of natural law, the ideas of the American revolution — incidentally to a much greater degree than those of the French — that Lassalle, Bebel, and Bernstein, and above all the disaster of the Hitler era, have left just as deep an impression on my conception of democracy and the state as Kant, whose works we are celebrating here today.

15

A Plea for Honesty and Tolerance: Speech at the Cologne Synagogue

(November 9, 1978)

Those are the words of the prophet Isaiah:

"How the faithful city has played the whore, once the home of justice where righteousness dwelt — but now murderers!"

Mr. Federal President,
Dear citizens of Cologne,
Dear Jews, Christians, and Free-Thinkers in Germany:

The German night whose observance after the passage of forty years has brought us together today remains a cause of bitterness and shame. In those places where the houses of God stood in flames, where a signal from those in power set off a train of destruction and robbery, of humiliation, abduction, and incarceration — there was an end to peace, to justice, to humanity. The night of November 9, 1938, marked one of the stages along the path leading down to hell.

I

Let us first turn our thoughts in this hour of remembrance to the events and deeds, to the dire fates and iniquities whose enormity surpasses description every bit as much today as it did then.

As at all times of history, the synagogue of 1938 was a house of God and a

This talk was delivered on the occasion of the memorial celebration in remembrance of November 9, 1938, in the Cologne Synagogue.

chamber of prayer for the community. Yet since the spring of 1933 and the Nuremberg race laws of 1935 as the Jewish minority became more and more sorely afflicted, the synagogue had been a symbol of Jewish life in Germany, even for those who took no part in religious life. When the synagogues were laid waste, that life began to fade.

Three years later, the rulers resolved on the "final solution of the Jewish question," on mass slaughter which they then carried out with cold vigor and single-minded brutality within their sphere of domination.

Those who ask for peace and, beyond that, for reconciliation, must be truthful: they must render themselves capable of truth. What is that truth? Forty years ago today, thirty thousand Jewish citizens were taken into custody; the overwhelming majority of them were thrown into concentration camps; ninety-one Jewish people were murdered; and a great many suffered torture. The truth is also that 267 synagogues were razed to the ground or destroyed; thousands of shops and dwellings were devastated.

I hesitate to avail myself of that word, so often repeated and sometimes so thoughtlessly in these days, to play down the events and the crimes committed that night.

The truth is that a great many Germans disapproved of the crimes and wrongs; by the same token, there were a great many others who learned of nothing or almost of nothing at the time.

The truth is that all this nevertheless came to pass before the very eyes of a large number of German citizens and that another large number of them gained direct knowledge of the events.

The truth is that most people, faint of heart, kept their silence. The truth is that the churches, also faint of heart, kept their silence even though synagogue and church serve the same God and remain rooted in the spirit of the same testament.

II

Twenty-five years ago, the German-Jewish philosopher Martin Buber spoke in St. Paul's Church, Frankfurt, and posed the question: "Who am I to presume the right to forgive?" In a later passage in the same speech, he also said: "This heart of mine, well aware of the frailty of man, refuses to condemn my neighbor because he failed to find the strength to become a martyr."

Of course, there were martyrs at a later date—in the churches and in the workers' movement, among the middle classes and the nobility.

One of them, General Henning von Treskow, when learning that the uprising of July 20, 1944, had failed, said: "If God once promised Abraham not to lay Sodom waste if there were but ten just men there, so it is my hope that God will spare Germany for our sake."

Countless Germans were put to death because of their resistance. Yet how could this monstrous collective crime happen? What had taken place before to enable such atrocious concerted wickedness by so many perpetrators to pass off so smoothly? What was it that set in motion in the Reich that process of alienation between Germans and Jews which preceded the crime?

III

We know that the relationship between the Jewish minority and the non-Jewish majority in Germany was never free from tension. Yet how it came to pass that the tension inherent in this relationship degenerated to such an extent as to bring about the final catastrophic events—that is a question of both Jewish and German history. An inquiry into this subject leads on to fundamental problems underlying the situation of the Jews and the Germans—and, over and beyond that, perhaps to fundamental problems inherent in the human soul.

After the Age of Enlightenment in the eighteenth century and the Jewish emancipation which followed in its wake, there were probably only a few nations in Europe where the Jews felt more at home than among us. There was hardly any nation in which the role played by Jews in society and the state, in art, literature, philosophy, and science was greater than among us. I need only list a few names to illustrate this: Moses Mendelssohn; the model for Lessing's Nathan, Heinrich Heine; Arthur Schnitzler; Franz Kafka; Franz Werfel; Stefan Zweig; Karl Kraus; Lassalle; Marx; Oppenheimer; Scheler; Gundolf; Buber; Mannheim; Franz Marc; Max Liebermann; Arnold Schönberg; and finally Albert Einstein.

Despite the writing on the wall smeared by anti-Semitic court chaplains over a century ago, these men and most of the 700,000 Jews in Germany did not feel themselves to be members of an autonomous national minority, but to be Germans. And they were mostly regarded as Germans. They made up an inseparable part of the fabric of our cultural heritage.

We are every bit as indebted to them as to all our intellectual forefathers. We ought to be aware that the expulsion of the Jews and the murder of innumerable Jewish citizens robbed our nation of creative minds who to this day have not been replaced and who remain irreplaceable.

IV

But if we are to ensure that the Germans' willingness to perform their duty, to practice obedience, and to strive for ideals is not perverted into servile compliance and deceived into perpetrating concerted criminal acts, then it is not enough for us simply to have incorporated the right of resistance in our constitution, the Basic Law. Indeed, we must educate the young people of our nation by imparting a knowledge of historical facts and by furnishing them with our own example so that they will put the question as to the moral and human value and the meaning of their actions—even where they seem prescribed by allegiance or obedience to an "idea" or law.

If we wish to do things better than former generations, we must be aware of what they did wrong and why they failed. The former generations were unable to prevent the catastrophe of an antihuman dictatorship in 1933, 1935, or 1938 because the democracy proclaimed in 1918 had slipped out of their grasp even before they had consciously accepted and developed it.

The political legacy unexpectedly bequeathed on November 9, 1918, had been devoid of any generally accepted spiritual basis; the cultural legacy stemmed in many cases from an antidemocratic cultivatedness aptly described by Thomas Mann as "soulfulness protected by power."

The "Untertan" mentality had by no means been overcome—the mentality into which the bulk of the middle classes had slipped after relinquishing their will to achieve political freedom in the second half of the last century.

The striking antithesis between the technico-economic modernity of the old imperial Germany on the one hand and its politico-social reactionary spirit on the other had by no means been overcome when that authoritarian state suddenly collapsed in 1918. With their lack of democratic education and political preparation, the middle class and the peasantry alike found themselves confronted with the opportunities and hazards of parliamentary democracy and open society. There were many who saw in democracy merely a technique and not an ethical stance inspired by the dignity of man as its paramount rule of action.

Notwithstanding, democracy proved incapable of contending with its internal foes or resolving the enormous economic and social problems attendant upon the Treaty of Versailles and compounded by the first world economic crisis.

Many Germans in that era, divested of the protecting walls built up around their old accustomed privileges, bereft of their glittering idols and profoundly disconcerted by the outcome of the war, by the futility of the sacrifices rendered and the diminution of the Reich, were moved by hatred and contempt for democracy and democrats as they searched for a guilty party on whom to vent their fury.

This was also true of many officials and soldiers and judges. Enemies of a democratic constitution remained or became public prosecutors, judges, and duly appointed teachers of constitutional law. Commencing in the Kaiserreich and stretching from Weimar to the exculpation of the murders committed in the Röhm affair, the justifiction sought for breaching the constitution, or the acceptance of the unlawful commands arbitrarily issued by the Führer right up until the People's Court, there took place a catastrophic but predictable decline in political justice.

The words spoken by the prophet Isaiah came true: the faithful city did indeed become the home of murderers.

Those who resorted to hatred found their victims: democrats, trade unionists, artists, poets, and scholars, and anyone who acknowledged his faith — they were all driven into exile or the concentration camps.

But the blow struck against the Jews went to the heart of enlightenment and freedom-loving emancipation. The fortunes of the Jews in Germany had been marked in essence by intellectual, social, and political emancipation — by a human and a humanitarian emancipation. Yet those who deemed all striving for emancipation to be damnable were easily tempted to see in the Jews a scapegoat for their own anxieties and frustrations and to vent their anger on them.

It was Hitler and his henchmen who, driven by unprecedented iniquitous energy, led Germany and its Jews and our neighboring countries into a catastrophe: but the ground had already been prepared for this. The education to promote democracy, to form a judgment of one's own, to embrace *humanitas,* to respect the dignity and freedom of the individual — all this education had been inadequate for generations.

Alone the workers' movement, the Centre Party, and a few narrow strata of the middle classes had imparted such education. It became manifest between 1919 and 1930 that these forces were not strong enough to resolve in commensurate manner the central task of teaching on a profound and wide scale the need for liberality and *humanitas.*

V

Why do we cast our minds to all this today? Not in order to dissociate ourselves from our own history and not in order to point our finger at others who had become guilty. No, we look back because our generation and the generations to follow wish to learn how Jew and non-Jew can live peacefully together in Germany.

We look back to learn. We look back in an attempt to comprehend and to appraise so that we can draw our conclusions and act accordingly. We look back so that those who were children at the time or born later — and that makes up over two-thirds of the whole population — may find a way to consort with each other, free from restraint and prejudice. We commemorate in order to learn how people ought to behave toward each other and how they ought not to behave.

There can be no question of casting our people into the debtors' prison of history. Let me repeat what I said in Auschwitz. Most of the Germans living today are individually free from blame. But we have to bear the political legacy of those responsible and we have to draw our conclusions. That is where our responsibility lies.

It would be highly dishonest and moreover hazardous to attempt to burden the young generation with guilt. Yet they have to sustain our history together with us and, like ourselves, they form part of our history. That participation renders both us and them accountable for what happens tomorrow and the day after. But may I add with every emphasis: young Germans can become guilty, too, if they fail to recognize the responsibility for what happens today and tomorrow deriving from what happened then.

Our young Germans should recall that it all started with the search for scapegoats. It continued with the use of force against writings, against books, and against property. The use of force against human beings was then a natural consequence of these preparations.

It began with contempt for the dignity of our fellowmen, with the shouting down of people voicing a different opinion. It continued with a sweeping condemnation of the whole democratic system. The natural consequence of these preparations was finally murder itself.

The parallelism of all terrorism must be made manifest if we wish to learn. The inescapable consequence of antihuman behavior must be comprehended if we wish to learn.

The abomination of all sweeping condemnations must be experienced if we wish to learn: that holds true whether they be directed against "the Jews," "the Germans," "the Communists," "the Capitalists," "the System," or "the Establishment." There must be a strengthening of the capacity to make an independent, individual, and critical judgment of one's own.

People must learn how important it is in our divided world and in every society to comprehend freedom as a sphere of action encompassed by firm legal and moral limits to the freedom of the individual and of groups.

The educating of democrats means equipping young people with a yardstick for freedom and commitment, enabling them to recognize and respect the dignity and inviolability of the other person and teaching them to understand *humanitas*, the *res publica*, law, and freedom as the limits to the pursuit of their own interests and the indulgence of their own conflicts.

A democratic education means educating people to assume responsibility for the consequences of their own actions. Assuming responsibility for the consequences of one's own actions or failure to act at all also means that we must take anxiety seriously whenever we encounter it. It may be imagined or self-induced. We must understand and overcome it; or we must find a remedy. For anxiety can lead to mania and hysteria and aggressiveness—that is what we can learn from the period between 1918 and 1930! The mania of believing that the blame for one's own grievances rests among others. The hysteria of making others the scapegoat. The resort to hatred and aggression—these are not hazards facing one generation alone or one nation alone. We must step forward to meet these dangers, by providing education and by setting a personal example.

We Germans of today, engaged as we are in the search for understanding, conciliation, and peace with our neighbors and inspired by the wish to attain social balance and peace in our own country in keeping with a free constitution, must stand up and be measured by these claims.

We share many of the worries and alarms of a great number of our fellow citizens, be they Jew or non-Jew, when the signs of an imagined return of National Socialist ideology emerge or when bloodthirsty terrorism recalls the murders committed during the early days of the first German Republic with Rathenau, Erzberger, Luxemburg, and Liebknecht as victims. We share their wrath.

But we have also disciplined ourselves to use constitutional moderation and commensurate measures in averting such dangers.

We shall adhere to this self-discipline. For we have no wish to drive out the evil of anarchism with the evil of an antiliberal superstate and merely exchange one for the other.

But we also fervently call upon the Jews throughout the world and upon all our neighbors not to measure our second German democracy in terms of the few muddled extremists and terrorists who, in other states as well, are impervious to reason and can hardly be prevented from emerging.

At this point, I would like to voice my gratitude to the Central Council of German Jews for always sharing, in public, our confidence in this matter. The right-wing extremists will certainly not find a home among us—nor will the left-wing extremists.

VI

We shall soon require the advice of our Jewish citizens in another question which will summon each of us to assume personal responsibility. The statute of limitations applicable to murder, after thirty years have elapsed, presents us with a momentous problem in 1979: It requires a decision in which significant moral principles are bound to clash.

We politicians and legislators shall listen to what our Jewish citizens, our friends in Israel, and our neighbors have to tell us. Each of us will pray that his conscience may guide him in finding the right action in this question.

It is our hope that we shall obtain advice and participation from many sources. That includes advice from our churches. For we remember with gratitude the Stuttgart Declaration made by the Evangelical Church of Germany in 1945 and the moving words spoken by Pope John XXIII during the Second Vatican Council—words with which the two churches asked the Jews to reach out their hands in reconciliation. And the statements which the two churches have published on this day seek that reconciliation: they were voiced in the spirit of understanding.

Everyone should bear in mind that we all stand on the same fundament and that we are inspired by the same scriptures: the Jewish Bible — the Old Testament of the Christians.

VII

The Egyptian Anwar-el-Sadat explained to me in the course of long, impressive talks his views on the common spiritual and historic roots of Judaism, Christianity, and Islam. He drew attention to their common home, the Sinai Peninsula, and to their common prophets. He asked with fervent conviction: Can it really be impossible there to be peace between these three? Let me add Albert Einstein's rhetorical question: Who doubts that Moses was a better leader of mankind than Machiavelli!

I know that Begin and Sadat have the same deep roots in the religious traditions of their peoples. I am convinced that these two men desire peace for their own peoples and for the neighboring nations. I know that is true of many statesmen in that region.

We Germans cherish a heartfelt wish: that Jews, Moslems, and Christians, that Israelis and Arabs alike will learn to live with each other in a just peace.

In keeping with the commandment to respect truth, we advocate the right of self-determination for all nations in the Middle East. We know of the need for life to be free from indigence and oppression if people are to be able to keep peace. As the German federal chancellor, speaking today at the same time to all Jews in the world and for whom the Cologne Synagogue symbolizes all synagogues throughout the world, I would add the following wish: May all those people in the Middle East who have so far stood aloof turn their gaze to the peacemaking initiatives of these days! May every people and state furnish its contribution to peace.

May they all recognize that peace is a victory by *"homo humanus"* against *"homo anti-humanus"* — to quote Martin Buber again. May they all perceive and take to heart that peace is impossible without the universal wish to find a balance and compromise! May they all recognize that Moses is indeed a better guiding-star than Machiavelli!

VIII

Let me revert to us Germans and observe that it is not for us to call upon the Jews of the world to achieve reconciliation, but we may perhaps ask them for reconciliation with us.

Anyone desirous of reconciliation, of holding out his hand and living at peace with his neighbors must raise his head and look the other in the eyes. Let us therefore promote meetings between Jews, Catholics, and Protestants, between believers and free thinkers and also between Israelis and Germans wherever that is possible. The unusually large number of meetings between young Germans and young Israelis fills me with joy. Christian-Jewish cooperation fills me with confidence.

When the federal chancellor looks at his Jewish fellow citizens in this state and in this city on the occasion of this special day, when he thanks them and asks them for their further cooperation in the state and society, he does so in the name of the overwhelming majority of the Germans alive today.

And when two classes of school children from Cologne also come to the synagogue today, they do so on behalf of the overwhelming majority of young people in our nation.

IX

I know that the great majority of people in our state have come to the same conclusions as I have attempted to formulate today.

Our Basic Law and our state were established on the same fundament thirty years ago. They marked a fresh start and a good start. We are proud of this state of ours, proud of our open society, proud of our traditions. We resolutely defend this state and this form of society. It is the most free society we have had in our history. We shall resist its enemies. We shall pursue the good traditions of this state.

We learned the following some considerable time ago from a great socialist and French neighbor, Jean Jaurès. The observance of tradition does not mean keeping the ashes. The observance of tradition means keeping the torch alight. The torch signifies love of mankind and respect for the dignity of everyone. The torch signifies the supreme value of our Basic Law: human dignity and human freedom.

16

Excerpts from an Interview on ABC News "Issues and Answers," Conducted by Peter Jennings

(November 16, 1980)

Q: Chancellor, Americans, as I guess you know, often see a contradiction in Europe. When there is perceived to be a weak American president, you cry out for American leadership. When there is a strong American president, Europeans seem to complain that they are being pushed around. Can you be specific—exactly what kind of man do you want to see in the White House?

A: I do not remember a situation where Europeans in unison complained about being pushed around. I don't remember any such situation. But you know, one of the necessary components of leadership is to act as a leader but not to show it off too much. It's a very difficult task.

Q: There are some people who would argue, Chancellor, that there is a real danger of your relationship with Mr. Reagan's team getting off on the wrong foot. There are complaints in the United States already that your country is not going to meet its 3 percent defense commitment to the Alliance this year.

A: I do not think that there is any danger of getting off on the wrong foot. For instance, many of those gentlemen whom Governor Reagan appointed for his transition team are people with whom we have cooperated during long, long periods of years. At least from my side there is not the slightest apprehension that anything might go wrong in the beginning.

As regards this 3 percent issue, it must not be overexaggerated. I have been chancellor for almost seven years, and my country has over the last decade increased its defense budget (annually) by 2.7 percent in real terms. And we will keep on that road. In 1980 it will be 2.8 percent. I admit, it's not quite 3 percent. . . .

I would like to take this opportunity to tell your American audience that I have no doubts that, as hitherto, as in this year 1980, also in 1981 Germany will live up to its commitments.

Q: The insistence, the move in the United States toward increased defense spending, which is generally anticipated to be higher, of course, in the United States next year than in Germany, is being seen by many people as a mark of loyalty or shorthand of loyalty within the Alliance. Senator Howard Baker is quoted in one of your newspapers this morning as saying that Bonn has an extremely ambivalent attitude toward an increased military presence in the Persian Gulf, and is refusing to prepare any troops for this plan. And on the other hand, Bonn is also opposed to American plans to move U.S. troops from Europe to the Persian Gulf region. Is that a correct analysis of the Bonn position?

A: No, it's not. And I wonder whether Senator Baker is being quoted correctly. I'm going to see him next week, I hope. So there would be no misunderstanding left afterward.

The truth is: Number one, we cannot send troops into the Persian Gulf. We have constitutional inhibitions. Number two, we have no inhibitions on seeing American troops being moved from Europe to the Persian Gulf. On the contrary, I have said—and I'm on public record for having said so—that there should be a division of labor in the Western Defense Alliance, and that if somebody has to take up new roles, somebody else might be forced to take up those jobs which he has to leave now in order to be able to take up new jobs. So, there is no inhibition from the German side to see American troops moved from Europe, let us say, to some place.

Q: And would Germany take up the slack, is that what you're saying?

A: Not only Germany. But certainly Germany is prepared to be helpful.

Q: Chancellor, you were saying a little while ago that policies often change between the campaign trail and the office itself. Could we talk a little bit of the policies. What is your view of President-elect Reagan's intention to attempt to renegotiate the SALT II agreements?

A: Well, I think SALT II is necessary. I think he is quite right there, that the SALT process ought to be continued. It's, I think, a fundamental must for both superpowers to continue the SALT process. Otherwise the world would lapse into a deep-going, very broad and frustrating and dangerous arms race. . . .

You see, I'm more or less believing that not only SALT II but SALT III will come in the end to a success, whatever is going to be altered in the meantime. And I think it's necessary. I deeply believe in a balance of military power in the world, especially in Europe. And a balance of power in the long run cannot be kept by any arms race, it can only be kept by mutually agreed limitations in strategic weapons as well as in conventional weapons.

Q: Most people are aware, sir, that you are a long-time advocate of a mutual balance of power. President-elect Reagan has campaigned on America's military superiority. Doesn't that put you and him at odds?

A: Well, I wouldn't concede that. But I want to see what it means in practice. If it means in practice, second to none, I am fully in agreement. I have been a defense secretary myself. By our own constitution, the German defense secretary is the supreme commander of the German forces. I know what the Soviet forces can do, what their military power and weight do mean. I also know what our forces can do, what our powers are. I know what the American forces in Europe — good forces — can do. I know what the German forces can do, good forces as well. I am not one of those who are in fright of the Soviets all the time. I'm rather self-confident.

Q: You would agree, however, I think, that there is a certain feeling abroad in some nations, including the United States, that West Germany sometimes seems to be more interested in the East than it is in the West. How does that impression get around?

A: That's not right. That's not correct. There are differences. For instance, we feel it necessary for us to maintain conscription. In our country every young man has to serve in the forces. In yours he has not. That's a basic difference. We ask a higher sacrifice from our people than right now you do from yours. I understand why you did away with conscription. It was my friend Melvin Laird who did it at the time of Nixon.

I just want to mention this in order to make it felt in the United States what we are really doing, what we feel is necessary for being able to defend ourselves or for maintaining the military balance. I am satisfied that all American generals who have closely observed the German forces are quite impressed by what our forces can do. It's not so much necessary to put the dot on the i's, that you spend as much money as you can. What is necessary, in the first place, is that you have motivated men; secondly, well-trained men; and then, in the third place, well-equipped men.

Q: Speaking of money, you have recently argued that Germany's leadership role in the world derives from its economic strength. You were predicting this year zero growth in Germany. What is that going to do to your leadership role?

A: I have never talked of a German leadership role. Others have done this, outside Germany. I do not speak of and I do not think of a leadership role of Germany. I think that would be a false concept of Germany's role in the world.

Q: On the point of money: you have made a very significant contribution . . . on the financial basis, to Portugal, to the economic improvement in Turkey and Greece.

A: And in Poland.

Q: And in Poland as well. Without the economic well-being that you are predicting this year, how is that going to be effective?

A: And also in Pakistan. We could mention quite a number of nations. Also to some countries in the Third World.

Q: All of that is going to be seen in more dramatic terms?

A: Yes. But on the other hand, if we have a year with lesser growth, maybe very small growth, this does not mean that our financial abilities are withering away. There are ups and downs in all economies, like in yours, like in other people's economies, also in ours. That does not detract or diminish our basic capabilities. There will be ups afterward.

Q: What would you do if the Soviet Union invaded Poland?

A: Well, I don't like to answer hypothetical questions, at all, I never do it. This is a very dangerous hypothetical question. I guess that any answer could be misconstrued as interference in Polish domestic affairs. I highly desire that we do not interfere in domestic Polish affairs. But I would like to mention that we have given financial support to Poland during the Gierek administration, as well as now under the Kania administration, because we feel that the economic well-being of Poland is of great importance not only to the Polish nation but also to other nations in Europe, including Western Europe. We are not the only ones who give help to Poland. The United States are giving help to Poland. I dearly hope that the Poles will be able to cope with their own difficulties.

17

An Interview with
The Economist

(September and October 1979)

Q: In the early 1970s it was said that Germany was an economic giant but a political dwarf. That, we would venture, is less true today.

A: It's not an economic giant and it's not a political dwarf either.

Q: What has changed to make it less of a political dwarf, would you say?

A: Three things. In the first instance, the *Ostpolitik,* not because it was intended to but as a by-product, gave us a much greater freedom of action. Second, our economic success. Third, domestic political stability. Quite a number of things have led to a situation in which the political weight of my country has become a little greater than it was in the early 1970s or late 1960s. I didn't like that development too much, but it was more or less unavoidable.

Q: Do you see it continuing?

A: It very much depends on how, politically and economically, other countries of Europe perform. If Germany's weight has grown, it has mostly been due to a better performance, relatively speaking, in comparison with others. Others had a chance to perform much more effectively than they did.

Q: All German politicians, you notably among them, have been reluctant to take on this political growth, the consequences of the economic success leading to political growth. Is that a reluctance that you still feel?

A: Yes, yes, I do.

Q: But in, for instance, the Turkish situation you weren't slow to put yourself forward as a convenor.

A: That's an impression you can only have because you were not present in Guadeloupe. I was hesitating. But I had to accept that possibly we could get

Reprinted by permission from *The Economist*, September 29, 1979, pp. 47–50, and October 6, 1979, pp. 47–54.

along with the Turkish government better than other Western governments could at the time, and therefore we undertook that mission.

Q: This reticence of yours is based on the past. How long does the past go on?

A: As long as I live and a little longer.

Q: But you see it ending sometime?

A: No, I am not so sure. The greater the relative success of Germany, the longer the memory of Auschwitz will last.

Q: Basically, even with Turkey as an example, you would want to continue seeing Germany not out in front, and always acting in a multi-polar way?

A: Right.

Q: Even if that were to extend at some future date, let's say, into the Middle East where you have very large interests?

A: We have no larger interests in the Middle East than have France or Britain or Holland or others who depend on oil.

Q: Oh, yes you do, actually, because you're a very large exporter there. Much larger than us.

A: Well, we are not any more export-minded than you British ought to be.

Let me tell you something about our exports. I might well like a situation in which we have deficits on our overall current account. And why not? We have enormous reserves.

Q: We'd adore that.

A: Yes, you should do something in order to bring about that situation by exporting a little bit more.

Q: It's going to take a while, we're afraid.

One very tangible area, though, where German political influence shows is one directly connected with its economic success: namely the international effects of your economic policy. For example, if your interest rates go up by .5 percent here, there is a great deal of attention in the world in a way that ten years ago there might not have been. Whereas the British are able to put up their interest rates by 2 percent and nobody pays any notice. We exaggerate: but are you having to learn, as a German government, to become less sensitive to the immediate cries of pain that go up in the world's treasuries and central banks when Germany moves?

A: No, we don't have to learn that. I think we were the first government in the world who learned really about economic and financial interdependence. Rather earlier than some others did. We don't need to be given any lessons there.

We were also the first to understand that you cannot cure the world's

economic structural crisis by printing money. We'll not give up our conviction
in that field. Others are on the verge of giving it up, some don't have the
strength to do it although they understand its being necessary. No, we will
not accept wrongly so-called Keynesian recipes for a totally non-Keynesian
situation.

THE DISCIPLINE OF EMS

Q: Do you see EMS, the European Monetary System, as a method of
teaching that lesson to your partners in Europe?

A: No, I see it as an instrument to let the countries of the EEC grow together
more quickly than hitherto. I see it as an instrument also to strengthen the EEC
institutionally, and I see it as an incentive for the Americans to understand that
they must not let the dollar go down the drain.

Q: If the dollar were to recover its standing, does the EMS not become
slightly redundant? Is not EMS largely a function of the problems of the dollar?

A: No, not really. I think it will have to be maintained even if the dollar
regains its strength but this latter condition doesn't seem to be real, at least not
in the very near future. I hope it will, but it doesn't look likely.

Q: Surely if EMS were to work, that implies a certain amount of discipline
on the member states?

A: That's one of the ideas behind it. When I said it was devised as an instrument for getting the economic behavior of the nine members of the EEC closer
together. . . .

Q: But is that not really a question of German reserves being put behind
financial discipline in, say, France?

A: It's not only German reserves. France has got quite a bit of reserves,
England nowadays has some reserves as well.

The EMS changes the situation of any participant government vis-à-vis its
own currency. If you have no fixed parities, neither vis-à-vis the outside world
nor vis-à-vis the other eight European countries, you can just let your currency
go downwards or upwards, just let it happen and leave it to the exchanges. But,
if you have fixed parities even within a community of only nine countries, you
have to take your own decisions. You don't like to devalue your currency, and,
possibly, somebody else doesn't like to upvalue his currency. In order to avoid
such uncomfortable decisions I hope one takes in time the right steps to correct
one's budgetary situation or one's monetary situation.

Q: And if necessary change the parity?

A: If necessary, yes, but not every Monday, not every weekend, I hope.
Rather seldom. Fixed parities, even if only among nine countries, make for

some discipline vis-à-vis one's own balance of payments, in the economic behavior of a government—and this is what I would like to be brought about.

Q: What is the desirability—long-term, not immediate—of the pound coming into EMS . . . particularly given its vulnerability to very sharp fluctuations?

A: The pound is not more vulnerable to fluctuations than is the Italian lira. That's a problem made up in the minds of the British rather than in reality.

Q: What about the residue of sterling's reserve role?

A: If the British public believes that they do Europe a favor by joining EMS then they had better stay out. If they do not understand that it is in their own best interests, then they had better stay out.

Q: We were also asking you a more technical question which is that, even with the best will in the world toward EMS and toward Europe, which does exist to some extent in cabinet circles and in the British prime minister's mind, sterling is, because of British economic weakness, and because possibly of the residue of sterling's reserve role, a more volatile currency than some.

A: The most volatile currency may be the deutsche mark.

Q: With your capital flows we quite see that. But you don't see sterling's volatility as a problem?

A: Yes, I see it as a problem, one among many others, but not as a problem of overriding weight. I am not an entrepreneur, I am not a trade-union leader, either; just a little political animal. From the political point of view, from my point of view, it would be a sign of self-confidence if the British joined, and it would serve as a signal to anybody that they felt strong enough to enter and stick to it. And this in itself would add additional psychological strength to the British economy. But I repeat, if the British feel that they ought to join just for the sake of Europe, then they should rather stay out.

Q: Could you not argue, as a primary creator of EMS, that the presence of sterling—not of Britain, but of sterling—would make it harder to make a success of EMS?

A: No, no I don't see any such thing.

Q: Would you think that it might be advisable to have the 6 percent band for Britain?

A: No, I think the 6 percent was wrong for Italy.

Q: You do?
A: Yes.

Q: And you think it would be wrong for Britain?
A: Yes. Italy would have felt even better if it had not asked for that 6 per-

cent as a margin. It was necessary for overcoming domestic Italian doubts and hesitations.

Q: It's been used, also, hasn't it? When you think of the French pattern where they're pursuing if anything an even narrower band, of less than 1 percent. . . .

A: Not too narrow. I think the EMS as it's now construed or constructed is a little bit complicated, but not bad. It will work.

Q: But the difficulty, as you know as a politician, is that this sort of financial discipline inherent in the system often has political consequences. In Italy it happens to have been convenient for the Italian government and the Italian central bank to cite their European existence in EMS as one reason for carrying out really quite an impressive performance of discipline.

A: The Italian economy is being run better than people in Europe think.

Q: We quite agree.

A: And it's more effective than many people are aware. Some may be caught by surprise within two years, and may be overhauled by the Italians. The instinct of Giulio Andreotti to join the EMS from the beginning was a very clever political and economic instinct. He was right.

Q: But you would probably concede that in a country like France, and even more in a country like Britain, the reverse side of that coin is that you get political pressure or a political campaign saying "just because we're a member of this thing which is a . . . ."

A: Oh yes, certainly. But governments do not exist in order to avoid campaigns. They have to launch their own. They have to stand up against campaigns which are directed against the policy of government. Government does not exist in order to avoid any difficulty. There are quite a few countries in Europe in which the necessary recipes to put their economic houses in order, or to correct their balances of payment, or to correct inflation of their prices or their rates of interest, or to correct their unemployment . . . where the recipes necessary for curing all these malaises may very well in the first instance lead to greater difficulties in order to get improvement in the second and third instance.

Q: Particularly given the electoral cycle. If you take the French case, with an election not that far away, with the Barre plan very courageous but having some quite harsh consequences: is that not going to lead to political tension between France and Germany, not on the part of France's president, but on the part of the other politicians?

A: No, certainly not. The French are taking their own economic and financial decisions. We do not interfere, nobody could, in his good senses, assume that we try even to interfere. We don't do it. It's for France to take its own decisions. Despite his being prime minister now for three years, Barre started his new economic policies, financial policies, only eighteen months ago, in spring 1978. It's just too early to expect great success.

Q: You don't see the sort of discipline necessary, and combined with recession, leading to deeper recession and, say, anti-German feeling in France?

A: No. I don't see that, either. They are not angry about me, they are angry about Raymond Barre and they are wrong. He is doing a good job and he knows, and so does the French president, our friend Giscard d'Estaing, that the benevolent effects of such a policy cannot be brought about within eighteen months. It may take a couple of years. It took us five years to get down from an inflation rate of nearly 8 percent to 2.5 percent.

It took us five years of hardship. It took me five years of moral suasion with our entrepreneurs, with our trade unions. I have been talking to trade unionists and the leaders of industry and banking 200 hours a year on an average. It has been an enormous undertaking in a Keynesian sense and in terms of moral suasion. There is no way to get out of economic difficulty without shouldering the difficulties.

BRITAIN AND EUROPE

Q: You showed very considerable powers of persuasion in your speech to the Labour Party conference in November 1974. You showed leadership in helping to keep Britain in the Community at that time. Do you think that you're going to have to show similar leadership in the Community this time in terms of Britain's EEC budget contribution and the CAP [Common Agricultural Policy]?

A: I hope not. I have hoped for a greater role of Britain within the EEC than has emerged so far. I still hope that Britain is going to play her proper role.

I was brought up as an Anglophile, to some degree emerged into an Americanophile and, in the ten years that I am in government now, I have turned into a Francophile. Still I have not forgotten my youthful leaning toward Great Britain, toward England. I have not so far really been satisfied by England's role in Europe. I hope there's going to be a greater amount of satisfaction in the future.

As for the EEC budget question, I think that the total budget is growing too fast, growing much faster than any single nation's budget. It's just too much, and I think it's good that for the time being the budget is being limited because the value-added tax component of the Community's revenues is being limited to 1 percent. I think it's a good limitation and it should be kept and not be violated.

Q: That's going to impose limits on agricultural spending and agricultural prices.

A: Not only there, but mainly there.

Q: Is the Federal Republic ready to play its part in keeping agricultural prices down?

A: I hope that the British will play the role for which they are world famous, namely going forward in a pragmatic way, muddle through, and get away from some of the most ridiculous exaggerations in the field of common agricultural policies. I build very much on the British common sense in that field.

Q: So what do you mean? That the British exaggerate the iniquities of the CAP?

A: I am not talking about the iniquities. I think that agricultural policies as a whole have run out of control, and ought to be brought back under control. They are consuming now, I think, over two-thirds of the finances of the EEC. This is ridiculous.

THE VIRTUE OF PARAGONS

Q: There's a paradox that the two paragons of behavior economically, Germany and Japan, are the ones that therefore come under criticism from those of us who are less effective. We're going into a recession. Do you foresee Germany and Japan doing more economically to offset the American recession?

A: The answer is no. The American economy is three and a half times as big as the German economy. How could we do something in order to offset any shortcomings of that giant? No. The fact that the economic performance of my country relatively speaking is not so bad must not mislead people to think of ourselves as economically gigantic. We are not a giant. It's an economy of roughly speaking $600 billion. The American economy is about $2,000 billion. The Japanese is about $1,000 billion — in that order of magnitude.

The Japanese economy has a very specific structure, not easy to be compared with other Western economies' structures. It has been very specifically structured for a couple of decades. I deplore the fact that the Japanese are from time to time accused of failures which have in fact been accomplished by other Western economies in their own spheres.

I think that this ridiculous little "locomotive theory" has withered away now. And correctly so. We flatter ourselves that we have played our little part to keep the world economically together in a time when, rather easily, the greater economies could, with wrong leadership by their respective governments, have lapsed into the beggar-thy-neighbor policies of the early 1930s. It could happen, it could very well have happened. It could still happen.

There are still enormously strong tendencies for protectionism of all kinds, not only in the trade field, also in the monetary field — beggaring-thy-neighbor in the monetary and the balance-of-payments fields.

The so-called economic summit conferences helped avoid that. They didn't bring about much, but what they avoided was of enormous importance. If they had not taken place I don't know what would have happened. The world can still go to pieces economically if oil prices are managed again in the way that they have been managed by OPEC countries this year; the world will not be able to digest easily another oil price explosion such as we experienced in 1979.

The British are not very aware of that danger, because they have got their own oil (and if they sell some they sell it at the highest OPEC prices which I don't think is prudent). But most countries, including quite a few communist countries in East Europe and, what's more important, including almost anybody in the developing world, are suffering enormous effects on their economies. Take a country like Turkey which needs about 90 percent of its export proceeds in order to pay for its little bit of petrol, or take a country like Brazil which nowadays needs more than one-half of its export proceeds in order to pay for that little petrol. And these are just two examples—I could name a long list of countries which have been put in the greatest trouble.

The repercussions of that economic trouble will also hit the British, the Germans, the French, and other Europeans. The oil producers' cartel is nowadays as great a menace to the functioning of the world's economy as is the menace of governments going it the easy way by printing money and parliaments asking for more spending and less revenue. This is the way by which you are ruining empires, states, world powers.

When I was a young man we had to pay DM 4.20 for one American dollar. Nowadays it's DM 1.80, or something. I would like to get back into a world in which it would be two marks again and stable at that point. The world needs stability much more than anything else. But in the first instance trade unionists and entrepreneurs, and in the second instance parliaments, and in the third instance governments, all have given in to that idea of printing money.

A SWING TO THE RIGHT?

Q: Do you think that the apparent swing to the right in a number of countries—if you take Britain, Canada, Australia, even France, you could argue Italy—is a sign, within the rather limited institutions that we all have, of people wanting to follow the sort of policy of stability you have just outlined?

A: I don't have the impression that right-wing governments have been more prudent in the past than left-wing governments, and it's not my impression that there is a swing to the right.

My impression is that there is a swing toward opposition parties in such countries where the economy has not been managed correctly. If you had a left-wing government then people switch to the right. If you had a right-wing government then people switch to the left. In a country where people have had the feeling that the economy was more or less managed correctly, then the previous government was reelected.

Q: No matter what color?

A: Yes. Like in Austria, like in Germany.

Q: You said earlier this year that "never before have we been so secure." What did you mean by that?

A: When I used that phrase, "we" was not meant to be "we," the West as a whole. It was meant to be "we," the Germans. I am trying still to make it understood to my own people that we, the Germans, the Germans in the Western Federal Republic of Germany as well as the Germans in the German Democratic Republic, as well as the Germans in West Berlin, that we are securer nowadays than we were in the 1960s and 1950s and 1940s.

My reasoning is rather simple. We saw many Berlin crises in earlier decades, the Khrushchev ultimatum, the building of the wall in the early 1960s, the intervention in Czechoslovakia in the late 1960s. Today, on the basis of a continuous equilibrium of military forces which results from those forces inside Europe, and those working upon Europe from the outside, we have created a policy of cooperation between Western and Eastern Europe. A policy of what one calls détente, a policy of calculability on both sides.

Eastern policies in Europe are more calculable nowadays. Western policies are calculable for the East. Nobody foresees a Berlin crisis around the next corner, as one had to in the 1950s and the 1960s. This is what I meant by saying that we are living in more secure circumstances than in the first twenty-five years after the war.

Q: Do you therefore base that feeling of security in West Germany — as distinguished from the West as a whole — on your interpretation of what Russian intentions are?

A: I do not accept your distinction. But on substance I would base an increased feeling of security in Europe not only on Russian intentions, but on Western intentions as well. I base it on the treaties and agreements that have been concluded. For instance, the treaties between my country and the Soviet Union, the People's Republic of Poland, the German Democratic Republic, the four-power agreement on Berlin, all of which were the prerequisites for the all-European Final Act of Helsinki in 1975. I base it on all these, not just on Soviet attitudes. Soviet attitudes are important, but also the Soviet Union has bound itself by all these treaties.

Q: But you're talking about agreements which were reached in the heyday of détente. Since then a strong streak of opinion in America, a strong streak of opinion in Britain, has not so much gone back on détente but has begun to worry again about Russian intentions.

A: If you want to have continuity of détente you have to have continuity of the balance of power, the equilibrium. Continuity of détente cannot persist if you let the military equilibrium deteriorate. You must not let that happen.

Some of those streaks of opinion you are quoting are more streaks of unrest about the West's own ability or effectiveness in maintaining the balance of power than they are streaks of uncertainty about a potential Soviet capability to exploit a deterioration in that balance or in that equation. It's in the first instance necessary that you maintain the balance. It's wrong just to point to the Soviet side. If one has the feeling of the balance being tilted, one has also to mend one's own defenses.

Q: Yes, but this feeling of alarm is also based on the degree of Soviet buildup, is it not? Something which you yourself have referred to.

A: Well, I don't like the word "alarm" but of course you have to watch. . . .

Q: We're not talking about your alarm, we're talking about alarm elsewhere in the West.

A: Well, I don't like the word "alarm" at all. There is no need for alarm. Some people are taking alarmist attitudes because they want to fight their own government or their own administration. Some people have to drop their alarmist attitudes once they have come from opposition into office. And they certainly will drop them. You have to watch what the other side does and the other side will have to watch what we do. It's a necessity for both sides to establish a continuous equilibrium.

This more or less is the moral, the rationale, of SALT I and SALT II, at least in the one field of global strategic weapons, intercontinental strategic weapons. Other fields in which military power plays a role haven't so far developed into the same maturity, the same established, agreed equilibrium as is the case in SALT II. So in these fields there is room for criticism. That's okay, it's necessary.

Q: You're talking about Eurostrategic weapons?

A: Not only, also conventional weapons.

Q: We nevertheless do face a situation where Western strategic superiority has gone.

A: It was never a Western strategic superiority. It was an American superiority in intercontinental strategic nuclear weaponry. It was never a superiority in the early 1970s or the 1960s in global military capabilities.

Q: We were talking about strategic superiority.

A: I do not like that. I think it's wrong to use the word "strategic" only in the context of intercontinental nuclear weaponry. It's a wrong perception of strategy. I use the word "strategy" in the sense of the late Captain Liddell Hart's grand strategy which embraces not only all the military fields but of course also the political, the psychological, the economic fields.

BEYOND EUROPE

Q: Yes, but then even in the wider sense that you're defining it, we've gone into a period where, after Vietnam, there has been a loss of superiority in the West or, if you prefer, in America.

A: Superiority is never, can never be, appropriate. If one talks of equilibrium, superiority has no place. It's the wrong perception.

Q: In places like Africa, let us say. . . .

A: There is no equilibrium in Africa, there hasn't been superiority in Africa.

Q: There was at one time.

A: Well, in the 1950s, before decolonization.

Q: If one takes the Gulf area, for example: the equilibrium, wouldn't you concede, is less stable now than it was?

A: Right, right. Not so much due to Soviet activities. Iran hasn't collapsed because of Soviet activities. There are some Soviet activities in the southern part of the Arabian peninsula.

Q: And the Horn of Africa?

A: The Horn of Africa, right.

Q: Now, it's a common perception that in all these areas there is an imbalance to the extent that the Soviet Union or its surrogates are willing to be involved militarily but the West or America and its allies are not ready to be involved. And you don't seem to us to be worried by that.

A: I am worried, but I am not one of those people who always sees only the negative developments. I also see positive ones. There was a time, not so long ago, when you had plenty of Soviet troops and military influence in Egypt and there is none right now. This is quite something.

I personally do not believe that in the end the complex of Middle East questions can be settled without some participation of the Soviet Union. But I do not maintain that Soviet influence as regards the Palestine question or the complexities between Israel and her neighbors is greater than it was five years ago. It's smaller, indeed.

Q: What role does or could Europe play in that sort of area in, say, the Horn of Africa or in Africa itself?

A: A rather small role because there isn't much that Europe could provide. What could the Europeans give or guarantee? Could they guarantee military assistance? Could they give a great amount of finance? Could they guarantee the flow of oil into Israel? Obviously they can't. They can, of course, be helpful in a limited way. But it is more or less a fact, whether you like it or not—and I don't like it too much but I have to accept it as a fact—that the Americans are the ones who have the influence there and, to a lesser degree, the Soviets. There is no European Sixth Fleet in the Mediterranean, nor is there any such thing in the Indian Ocean, nor in the Gulf—nor would there be any such thing.

Q: Not in the foreseeable future, you think?

A: No, no.

Q: Is SALT II vital to maintaining the nuclear strategic balance?

A: Yes. It gives some stability to that balance. Only in that one field, not in other fields. If agreements were limited just to intercontinental nuclear weaponry it would not be enough to stabilize the strategic situation as a whole.

Q: Would it be a serious matter if SALT II now were seriously amended or went into cold storage?
A: I don't see any technical, diplomatic possibility for effectively changing the substance of a treaty which has been concluded between governments. I have never seen this happen in modern times.

Q: The Treaty of Versailles?
A: It was not amended afterward. There is no possibility of changing by parliaments the substance of treaties which have been concluded and signed by governments. That's a rather naive conception.

If SALT II was not ratified as it stands, it could — and this would be my apprehension — create a broad feeling of uncertainty. This treaty has been negotiated by three American presidents, Nixon, Ford, and Carter, by three American secretaries of state, Rogers, Kissinger, and, nowadays, Vance, and their aides and security advisers and so on. If, after such a long period of negotiation and agreement, in the end parliaments refused to ratify that sort of treaty, the world becomes rather incalculable. How could you in the future depend on a policy carried out by an American president? It would be a disastrous blow to the necessary leadership of the United States as regards the West as a whole. I rule out amendments which would require renegotiation.

Now, having said this, of course the Americans, whether it's the administration or the Senate, can embed a treaty which they ratify into an environment of other things which they do at the same time: not violating the treaty, not amending the treaty, but adding to the general strategic setting. And of course they can do that and obviously they will.

Q: You think it's useful, therefore, the way the SALT debate seems to be acting as a catalyst for larger spending on nuclear strategic systems?
A: I am the representative of a non-nuclear power. That is not my business and I do not want to appear to regard that field to be my business.

Q: Coming to the Eurostrategic field, since Russia's deployment of the SS-20 there has been a debate which you have participated in quite vigorously yourself about the stationing of Pershing or cruise Eurostrategic weapons on German soil.
A: This is a long history that does back more than twenty years.

It was in 1960 that a great American soldier who had just left active service, Maxwell Taylor, published a book called *The Uncertain Trumpet.* He was one of those who foresaw at that time that situations might arise in the future in which one could not and would not actually apply one's superiority in the intercontinental nuclear strategic field in order to make up for deficiencies in other military fields.

I myself wrote a book many years ago, the English title of which was *Defense or Retaliation?*, in which I put forward the thesis that one could not rest assured on the theory that it was just enough to be able to retaliate afterward and that one had to be able to defend oneself if attacked. Ten years later, I published a second book, *Balance of Power,* in which I again depicted the obvious development of the 1970s by which it was more or less bound to become unthinkable that the Americans would apply their diminishing, shrinking, withering intercontinental superiority in order to correct all situations which might arise in the future in other fields. Already in 1969 I asked for an adequate equilibrium, military equilibrium, on other levels and in other areas of defense.

This is not new for me, it has been my thinking for twenty years, remained as my thinking when I was defense secretary of this country and still is my belief as chancellor. It's nothing new. Nobody needs to be alarmed about it. It did not start once we heard for the first time of the SS-20s or the Backfires. It has been my thinking all along the past twenty years. Backfires and the SS-20s are just a confirmation of what one saw as likely to develop.

In the late 1960s, American governments started to think in terms of parity in the intercontinental strategic field which should have, by pure logic, led them to understand that, if they engaged in negotiations which were meant to lead to a situation of parity in the intercontinental field, they should also have to do something about the field in which they were inferior, like the field of the SS-4s, SS-5s, nowadays SS-20s. There were Western medium-range ballistic missiles and intrarange weaponry in the late 1950s but they were dismantled by 1963, which I think from hindsight was a wrong step. They should have been modernized rather than dismantled.

Q: So that does raise the question you are now raising yourself, namely of stationing in Europe of Eurostrategic weapons so that there is a Eurostrategic balance, not one that is just covered by an intercontinental balance.

A: I wouldn't necessarily ask for parity, I would ask for a sufficient counterweight. And I would ask for a serious undertaking on the basis of mutual agreement to limit the number of weapons or warheads in that field, both for the East and the West.

Q: That's SALT III?

A: Could very well be under SALT III, yes. I would prefer it to happen under SALT III.

Q: Does that mean that the Federal Republic as a non-nuclear power, plus Britain and France as nuclear ones, should be directly involved in SALT III?

A: France would certainly not wish to be involved. We ought not to be involved because we are not a nuclear power and don't want to give the impression that we are striving to become one.

Q: The Federal Republic, as I understand it, has said that it is not happy about having Eurostrategic weapons stationed on its soil unless other countries in the NATO alliance also agreed to do so.

A: Other *non*-nuclear countries. Britain and France are nuclear powers in their own right, and I don't want by any means to have my country compared with those.

Q: It has been said in West Germany that the increase in Russian military strength was primarily or purely defensive. Is that a notion which you subscribe to?

A: I will not comment on what others have said. I myself believe that the Brezhnev leadership is fundamentally not aiming at war in Europe, not aiming at offensive moves in Europe, but aiming at maintaining a stable and secure situation. I have to add that, as it was in the past, so also in their perception of stable security in the present, the Russians always want to be on the safe side, having a little more in any field than others, a little better. Well, that is their inbuilt instinct.

They overdo it in some fields. Therefore the West has to respond, to tell them that this is being overdone. But one has either to limit the figures on both sides by agreement or by tacit agreement, or one has to accept that the West acts as well in order to keep up the equation.

But there is, so far as I can see, no tacit hidden offensive attitude behind Russia's policy. This I say for the present leadership in the Soviet Union. I am not making any prophecies for the rest of the 1980s.

Q: There is always a question of succession in the Soviet Union.

A: Not only in the Soviet Union, also in the West. Questions of succession play a much greater role than is being anticipated by today's political analysts, and a much greater role in the East than is being foreseen in Marxist theory. Personalities do matter sometimes, and, to be quite frank, I would hope that the attitudes of the present leadership in the Soviet Union will be respected and further developed by their successors.

Q: We've got the nearest we're likely to see to an election campaign in the Soviet Union coming sometime in the next few years. It happens rarely there, therefore it makes more of a splash when it does happen. We're used to the idea that Schmidt will be up for election or Giscard will be up for election. We're not used to the idea of frequent changes in the Soviet Union. Does the prospect of a change in Russia in the nearish future disturb you?

A: I wouldn't say "disturb," but it should be borne in mind and understood in the East as well as in the West as an incentive to settle the business which has been prepared for settlement by the present Russian leadership.

Q: Like SALT II?
A: Like SALT II, yes. And the engagement into SALT III.

Q: What about Russian intentions outside Europe, which seem to us to be much less just a question of containing and preserving the status quo?

With Mao Zedong in the People's Republic of China, October 1975.

A: They are exploiting the situation in some places which the West has by negligence, and as a result of the psychological aftermath of Vietnam, allowed to open up. But even so, I do not think that the present leadership in the Soviet Union would risk any showdown in any place of the world. I think that one could see this clearly with the Vietnamese request for Soviet help vis-à-vis the so-called Chinese operation of punishment. The Soviets behaved rather cautiously.

Q: You made it very clear at the time, as we understood it, that you were happy about the restraint that the Soviets showed.

A: I praised them because of their self-restraint, yes, that's right.

Q: But you also were fairly critical of the Chinese move and indeed of the playing by America and others of the Chinese card.

A: I was critical of the Chinese. They don't have a right to punish somebody, nobody has a right to violate the territory of somebody else, to violate somebody else's sovereignty.

Q: Even if there's somebody else doing a rather ugly thing?

A: The Vietnamese had no right to intervene in Cambodia even if Pol Pot was a criminal murderer.

Q: But they did. So then what does China do?

A: Neither the Vietnamese had the right to intervene, nor had the Chinese the right to intervene. Nobody has a right to intervene.

Q: No. But if the Vietnamese have already done it? You only have to speak to Lee Kuan Yew or anybody down in that area to know they were rather satisfied that the Chinese came in.

A: Well, I can imagine, in pragmatic terms, that one could be satisfied. But the morale of the world is going to go under if from time to time we praise intervention into sovereign territory and from time to time we criticize it. I am criticizing it all the time, whether it's in Southeast Asia or whether it's in eastern Africa.

Q: It must be said you're sounding somewhat as you were represented after Brezhnev's visit here in May 1978. There was speculation at the time that there was an understanding between the two of you that the Federal Republic and its leadership would become the explainer and the advocate of Soviet attitudes within the Alliance.

A: We are not the advocates of the Russians. We are not even the interpreters of the Russians. They are a great power, one of the two greatest powers of the world, who can and do speak for themselves. We are a member of the Western Alliance, we want to see this alliance maintain its strength, maintain its operability, maintain its defensive capabilities, be regarded as a strong alliance — not only to appear like a strong one — be respected as a strong alliance.

We contribute quite a bit to the defensive abilities of that alliance. To think of the Alliance without Germany is to think of fairly little. As in the past, so in the future we shall contribute what is our duty, not because it's our duty, but because we feel it's necessary. We do it for our own sake, out of our own necessities.

On the other hand, one of the necessities of the Alliance as well as for us Germans is to get along with the Eastern power. We don't want to get back into the cold war. There is nothing to be gained for the Germans in a cold war, divided as our nation is, divided as our capital of Berlin is, nothing to be gained from a new cold war period. A return to the cold war is still thinkable: I hope it doesn't occur, but we have not passed the point of no return as yet.

More important than strategic thinkers yet understand is economic cooperation. There is no possibility for the Soviet Union or other European powers in the future to exist economically on their own. They need exchanges with the West, they need capital goods, they need investment goods, they need export markets for their own produce, their own raw materials especially. They are much more intertwined in the world's economy, as a whole, than in the past. They have come to understand it. It's good that they understand that, it's good that we in the West respond to that.

They are much more dependent on the Western world economy than the Western world is dependent on the economy of the East.

DIVIDED AS OUR NATION IS

Q: All right. Greater independence. Greater security than twenty or thirty years ago. Very much greater German success economically, and stability inside Germany. All these things have raised questions about how firmly embedded Germany is in the Western Alliance, the whole question of reunification. Heine's famous words: "If I think of Germany at night I cannot sleep."

Where do you think the reunification debate and the reunification matter between yourselves in negotiation with the Soviet Union goes in the next year or two?

A: I'll tell you the same thing which I tell anybody, whether on German television or in conversation with Leonid Brezhnev. I always let people remember the Polish example.

Historically there have been three divisions of Poland: after the third division at the end of the eighteenth century nothing was left of Poland. All the Polish nation and the Polish territory was divided between three great European powers at the time: Russia, Prussia, and Austria. And then again, in 1939, there was a fourth division of what then again had been created as a Polish state between Stalin and Hitler. But nevertheless, the Poles, over a period of now 200 years, two centuries, did not give up the will, not give up the hope to get together one day in the future. They didn't know when.

Q: They've had a fairly nasty time along the way.

A: Yes, they have. But they didn't give up. And the first line of the Polish national anthem since the early nineteenth century has been "Poland is not lost as yet" and so far they have been proved right.

I do not foresee under what auspices and conditions the Germans will get together again, but they will. Maybe only in the twenty-first century. I don't know. It would obviously be wrong for any European nation to believe that the nation state is normal for any nation but not for the Germans.

Q: What's the implication for the Alliance then?
A: There is no implication for the Alliance, no.

Q: No *immediate* implication. In the long run there must be.
A: I don't know, I don't know. I do not think that the present alliances will last for centuries. For the time being the Alliance is a totally indispensable instrument for maintaining peace in Europe. Therefore the Alliance is good for the Germans and they'll stick to it. There is no need and indeed no reason for philosophizing about Germany's adherence to the Alliance. I would just repeat

that, if every great nation in the West would contribute to the defensive strength of the Alliance as much as we do, the Alliance would be better off.

Q: How live is the feeling for reunification among the younger generation here? There have been opinion polls showing that they'd prefer to go on holiday in Spain and they no longer terribly care about reunification.

A: Yes? The Poles waited for two centuries. Nevertheless the matter was very vital deep in their souls. It's not necessary that you advertise it every Sunday.

One Germany is not something which anybody thinks of as being right around the next corner, or even the corner after the next. It's some way in the future but it does exist. It's a real desire in the soul of the German nation, whether in the West or the East, and one must not delude oneself by young people going to Ibiza or Majorca.

Helmut Schmidt:
A Biographical Political Profile

Hans Georg Lehmann

On May 6, 1974, Willy Brandt resigned as federal chancellor; ten days later, his minister of finance, Helmut Schmidt, assumed the office. This was an unforeseen change of leadership, since Willy Brandt was the undisputed head of the governing coalition between the Social Democrats (SPD) and the Free Democrats (FDP) that had been forged in 1969 and there was no indication following his overwhelming victory in the November 1972 elections that he would vacate his position voluntarily. Contrary to expectation, however, and despite the large majority that the coalition government enjoyed in the Bundestag, Brandt's aura as a chancellor committed to domestic reforms had paled visibly and the wave of public support for his personal and political qualities had receded. The arrest of his personal assistant, Günther Guillaume, who was unmasked as a spy for the German Democratic Republic (GDR), was the last act in a political and personal drama that led to his decision to resign.

Although Brandt's resignation could not be anticipated, there was no doubt about who would succeed him. In terms of temperament, Brandt and Schmidt, both North Germans and only five years apart in age, are a study in contrasts. While Brandt preferred cautious decision preceded by long discussions and occasionally exhibited visionary traits, Schmidt embodies the more resolute, sober type who sets to work quickly, pragmatically, and precisely, a trait that has earned him a reputation as a manager and a technocrat. The course of their lives also reveals striking differences. Brandt emigrated during the period of National Socialism and was deprived of his German citizenship; he is thus an exception to the rule, an atypical German of his time. By contrast, Schmidt belongs to the "war generation" that, out of an often wrongly understood Prussian sense of duty, served in the armed forces. He consequently personifies the fate of the average German who remained in Germany and participated in the war, although he cannot for that reason be identified as sympathizing with National Socialism.

A BORN HANSEATIC

Schmidt was born on December 23, 1918, in the workers' district of Barmbek in Hamburg, Germany's "gateway to the world." His grandfather was employed in the port. His father, Gustav Schmidt, was the first member of the family to gain entrance into the bourgeoisie by becoming a certified teacher of commerce. Severe Prussian discipline that brooked no contradiction predominated in the patriarchal, Protestant family. It was somewhat tempered by Schmidt's mother Ludovica, whose musical talents were inherited by her two sons, Helmut and Wolfgang. For Helmut Schmidt, Hamburg incorporated a "splendid synthesis between the Atlantic and the Alster, between Budden- brooks and Bebel, between live and let live," as he wrote in 1962. "I love this city with its scarcely concealed Anglicisms in form and gesture, its ceremonious pride in tradition, its mercantile pragmatism that is accompanied by an endear- ing provincialism." The influence of Hamburg's stimulating atmosphere left a lasting imprint on Schmidt.

After completing the *Volksschule*, he attended the *Lichtwarkgymnasium*, a rather modern German high school that rejected one-sided intellectual training and stressed the artistic and emotional development of its students. In contrast to other schools in Germany, emphasis was placed not only on Spartan discipline and dutiful accomplishment, but also on the development of critical, open-minded, and broadly educated individuals.

The discipline of Protestantism, Prussianism, and Puritanism; the cosmopolitanism, tradition, and pragmatism of the old Hanseatic city of Ham- burg; and the courage of his convictions, his artistic nature, and the in- dividualism inculcated by the Lichtwark pedagogy — all these various elements, however contradictory and ambivalent, became part of Helmut Schmidt's per- sonality. He admired Albert Ballin, the Hamburg shipowner and head of Hapag Lloyd; he wished to emulate the great Hamburg architect Fritz Schumacher by studying architecture, he enjoyed Marcus Aurelius's *Reflections* and was interested in reading about the Roman emperors and stoic philos- ophers; he considered Thomas Jefferson the model politician; he admired the modern art of Emil Nolde and Ernst Barlach; and he revelled in baroque and church music, especially Bach. Playing the organ, reading, sailing, and playing chess remain among his favorite leisure occupations. Schmidt was a very good student, as his grades attest. He completed his examinations in the spring of 1937. Immediately thereafter he had to fulfill the prescribed military and labor service.

MILITARY SERVICE AND THE WAR YEARS

Schmidt's politically uncommitted parents were skeptical about the National Socialist Party and did not vote for it. Through the school rowing club, Helmut

Schmidt joined the navy segment of the Hitler Youth in 1934, taking pride in his appointment as group leader. But he inwardly broke with the Nazi regime when the German Expressionists whom he revered—among them Emil Nolde and Ernst Barlach—began to be castigated. Because of his opposition to ideological regimentation, and because he had refused to give the Hitler salute in school, he increasingly became known as a "complainer," and in the fall of 1936 he was expelled from the Hitler Youth.

After graduation in 1937, Schmidt served in the work corps before being recruited into the 28th anti-aircraft regiment of the German air force. At the beginning of World War II, Schmidt was temporarily assigned to the air defense of Bremen and then in the summer of 1941 was transferred as lieutenant to the 83rd anti-aircraft section of the First Tank division, assigned to the Russian Front. The horrors of the Eastern front left him with indelible impressions of suffering. Even today, Schmidt's resolve to prevent conflicts from escalating into war is strengthened by his frontline experiences.

Schmidt returned from the Eastern front in 1942, serving as training adviser to the Ministry of Air Transport in Berlin from mid-1943 until the end of 1944. In June of 1944 he married Hannelore Glaser, whom he had met and fallen in love with while still at the *Lichtwarkgymnasium*. They had two children—a son who died during the war and a daughter, Susanne, who was born in 1947. Hannelore ("Loki") Schmidt worked as a teacher until 1967.

Schmidt was on the Western front when the war ended, having been sent to Belgium as a first lieutenant and battery commander at the end of 1944. The conflict of defending the fatherland and simultaneously serving a criminal regime became increasingly unbearable. Yet Schmidt, who had attracted attention in Berlin because of his sharp tongue, and who had been sent as a spectator to witness the trial of the conspirators against Hitler, could not bring himself to oppose the regime actively. In April 1945, he was taken prisoner by the British during the German retreat through the Lüneburg heath.

THE EARLY POLITICAL YEARS

Schmidt's political awareness developed in a British prisoner-of-war camp in Belgium. Affected by the comradeship and solidarity of the war experience ("socialism of the front") and by some older officers (especially Hans Bohnenkamp), he became a social democrat. He sought to master the bitter experiences of the National Socialist era and the war by becoming politically active.

As an "anti-Nazi" he obtained an early release from imprisonment, and at age 27, as a first-year economics student at the University of Hamburg, he helped found a group of socialist students. From this time on, politics and his professional life were inseparable. In March 1946 he joined the Social Democratic Party of Germany. He and his associates were thoroughly imbued with the skepticism and pragmatism of the war generation and much less attracted to the long-term ideological goals of an earlier Marxism.

Schmidt's course of study was characterized by dire necessity and was free of any wishful thinking. Instead of his original choice of architecture, he chose to study economics because the program of study was shorter, cheaper, and more practical. Nonetheless, he took full advantage of all the opportunities offered at the university for expanding his knowledge of history, law, and politics, acquiring a comprehensive fund of knowledge that continues to serve him well.

The core of the Socialist German Student League (SDS) grew out of the student group that Schmidt had participated in founding. In 1948, he was elected chairman of the league, his first office as a political leader. Schmidt and his group of friends to some extent considered the SDS a forum for self-development. Their task was to train the members intellectually and to support their quest for a political homeland.

After completing his studies in 1949, Schmidt obtained a position with the city of Hamburg's Ministry of Economics and Transportation, headed by Karl Schiller, who subsequently became Willy Brandt's "super-minister." The recent economics graduate was initially preoccupied with questions of business and transportation policy. He was promoted in the spring of 1951 to head the division for economic policy and a year later to head the Department of Transportation.

Although his career progressed rapidly, Schmidt was not attracted by the prospect of remaining a bureaucrat. He had an urge to be active and wanted the responsibility of making rather than implementing decisions. He became a candidate for the SPD in the 1953 Federal elections in Northern Hamburg. Although he lost as a direct candidate, he was elected to the second German Bundestag as a result of being on the party list.

As a member of the Bundestag, "Schmidt-Hamburg" (as he was called in order to distinguish him from other deputies having the same name) was primarily concerned with transportation policy, building in Parliament on his previous professional experience. His success as a transportation expert gained him recognition among his colleagues but not among the public. If he wanted to make a name for himself, he had to enter new territory, an opportunity he perceived in the field of defense policy. At that time, defense policy constituted an extremely contentious and emotional issue for the SPD, but it offered Schmidt the opportunity of becoming known, and gradually the transportation expert became the defense expert of the SPD.

Helmut Schmidt made headlines for the first time in late March 1958 during a heated four-day debate on defense issues in the Bundestag. He delivered an inflammatory address opposing a government proposal to supply the armed forces with nuclear armaments. His highly-charged rhetoric triggered a wave of enthusiasm among the SPD and outrage among the CDU/CSU.

When Schmidt later volunteered to participate in an army reserve exercise, he was expelled as an alleged turncoat from his party's parliamentary leadership by his disappointed colleagues. Actually, Schmidt's action had been prompted by his desire to demonstrate his unbiased attitude toward the armed forces. His book, *Defense or Retaliation*, was published in 1961, making a widely noted German contribution to an examination of the strategic problems of NATO, and making the author an acknowledged expert on questions of security and defense.

Frustrated by the SPD's opposition role in the Bundestag, Schmidt readily accepted the offer made by the City of Hamburg at the end of 1961 to become "senator" of the Internal Affairs Department, which had been created at his suggestion. He had hardly been in office three months when a natural catastrophe more severe than any since the Middle Ages afflicted Hamburg. On February 16 and 17, 1962, high waters caused by a hurricane beat against and over a protective dike, causing it to break. Floods covering extensive parts of the city-state killed more than 300 people and caused extensive damage. The young senator of internal affairs took control: he sent First Mayor Nevermann home and in military fashion assumed command of everything—the police, army, assistance personnel. His name was on every tongue: he had proved his ability to get things accomplished, to govern with resoluteness, and to command with authority.

Schmidt returned to Bonn as one of the SPD's "big hopes" in the fall of 1965 following the federal elections—once again, contrary to expectations, as a deputy of the opposition. But a change of administration occurred sooner than expected just one year later. After Chancellor Erhard's failure to agree with the Free Democratic Party on budget deficits and tax increases, the grand coalition headed by Kiesinger (CDU/CSU) as chancellor and Brandt (SPD) as vice-chancellor and foreign minister came into being on December 1, 1966.

Schmidt was offered the cabinet post of minister of transport, since the former foreign minister, Gerhard Schröder (CDU), had been appointed minister of defense as part of the political maneuver to cement the coalition. Unwilling to accept a position chosen for him by someone else, Schmidt preferred to substitute for the ailing leader of the SPD parliamentary group, Fritz Erler. Following the death of Erler in February 1967, Schmidt became his successor.

Schmidt's relations with Rainer Barzel, then head of the CDU/CSU parliamentary group, remain to this day characterized by "respect and trust." As coalition partners in Parliament, they accomplished more than the cabinet, which, as a mediation committee under Kiesinger's leadership, was capable of functioning only to the extent that it adhered to the policy guidelines previously established by Schmidt and Barzel. Schmidt considered the three years spent as head of his party's parliamentary faction more strenuous, but also more instructive and multifaceted, than his later activity as a cabinet minister. As leader of the SPD caucus, he had again proved himself as a crisis manager, this time backstage, within the party caucus in the Bundestag.

THE FIRST SOCIAL DEMOCRATIC DEFENSE MINISTER

After the formation of the SPD/FDP coalition of Brandt/Scheel in October 1969, it came as a surprise that Schmidt was not eager to be the first Social Democratic minister of defense since Gustav Noske (1920) but preferred to remain leader of the parliamentary group. After long hesitation, he finally yielded to his friends' entreaties and a sense of duty and assumed the office. In his book *Balance of Power,* published in 1969, he had analyzed the military and foreign policy situation of Europe between the two blocs and outlined the main characteristics of a policy of détente based on the balance of power.

Schmidt was primarily concerned with a "critical assessment," of the German armed forces, to be followed by reforms. Teamwork was to replace isolated decisions by individual ministers. He began to reorganize education and training, as well as personnel and procurement procedures — to this end, he invited industrialist Ernst Wolf Mommsen to join his ministry — he sought a more equitable conscriptive arrangement by shortening basic military training from eighteen to fifteen months, and he was much concerned with the idea of "inner leadership," the concept of the citizen in uniform. In instances of disagreements with general officers, he insisted on the primacy of political authority over the military.

BRANDT'S CRISIS MINISTER

In 1972, Schmidt was recuperating from an illness when a new position involving two functions demanded all his energies. Karl Schiller, who was both minister of economics and of finance and known as Brandt's "superminister," resigned in July over policy matters, and Brandt, looking for a "crisis manager," urgently implored Schmidt to take over both ministerial positions.

Despite the conflicts complicating the relationship with his former economics professor and employer in Hamburg, Schmidt, like his predecessor, also wanted to safeguard the social market economy. But he was more inclined than Schiller to attach greater importance to full employment and economic growth than to price stability, which would have been implemented at the expense of socially weaker groups.

The superministry held by Schmidt was divided in two after the victory of the SPD/FDP coalition in the federal elections of November 19, 1972, with Schmidt retaining the position as head of the Ministry of Finance, which had been enlarged to include a department dealing with currency policy. This was the era of crises in currency, business, and energy matters, triggered by, among other things, the drastic increase in oil prices. Schmidt soon gained an international reputation as a currency expert and crisis manager.

FEDERAL CHANCELLOR AS BRANDT'S SUCCESSOR

Surprised by Brandt's resignation and unable to persuade him to remain in office, Schmidt agreed to assume the duties of the federal chancellor in May 1974. There was dissension within the SPD, whose popularity with the electorate had diminished. The international economic crisis, accompanied by rising unemployment, was reaching a peak.

The motto of Schmidt's governmental program was "continuity and concentration," which meant that in an era of mounting problems he wanted to continue the policy of the social-liberal coalition, restricting himself to matters of the greatest importance and letting everything else wait. "No government can accomplish miracles. All strength must be used, however, for realizing the possible. We are now making a new start by concentrating on what is now essential and possible." Unlike Brandt, whose political perspective, especially in his policies concerning internal reforms and toward the East, was occasionally distorted by overly optimistic expectation, Schmidt's chancellorship signaled pragmatism in a difficult era and aimed at regaining a sense of equilibrium for the Federal Republic of Germany.

Schmidt built a good record for himself during the two and a half years before the next federal elections. Although continuing Brandt's main foreign policy achievement—a policy of détente toward the East—he steered a course of greater caution and restraint. As agreed upon with the Western allies, the Federal Government signed the final accords of the Conference on Security and Cooperation in Europe in Helsinki on August 1, 1975. One result of discussions with Polish party chief Gierek in Helsinki were agreements with Poland concerning questions of finance, insurance, and resettlement that had been an obstacle to further normalization of relations.

In domestic policy, Schmidt succeeded in mitigating the effects of the general international economic crisis within the Federal Republic, in closing the ranks of the SPD and young socialists who were embroiled in never-ending theoretical discussions, and in leading voters who had deserted the SPD back into the party. Reflecting a change in the general trend, reform plans had to be set aside, particularly since financial resources were lacking and many of Schmidt's aims (such as the improved economic productivity and the elimination of unemployment) could not be realized. In comparison with other Western industrial nations, the Federal Republic nonetheless succeeded quite well in its effort at meeting the challenges created by the worldwide recession; Schmidt was chosen "Man of the Year 1975" by the respected English daily, *Financial Times*.

Although the social-liberal coalition was again able to win the federal elections in October 1976, its majority shrank to ten seats — a margin almost too narrow for forming a stable government. Even in the parliamentary selection of the chancellor the SPD and FDP barely escaped defeat: Schmidt, like Adenauer in his first election, was chosen head of government by a one-vote majority.

This blow to Schmidt's prestige was directly connected to the "pension fiasco." Before the election, the government had promised to increase pensions by 10 percent starting July 1, 1977, but after the election called for a six-month postponement. There was a good deal of public consternation over this turnabout, and members of the SPD parliamentary group were unhappy as well. Schmidt was compelled to back down. This "debacle" was caused by erroneous economic forecasts predicting larger state revenues (on the basis of growth rates) than were actually realized. Schmidt later admitted that his administration had made a mistake, but his opponents still branded him a "political deceiver on pensions" in the 1980 federal electoral campaign.

After this bad start, a series of terrorist incidents threatened to topple the Schmidt government. The murders of federal prosecutor Siegfried Buback and banker Jürgen Ponto, the abduction of the industrialist Hans Martin Schleyer, and the highjacking of a Lufthansa plane to Somalia (aimed at liberating imprisoned members of the Red Army Faction) proved to be a severe test for the government. In case of failure Schmidt was prepared to accept the consequences and resign, but a special unit of the Federal Border Police was able to liberate the hostages in Somalia in October 1977.

Schmidt's star rose in the aftermath. According to opinion polls, his popularity rating was comparable to or even greater than that of Chancellor Konrad Adenauer in his best years. The stabilization policies initiated by Schmidt when he was minister of finance also contributed significantly to his reputation. Although he was unable to avert severe economic problems, inflation, hikes in oil prices, unemployment, and state indebtedness (especially since all these issues were strongly influenced by international factors), he was nonetheless successful in checking them. Although the government's record was uneven, Schmidt achieved significant progress in his efforts to stimulate Germany's economy.

Schmidt's prestige reached its peak in July 1978 at the economic summit meeting held in Bonn, which was attended by the heads of state of the most important industrialized nations. The most important topic on the agenda was how to construct an effective common policy for combating worldwide recession, and participants assigned the task of political leadership to the chancellor and the Federal Republic of Germany. While Brandt had imbued West German policy with a measure of flexibility by expanding Adenauer's commitment to the West with a dynamic policy toward the East, Schmidt tried to delineate and redefine the Federal Republic's changed role in international politics. In early January 1979 he was invited by the heads of state of the three Western powers to attend their summit meeting on Guadeloupe to discuss the worldwide political situation. In the estimation of its allies the Federal Republic of Germany, thirty-five years after the demise of Germany as a world power and until now ranked as an economic giant but a political dwarf, had assumed a new function within the Western alliance.

Schmidt himself considers the following his main accomplishments as chancellor: 1) he deliberately nurtured Adenauer's legacy — Germany's commitment to the Western alliance, to European integration, and to friendship with France, placing special emphasis upon cooperation with Giscard d'Estaing and the jointly initiated European currency system; 2) he continued Willy Brandt's and Walter Scheel's policy of détente with the East which, based on NATO and the European Community, served as a complement to Adenauer's Western policy; and 3) he assisted in steering the Federal Republic through the perils of the persisting worldwide economic crisis. Schmidt recognized that regarding the first two points he merely continued the original accomplishments of his predecessors. He perceived the third point as his own achievement, his personal contribution toward stabilization of an endangered world that was threatened by chaos. The fact that the Federal Republic of Germany managed to retain a large measure of economic stability amid the turmoil of the worldwide economic crisis undoubtedly is one of Schmidt's achievements.

CHANCELLOR IN CRISIS?

According to opinion polls taken in the spring and summer of 1980, approximately 60 percent of the electorate supported the reelection of Helmut Schmidt as chancellor. Such popularity prompted the SPD to predict an overwhelming electoral victory at the forthcoming federal elections. The results of the October 5, 1980, election, therefore, were disappointing, coming in the wake of a hard-fought electoral campaign that focused largely on the personalities of the two major candidates, Helmut Schmidt and Franz Josef Strauss. Although the SPD/FDP coalition increased its majority, the FDP gained on second-ballot votes, and the SPD stagnated except for a small increase in votes. The CDU/CSU, despite significant losses, remained the strongest party in the Bundestag. Unrealistic expectations had proved deceptive, and it almost looked as if Schmidt, despite his victory, had lost the election. Many SPD members faulted an electoral campaign that had been tailored to Schmidt's personality and consequently short-changed programmatic party objectives.

Schmidt's new administration got off to a bad start. Immediately following the election, the East German government drastically increased the currency exchange requirement for Western visitors, thereby straining relations with the Federal Republic. In addition, negotiations between the coalition partners, the SPD and the FDP, progressed slowly. The Free Democrats, conscious of being indispensable after their showing at the polls, exploited their leverage and exacted a number of compromises, largely in the area of economic and social policy, from Schmidt. The chancellor was caught in the middle. Pushed toward a more conservative stance by his coalition partners, he faced pressure from the trade union leaders, who perceived a threat to their co-determination rights in the coal and steel industries, and from within the ranks of his own party, whose members and officials criticized what they perceived to be the watering-down or even abandonment of social democratic principles in the government's program. The mass media began to portray the government leader as in "the dumps" and toying with the idea of resigning. Schmidt was reproached for speaking more about decisions than implementing them, with the suggestion that he had lost the political mettle for which he had always been noted.

By the spring of 1981, the Schmidt government had regained firmer ground, but it had undoubtedly lost in authority. Fiscal and economic issues, as well as the divisive issue of the planned stationing of modernized intermediate-range nuclear armaments in Western Europe, continued to plague the cohesion of the SPD/FDP coalition. The left wing of the SPD had for all practical purposes become a more effective opposition to the government's program than the official opposition, the CDU/CSU. In the past, the chancellor has proved himself many times in many ways as a crisis manager. In times marked by increasingly difficult problems, he will, more urgently than ever, have to act on the principle of "courage toward the future," the guiding theme of his government declaration.

Bibliography

MAJOR PUBLICATIONS BY HELMUT SCHMIDT

Schmidt, Helmut. *Verteidigung oder Vergeltung: Ein deutscher Beitrag zum strategischen Problem der NATO.* Stuttgart: Seewald Verlag, 1961.

————. *Defense or Retaliation: A German View.* Translated from the German by Edward Thomas. New York: Frederick A. Praeger, 1962.

————. Foreword to André Beaufre, *Die NATO und Europa.* Translated from the French by Walter Schütze. Stuttgart: Seewald Verlag, 1967.

————. *Beiträge.* Stuttgart: Seewald Verlag, 1967.

————. "Die Kriegsgeneration." *Die Neue Gesellschaft,* November-December 1968.

————. *Strategie des Gleichgewichts.* Stuttgart: Seewald Verlag, 1969.

————. *The Balance of Power: Germany's Peace Policy and the Super Powers.* Translated from the German by Edward Thomas. London: Kimber, 1971.

————. *Social Democratic Policy for Progress and Stability.* Edited by Günther Lehrke. Translated from the German by Diet Simon. Bonn–Bad Godesberg: Verlag Neue Gesellschaft, 1974.

————. *Bundestagsreden.* Edited by Peter Corterier. Bonn: Verlag az Studio, 1975.

————. *Kontinuität und Konzentration.* Bonn–Bad Godesberg: Verlag Neue Gesellschaft, 1975.

————. Foreword to *Kritischer Rationalismus und Sozialdemokratie.* Edited by Georg Lührs, Thilo Sarrazin, Frithjof Spreer, and Manfred Tietzel. 2nd ed. Berlin, Bad Godesberg: Dietz Verlag, 1975.

————. *Als Christ in der politischen Entscheidung.* Gütersloh: Gütersloher Verlagshaus Gerd Mohn, 1976.

————. Foreword to Jean Monnet, *Erinnerungen eines Europäers.* Translated from the French by Werner Vetter. München, Wien: Hanser Verlag, 1978.

————. *Der Kurs heisst Frieden.* Düsseldorf-Wien: Econ Verlag, 1979.

————. Interview in *Nach dreissig Jahren.* Edited by Walter Scheel. Stuttgart: Klett-Cotta Verlag, 1979.

————. *Pflicht zur Menschlichkeit.* Düsseldorf-Wien: Econ Verlag, 1981.

Schmidt, Helmut, and Willy Brandt. *Deutschland 1976—Zwei Sozialdemokraten im Gespräch.* Hamburg: rororo aktuel, 1976.

Schmidt, Helmut; Willy Brandt; Herbert Wehner; Egon Bahr; and others. *Zwischenbilanz: Zur Entwicklung der Beziehungen der Bundesrepublik Deutschland und der Sowjetunion.* Köln: Pahl-Rugenstein Verlag, 1978.

MAJOR PUBLICATIONS ABOUT HELMUT SCHMIDT

Blank, Ulrich, and Jupp Darchinger. *Helmut Schmidt—Bundeskanzler.* Hamburg: Hoffmann & Campe Verlag, 1974, 1977.

Böhr, Christoph. "SPD: Neuorientierung an Kant und Popper? Anmerkungen zum Politikverständnis Helmut Schmidts und der deutschen Sozialdemokratie." *SONDE. Neue Christlich-Demokratische Politik.* Vol. 9, Nr. 1 (1976):17–31.

Dönhoff, Marion Gräfin. *Menschen, die wissen worum es geht.* Hamburg: Hoffmann & Campe Verlag, 1976.

Grunenberg, Nina. *Vier Tage mit dem Bundeskanzler.* Hamburg: Hoffmann & Campe Verlag, 1976.

Hart am Wind: Helmut Schmidts politische Laufbahn. Introduction by Marion Gräfin Dönhoff. Hamburg: Albrecht Knaus Verlag, 1979.

Hermann, Ludolf. "Les 'cent jours' du second gouvernement Schmidt." *Documents. Revue des Questions Allemandes.* Vol. 32, No. 2 (1977):5–15.

Kahn, Helmut Wolfgang. *Helmut Schmidt—Fallstudie über einen Populären.* Hamburg: Holsten Verlag, 1973.

Koch, Peter. "Das Duell." *Stern-Magazin.* Hamburg: Verlag Gruner und Jahr, 1979.

Krause-Burger, Sybille. *Helmut Schmidt—Aus der Nähe gesehen.* Düsseldorf-Wien: Econ Verlag, 1980.

Mahler, Gerhard, "Die Sprache des Bundeskanzlers." *SONDE. Neue Christlich-Demokratische Politik.* Vol. 9, Nr. 1 (1976):72–86.

Pélassy, Dominique. "Helmut Schmidt, esquisse d'un temperament politique." *Documents. Revue des Questions Allemandes.* Vol. 33, No. 4 (1978):59–71.

Prittie, Terrence. *The Velvet Chancellors: A History of Post-War Germany.* London: Muller, 1979.

Rovan, Joseph. "Le chancelier Helmut Schmidt." *Études.* Vol. 350, No. 5 (1979): 599–606.

―――. "La politique interieure du chancelier." *Documents. Revue des Questions Allemandes.* Vol. 33, No. 4 (1978):39–46.

Sandoz, Gérard. "L'Allemagne d'Helmut Schmidt." *Documents. Revue des Questions Allemandes.* Vol. 33, No. 4 (1978):17–28.

―――. "Survivre à Brandt et Schmidt. Comment?" *Documents. Revue des Questions Allemandes.* Vol. 34, No. 2 (1979):43–49.

SPD, ed. *Wirtschafts- und Finanzpolitische Bilanz. Sozialdemokratische Politik, 1969–1972.* Bonn, 1972.

The archives of the Friedrich-Ebert-Stiftung (Godesberger Allee 149, D-5300 Bonn 2, FRG) contain an extensive collection of materials about Helmut Schmidt. Voluminous computer data is available at the German Press and Information Office, Gruppe Datenverarbeitung, D-5300, Bonn, Federal Republic of Germany.

Schmidt has also displayed his musical talents with the London Philharmonic: Wolfgang Amadeus Mozart, Concerts for Two and Three Pianos, K. 365 and K. 242 (Schmidt participated only in the latter). Pianists: Christoph Eschenbach, Justus Frantz, Helmut Schmidt. Under the direction of Christoph Eschenbach. London Philharmonic Orchestra. EMI Electrola 1 C 067-43 231 T. Recorded in London, December 1981.

Abbreviations

ASEAN	Association of Southeast Asian Nations
CDU/CSU	Christian Democratic Party/Christian Social Democratic Party
CSCE	Conference on Security and Cooperation in Europe
EEC	European Economic Community
EC	European Community
EMS	European Monetary System
FDP	Freie Demokratische Partei
FRG	Federal Republic of Germany
GATT	General Agreement on Trade and Tariffs
GDR	German Democratic Republic
MBFR	Mutual Balanced Force Reductions
NATO	North Atlantic Treaty Organization
OECD	Organization of Economic Cooperation and Development
OPEC	Organization of Petroleum Exporting Countries
SALT	Strategic Arms Limitation Talks
SPD	Social Democratic Party
UNCTAD	United Nations Conference on Trade and Development

Index

About the Book and Editor

Helmut Schmidt: Perspectives on Politics
edited by Wolfram F. Hanrieder

Helmut Schmidt, chancellor of the Federal Republic of Germany, is one of the most remarkable and prominent political figures on the contemporary world stage. His many years of public service in a wide range of government and party positions have coincided with the growth of the Federal Republic; one might say that he and West Germany have grown to maturity together. The various responsibilities that he has undertaken—as a member of the Bundestag, as senator of the city-state of Hamburg, as floor leader of his party in the Bundestag, as minister of defense, as minister of economics and finance, and as chancellor—have kept Schmidt in close contact with the major concerns of the Federal Republic. There is hardly an important issue in West German foreign or domestic policy in which Helmut Schmidt has not participated.

Chancellor Schmidt's masterful use of language, developed in the critical forum of parliamentary debate and sharpened over the decades as an instrument of explanation and persuasion, has made his public voice one of the most articulate of our time. The speeches, interviews, and essays collected in this book—the first such collection presented to an English-speaking readership—reflect the broad spectrum of Chancellor Schmidt's experience as well as his political temperament. Many of the chapters focus on practical matters of public policy, but in the more philosophical essays, the reader will find Helmut Schmidt speaking in a reflective, contemplative voice, providing insight into the underlying moral sensibility and personal view of public life that tie his world of thought to his world of action.

Wolfram F. Hanrieder is professor of political science at the University of California, Santa Barbara.